W9-CDT-037

On Modern Jewish Politics

STUDIES IN JEWISH HISTORY
Jehuda Reinharz, *General Editor*

THE JEWS OF PARIS AND THE
FINAL SOLUTION
*Communal Response and Internal
Conflicts, 1940–1944*
Jacques Adler

JEWS IN CHRISTIAN AMERICA
The Pursuit of Religious Equality
Naomi W. Cohen

ATLAS OF MODERN JEWISH
HISTORY
Evyatar Friesel

A SIGN AND A WITNESS
*2,000 Years of Hebrew Books and
Illuminated Manuscripts*
Paperback edition (co-published with
The New York Public Library)
Edited by Leonard Singer Gold

A CLASH OF HEROES
*Brandeis, Weizmann, and American
Zionism*
Ben Halpern

THE MAKING OF THE JEWISH
MIDDLE CLASS
*Women, Family, and Identity in
Imperial Germany*
Marion A. Kaplan

THE MAKING OF CZECH
JEWRY
*National Conflict and Jewish Society in
Bohemia, 1870–1918*
Hillel J. Kieval

THE ROAD TO MODERN
JEWISH POLITICS
*Political Tradition and Political
Reconstruction in the Jewish Community
of Tsarist Russia*
Eli Lederhendler

THE BERLIN JEWISH
COMMUNITY
*Enlightenment, Family and Crisis,
1770–1830*
Steven M. Lowenstein

ON MODERN JEWISH POLITICS
Ezra Mendelsohn

RESPONSE TO MODERNITY
*A History of the Reform Movement in
Judaism*
Michael A. Meyer

THE VATICAN AND ZIONISM
Conflict in the Holy Land, 1895–1925
Sergio Minerbi

ESCAPING THE HOLOCAUST
*Illegal Immigration to the Land of
Israel, 1939–1944*
Dalia Ofer

CHAIM WEIZMANN
The Making of a Zionist Leader
Jehuda Reinharz

CHAIM WEIZMANN
The Making of a Statesman
Jehuda Reinharz

COURAGE UNDER SIEGE
*Starvation, Disease, and Death in the
Warsaw Ghetto*
Charles G. Roland

LAND AND POWER
The Zionist Resort to Force, 1881–1948
Anita Shapira

THE TRANSFORMATION OF
GERMAN JEWRY, 1780–1840
David Sorkin

FOR WHOM DO I TOIL?
*Judah Leib Gordon and the Crisis of
Russian Jewry*
Michael F. Stanislawski

UNWELCOME STRANGERS
*East European Jews in Imperial
Germany*
Jack Wertheimer

THE HOLOCAUST
*The Fate of European Jewry,
1932–1945*
Leni Yahil

WILHELM MARR
The Patriarch of Antisemitism
Moshe Zimmermann

OTHER VOLUMES ARE IN PREPARATION

ON
MODERN JEWISH POLITICS

Ezra Mendelsohn

New York   Oxford
OXFORD UNIVERSITY PRESS
1993

Oxford University Press

Oxford   New York   Toronto
Delhi   Bombay   Calcutta   Madras   Karachi
Kuala Lumpur   Singapore   Hong Kong   Tokyo
Nairobi   Dar es Salaam   Cape Town
Melbourne   Auckland   Madrid

and associated companies in
Berlin   Ibadan

Copyright © 1993 by Oxford University Press, Inc.

Published by Oxford University Press, Inc.,
200 Madison Avenue, New York, New York 10016

Oxford is a registered trademark of Oxford University Press

All rights reserved. No part of this publication may be reproduced,
stored in a retrieval system, or transmitted, in any form or by any means,
electronic, mechanical, photocopying, recording, or otherwise,
without the prior permission of Oxford University Press.

The author has made every effort to obtain permission from copyright
holders to reprint or reproduce material for this book. In some cases
the copyright holders and/or their whereabouts were unknown.

Library of Congress Cataloging-in-Publication Data
Mendelsohn, Ezra.
On modern Jewish politics / Ezra Mendelsohn.
p. cm. — (Studies in Jewish history)   Includes index.
ISBN 0–19–503864–9 — ISBN 0–19–508219–9 (pbk)
1. Jews—Politics and government. 2. Judaism and politics.
3. Jews—United States—Politics and government.
4. Jews—Poland—Politics and government.
5. United States—Politics and government—1919–1933.
6. United States—Politics and government—1933–1945.
7. Poland—Politics and government—1918–1945.
I. Title. II. Series.   DS140.M45   1993
909′.04924082—dc20   92–32612

1 3 5 7 9 8 6 4 2

Printed in the United States of America
on acid-free paper

This book is dedicated
to the memory of my parents,
Fannie Soyer Mendelsohn
and Isaac Mendelsohn

PREFACE

In 1913 the Galician-born American Yiddish poet Moyshe-Leyb Halpern published a lengthy poem entitled *In der fremd* [In a foreign world]. Writing in harsh, inhospitable New York, the poet presents us with a glowing description of the good old days in Jewish Eastern Europe:*

> We had corners in their cities and we lived there together,
> And life was good, although taxes oppressed us.
> Although the king sent evil men to govern us,
> No one complained. We loved this spot of earth
> God granted us in our homeless wandering.
> And God's name was inscribed on every door
> Through which our children stepped.
> Rich men had poor men to their tables every day
> And blessed peace prevailed in streets and homes.

Unfortunately, this enchanting state of affairs, this "blessed peace," did not endure.

> But these quiet times were too good for us.
> The blind wheel spun around, and then
> A restlessness arose and, like a bad wind,
> Blew through old and young in every land throughout the world.
> And on a dark night, this restlessness descended on our street.
> A vile dispute began between the generations,
> And young and old became estranged, alien, cold,
> As if a message of a terrible judgement hovered over them.

*Moyshe-Leyb Halpern, *In New York: A Selection*, Kathryn Hellerstein, trans. and ed. (Philadelphia: 1982), p. 55.

Suddenly the sons and daughters talked and sang
Of a new light, like a delirious patient babbling in his sleep.

These lines may be read as an evocation of the origins of modern Jewish politics. The "restlessness," the "new light," above all the "vile dispute" (*beyze krig*) signified the emergence, sometime during the nineteenth century, of new and fateful divisions within the Jewish community. These divisions grew in intensity and complexity from generation to generation. Among other things, they led to the establishment of modern Jewish political movements whose aims and activities comprise the subject of this book.

The phrase Jewish politics as employed here refers to the programs formulated by these new movements, that is, the different ways in which they viewed the future of the Jewish people and their proposals for solving, once and for all, the celebrated Jewish Question—and the competition among them for hegemony on what was sometimes called the "Jewish street." The thorny problem of determining exactly which organizations qualify for admission to the realm of Jewish politics will be briefly addressed in the introductory chapter. I shall not be dealing with the early, formative period of modern Jewish politics, thereby avoiding the much-debated question as to when, exactly, it began.* Rather, this book will concentrate on the period between the two World Wars, when modern Jewish politics may be said to have come of age, reaching new heights of influence and achieving dramatic successes as well as suffering no less dramatic failures. As regards the geographic scope of this study, what follows is a discussion of Diaspora Jewish politics, excluding events in Jewish Palestine. More specifically, the focus is on Jewish politics in Europe—in particular non-Communist Eastern Europe—and the United States.

The book is divided into seven chapters. The first suggests a typology of modern Jewish politics. The second discusses the geography of Jewish politics. It raises the question as to why certain environments in which Jews lived were singularly conducive to the flourishing of particular kinds of Jewish politics and establishes core areas for the major Jewish political movements. It also tries to explain why different kinds of environments produced important variations on a specific Jewish political theme—why, for example, Zionism in Poland differed so sharply from its counterpart in the United States. Chapters 3 and 4 consider the dynamics of Jewish politics. They survey the fortunes of the various Jewish political forces that were competing for the allegiance of the Jewish community during the 1920s and 1930s and the underlying sources of their appeal. Chapters 5 and 6 recount the successes and failures of modern Jewish politics and attempt to place it in a comparative context. The concluding chapter examines the far-reaching changes in the political arena that have taken place

*On this see Eli Lederhendler, *The Road to Modern Jewish Politics: Political Tradition and Political Reconstruction in the Jewish Community of Tsarist Russia* (New York: 1989).

since 1939, changes that have transformed interwar Jewish politics in general into a phenomenon of the seemingly distant past.

For a number of years I have been working very closely with Jonathan Frankel and Peter Medding, my friends and colleagues at the Institute of Contemporary Jewry of The Hebrew University. Together we have edited the annual Studies in Contemporary Jewry, and have taught graduate seminars on modern Jewish politics. This book derives, in large measure, from our close working relationship (especially the first chapter, whose typology is based on a scheme worked out by all three of us). Had I not been able to benefit from their wisdom, encouragement, and friendship, it would have been quite a different book. I should add that I, like everyone else who works in this field, have been much influenced by Jonathan Frankel's *Prophecy and Politics,* the most important study to date of modern Jewish politics.

Although my book reflects the collective wisdom of all three of us, I hasten to absolve my colleagues of all responsibility for its shortcomings. The reader will soon discover that this is a highly selective, perhaps even eccentric study whose biases and peculiarities are mine alone. It is intended to be a kind of primer. I hope that it will serve as an interesting and informative introduction to what is beyond a doubt a formidably complex subject.

Jerusalem   E.M.
November 1992

ACKNOWLEDGMENTS

I wish to record my heartfelt thanks to my friend Aryeh (Arthur) Goren, who read part of the manuscript and brought several quotations and one picture to my attention. I also want to thank another friend, Deborah Dash Moore, for her encouragement. My colleague Milly Heyd was of great help in the preparation of the artwork that accompanies the text. Lisa Rubens was kind enough to photograph Raphael Soyer's drawing *Amos on Racial Equality,* and Daniel Soyer made a valuable suggestion regarding the Yiddish text in Ben Shahn's painting *East Side Soap Box.* Chone Shmeruk directed my attention to Isaac Bashevis Singer's short story about the unhappy pioneer who returns from Palestine to Poland.

I am grateful to Nancy Lane, senior editor at Oxford University Press, for her patience and encouragement, and to her assistant, Edward Harcourt, for his good advice. Henry Krawitz did a splendid job of supervising the editing process. Finally, I wish to thank the Littauer Foundation for providing a generous grant toward the completion of the book.

I am grateful to the artists Jack Levine, Larry Rivers, and Leonard Baskin for permitting me to reproduce their work. I am likewise grateful to Ms. Sophie Gropper for permitting me to reproduce several works by William Gropper, and to Ms. Rebecca Beagle for permitting me to reproduce Raphael Soyer's drawing *Amos on Racial Equality.* The verses from Moyshe-Leyb Halpern's poem appear with the permission of the Jewish Publication Society of America. The quotation from Delmore Schwartz's poem © 1954, 1959 by Delmore Schwartz; used by permission of New Directions Publishing Corporation.

CONTENTS

On Modern Jewish Politics

1

Varieties

In 1907 Israel Zangwill, a Jewish political leader as well as a celebrated writer (the author of the play *The Melting Pot*) published a remarkable story dealing with Jewish political life in Milovka, a Polish shtetl, shortly before World War I.[1] A young man, David Ben Amram (note his new-style, Hebrew-Zionist name), arrives in this town to organize a Jewish self-defense force as pogroms sweep over the land. His heroic efforts are ultimately frustrated by the incredible fragmentation of the small but highly politicized Jewish community. Not only have Jews adhered to various legal and illegal Polish and Russian organizations (this part of Poland was under Russian rule), but they are also divided among a large number of specifically Jewish organizations. David, a true believer in the holy principle of Jewish unity, a principle that for all-too-many Jews was honored more in the breach than the observance, encounters in this wretched backwater the following competing Jewish ideologies: integrationism or assimilationism (of which there were two or three distinct types), Orthodoxy (also divided into two types, Hasidic and anti-Hasidic), several varieties of socialist Zionism, Zionist Zionism, cultural Zionism, Mizrachi (Orthodox Zionism), Sejmism, territorialism, socialist territorialism, and Bundism. This awful divisiveness drives the young idealist to despair:

> He had a nightmare vision of bristling sects and pullulating factions, each with its Councils, Federations, Funds, Conferences, Party-Days, Agenda, Referats, Press-Organs, each differentiating itself with meticulous subtlety from all the other Parties, each defining with casuistic minuteness its relation to every contemporary problem, each equipped with inexhaustible polyglot orators speechifying through tumultuous nights.[2]

3

In the end, unable to prevail against the political consequences of Halpern's "vile dispute," David commits suicide.

A similar note of despair is sounded in Aron Zeitlin's drama *Weizmann the Second,* which takes place somewhat later, during the Nazi persecutions. Here Jews, hounded out of Europe by ferocious antisemitism and placed in a ship sailing to Palestine, argue endlessly about the proper political solution to the Jewish Question. They elect Albert Einstein as their president, and the great scientist, like Zangwill's David, is obliged to confront a bitterly divided Jewish world: "What a tumult, what a tumult! Oh, the opposition movements with their resolutions, their revolutions, their complaints and their just demands. How difficult it was to be president of Israel."[3]

Historians do not have to worry about unifying the Jews, a job likened in Zeitlin's drama to "organizing chaos."[4] However, acting according to the principle that order is a necessary prerequisite for understanding, I shall attempt an easier but still-complicated task, namely, I shall suggest a typology of Jewish organizations active in Jewish politics during the interwar period. A *Jewish* organization, obviously enough, is one that defines itself as such and that recruits its members from within the Jewish community. But matters are not quite so simple, and a few exceptional cases should be mentioned. There were, for example, the Jewish sections, also known as Yiddish-language sections. These organizations, very common within the socialist movement, were in fact subdivisions of non-Jewish political parties, as was the case with the celebrated Yevsektsiia, the Jewish section within the Communist parties of the Soviet Union, and with the Jewish section of the American Socialist party. Despite their subservient status it would be unjustified to ignore them because they did cater to an exclusively Jewish clientele and definitely possessed their own Jewish political "line." Also impossible to ignore are the so-called Jewish labor unions in the United States, such as the International Ladies Garment Workers' Union (ILGWU) and the Amalgamated Clothing Workers of America (ACWA). These large organizations did not define themselves as Jewish and did not cater to an exclusively Jewish membership. Nonetheless, it would be difficult to discuss the history of *Jewish* politics in America without taking them into consideration—just as no history of black politics in the United States would be complete without an analysis of the role of A. Philip Randolph's Brotherhood of Sleeping Car Porters, which was not defined as an exclusively black union, nor would a history of Ukrainian politics ignore the role of the Uniate (Greek Catholic) church, which never restricted its membership to ethnic Ukrainians.

Questions

How can one arrive at an acceptable if not airtight typology of the various Jewish organizations active in Jewish politics? I suggest posing a number of key questions, the answers to which will help one to divide the Jewish political world into a manageable number of schools or camps.

1. How are the Jews, taken collectively, to be defined? This question asks not *who* are Jews—an issue that keeps some rabbis and rabbinical seminaries busy and bedevils contemporary Israeli politics—but rather *what* are Jews? This is a somewhat different puzzle with a number of apparently mutually exclusive answers.

2. What should be the predominant cultural (meaning above all linguistic) orientation of the Jews? In simpler terms, what language (or perhaps languages) should the Jewish community of the future speak? Here, too, there exist a number of possible responses.

3. Assuming the existence of a Jewish Question, *where* does the solution lie—"here" in the Diaspora, where the Jews already live, or "there" in Palestine/Eretz Yisrael or in some other Jewish territory to which they will go and where the Jews will be allowed to establish a state of their own or at least enjoy some sort of territorial autonomy.

4. From a large number of potentially usable Jewish pasts, of Jewish historical pedigrees, which did the various Jewish organizations choose? In other words, from the vast expanse of Jewish history—over three thousand years—which Jewish personalities and which historical periods did they celebrate as inspirational and exemplary?

5. Which political forces in the non-Jewish world did these Jewish organizations identify with and seek out as allies? Whom did they perceive as their gentile friends and supporters?

6. What sort of political tactics did these various organizations favor? Did they think that the Jews, in the course of their campaign to further their interests and achieve their aims, should engage in high-profile or low-profile behavior, that is, in the politics of loud and open protest or in quiet, even secret diplomacy behind closed doors (among other reasons so as not to provoke the gentiles)?

7. The final question (the answer to which derives from the answer to question 3): To what degree were the various organizations under consideration optimistic or pessimistic with regard to the collective future of the Jews in the Diaspora?

In additon to seeking answers to these seven questions, some of which relate directly to the peculiar condition of Diaspora Jewry, it is necessary to consider the attitude of the various Jewish political organizations toward general social issues. Did they believe that the restructuring of society on socialist (or Communist) principles was essential to the solution of the Jewish Question? Or did they promote liberalism, conservatism, or even fascism? Are they to be located on the left, the center, or the right of the general political spectrum?

This Is Our Home, Our Palestine

In 1888 Simon Wolf, a leader of the veteran American Jewish fraternal organization B'nai B'rith, founded in 1843, announced with pride that the United States of America was "our Home, our Palestine; we have no other ambition than to prosper in this land of our adoption, to whose growth— material, social and intellectual—we have contributed our share. . . ."[5] Such a statement serves as an excellent summary of the worldview of one well-defined school or camp of modern Jewish politics. How did its adherents respond to the questions mentioned earlier? For them, as for many others, the first question was the most difficult as no one really possessed a definitive answer to the "What are the Jews?" conundrum. Bernard Berenson's remark, made in 1937, that Jews "are neither a religion nor a nation nor a race any more, whatever they may have been at one time"[6] exemplifies the widespread confusion and even bewilderment on this subject (this great art historian and connoisseur was by birth a Lithuanian Jew, a convert, and at the end of his life a bit of a pro-Zionist). Much better defined was the view of Eisenstein, a character in Henry Miller's *Sexus,* who insisted: "The religion is everything. . . . If you can't be a good Christian, you can't be a good Jew. We are not a people or a race—we're a religion."[7]

Eisenstein's interlocutor was skeptical: "That's what you say, but I don't believe it. It's more than that."[8] But for the Simon Wolfs of the Jewish world, Eisenstein's answer was the politically correct one. They would have agreed wholeheartedly with the sentiments of the composer Darius Milhaud, who begins his memoirs with the simple but ideologically significant statement, "I am a Frenchman from Provence, and by religion a Jew."[9] Religion was the thing that defined the Jew, and the Jews were, above all, a community held together by a common faith. Consider the words of Louis Marshall, the prominent American Jewish leader who founded, in 1906, the American Jewish Committee. Marshall is discussing another illustrious American Jewish leader, a banker and philanthropist:

> [Jacob Schiff] regarded Judaism as a faith, and not as a race, and that the ties which bound one Jew to another were religious and not racial.
>
> I entirely concur in this statement. . . . To my mind there is only one Judaism, and I consider all of its followers united by the bond of religion, and none other."[10]

This was the reason why Marshall preferred to be called a "Jew," meaning an adherent of Judaism, rather than a "Hebrew" or an "Israelite," terms that to his mind bore a certain "tribal significance."[11] By the same token it was highly significant that the leading German Jewish organization, founded in 1893, called itself the Centralverein deutscher Staatsbürger jüdischen Glaubens (The Central Union of German Citizens of Jewish Faith), and that a conference of Polish Jews meeting in 1919 referred to its participants as "Polacy wyznania mojżeszowego" ("Poles of the Jewish faith").[12] In the same spirit, in 1924 the former president of a B'nai B'rith lodge in Romania declared: "Religion is the only tie that still links us together."[13]

Assuming for the moment that what makes the Jews a coherent group is their adherence to the religion of Judaism, to which of the many varieties of Judaism should they adhere? Most of the organizations mentioned and most of their followers tended to favor some sort of reformed or "liberal" Judaism—in a word non-Orthodox or at least non-East European Orthodox. They were convinced that Judaism must adapt itself to the winds of change and not cling to outmoded and even grotesque "medieval" practices (including the special Jewish garb and such oddities as long beards and sidelocks). Although cleaving to its timeless, essential truths, its adherents must at the same time more closely conform to the norms of religious practice in the countries where the Jews resided. Some felt that Judaism must also be a religion with a message accessible to all, not the private property of a self-segregated separatist sect. Thus, the first seal of the Jewish Publication Society of America, founded in 1888, proclaimed to the world that "Israel's Mission Is Peace" (see fig. 1). Probably the most eloquent American spokesman for this standpoint was the founder of the reformed Jewish "church" in that country, Isaac Mayer Wise, who in 1895 declared: "Judaism is no tribal, nor racial religion, no conglomeration of antiquated customs and obsolete laws, it is the universal religion, progressive like reason, motherly humane, and like God's sun radiating light and life to all pilgrims of this sublunar sphere."[14]

If the Jews were neither a race nor a tribe and if theirs was a modern, universal religion with something to teach mankind, it followed that their standpoint must be militantly acculturationist. Which language should the Jewish community speak? Obviously not Hebrew—a language greatly esteemed by both Jew and gentile—the language of the book of books, of prayer and study, of the prophets and sages but for more than two thousand years not the spoken language of world Jewry. Even more emphatically not Yiddish, which was the spoken tongue of millions of East European Jews, both in Eastern Europe and in the lands of their dispersion. If Hebrew was honored by both gentiles and Jews as the language of the glorious Jewish past, Yiddish was often seen as an embarrassment, an object of scorn and ridicule. Many Jews regarded it as a misfit language (if a language at all). The pianist Artur Rubinstein, by origin an acculturated Polish Jew, advertises his contempt for it when he writes in his memoirs that it was spoken with "the singsong of the jargon."[15] Like many Jews he much preferred, though he was quite ignorant of, Hebrew. The Jewish "jargon" (or dialect) was regarded as a major cause of the infamous Chinese wall that, so regrettably, separated Jew from gentile. Thus, a character in the famous "Jewish novel" *Meir Ezofowicz,* by the Polish writer Eliza Orzeszkowa, expresses his amazement that the Polish Jews, resident in the land for a thousand years, are incapable of speaking Polish, "What! . . . they don't understand the language of the country in which

Fig. 1: Judaism Is for Everyone. Judaism is represented as the universal religion of mankind under whose warming sun perfect harmony prevails. ("Israel's Mission Is Peace," the first seal of the Jewish Publication Society of America. *American Jewish Year Book,* 15, 1913–14, p. 187. Reproduced with the permission of the Jewish Publication Society of America.)

they live?"[16] This most serious impediment to gentile understanding and respect would have to be removed, and the sooner the better.

A program of acculturation meant that American Jews should speak English and look "American," Polish Jews should speak (and look) Polish, and so forth. Unfortunately, matters were not always clear-cut. There were many regions where it was by no means apparent which non-Jewish language should be adopted by the Jews. Should the Jews of pre–World War I Bohemia speak German or Czech? Should the Jews of pre–World War I Vilna (Wilno in Polish: Vilnius in Lithuanian)—the historic capital of the old Lithuanian state—a city inhabited mostly by Poles and Jews and ruled ever since the late eighteenth century by the Russian Empire, adopt as their spoken language Russian, Polish, or Lithuanian? These were not merely academic questions. If the Jews of Vilna opted for Polish, would they not infuriate the Lithuanians? And if they decided to speak Russian, would they not be accused by the Poles of siding with the power that had trampled on Polish freedom and subjected them to slavery? A wrong choice in the language game in the ethnically confused corners of Eastern and Central Europe could and often did lead to unfortunate, even tragic consequences. These complications notwithstanding, the principle was clear—

the language (or languages) of the land, however defined, must be learned, and learned quickly. Cyrus Adler, a leader of the American Jewish Committee, noted in 1922, "A statement was given out only a fews days since, indicating that over 960,000 persons in New York City had Yiddish as their mother tongue."[17] Here was one excellent reason, Adler thought, why Americans, fed up with newcomers who were refusing to "melt," were turning against the notion of free immigration. The old, European-born generation could go on reading Yiddish newspapers and speaking *mame loshn* (the mother tongue). The new generation must Americanize, as it is seen to be doing in Raphael Soyer's well-known 1926 painting *The Dancing Lesson* (see fig. 2). It must fit in in every way, as does Oscar Straus,

Fig. 2: The History of Acculturation. Raphael Soyer, a noted Russian-born American artist, portrays the inexorable process of Jewish acculturation in the New World. The grandparents, whose picture (I presume) hangs on the wall, are old-style Russian Jews. The parents, who came to America as adults, seem somewhat disoriented—even depressed—as they watch their children learn how to dance American-style. The mother holds a Yiddish newspaper in her lap, but English is the language of this family's future. (Raphael Soyer, *The Dancing Lesson,* 1926. Collection of Renee and Chaim Gross, New York City.)

indistinguishable from the other U.S. leaders in a group portrait of Theodore Roosevelt's cabinet (see fig. 3).

Where is the Jewish Question to be solved? The obvious answer was "here" (in the lands of the Jewish dispersion), and not "there" (in Palestine or in some other territory set aside for the Jews). This principle was known in the Jewish political lexicon as *doikeyt*, a Yiddish word meaning (literally) "hereness," as opposed to the "thereness" of Zionism and other forms of Jewish territorial nationalism. It did not necessarily imply hostility to emigration, which was sometimes necessary, but it did imply a strong attachment to the land in which the Jews resided along with an even stronger objection to the idea that the Jews should establish an autonomous or sovereign territorial unit somewhere else in the world. The Jewish organizations I have mentioned loved to emphasize the Jews' deep roots in their "native land" and their outstanding contributions to its cultural and economic development (see fig. 4). On the eve of the Nazi revolution, German Jews were instructed by the Central-Verein to inform their gentile neighbors, "The graves of my forefathers are in German soil. I know that for more than a thousand years Jews have lived and worked in Germany. My mother tongue is German. I can speak no other language; Hebrew for me is a language of prayer, like Latin for the Catholics."[18] A Jewish member of the Hungarian parliament, presumably a serious man, boasted in 1920 that the Jews were present at the very creation of the first Hungarian state in the

Fig. 3: Blending In. Oscar Straus, appointed U.S. Secretary of Commerce and Labor in 1906—the first Jewish member of an American cabinet—embodies acculturation by perfectly blending into this group portrait of its members. (*Source:* Oscar S. Straus, *Under Four Administrations. From Cleveland to Taft. Recollections of Oscar S. Straus* [Boston and New York: Houghton Mifflin, 1922]. Photograph by Clinedinst.)

Fig. 4: *A Jewish Explorer.* This illustration sheds light on a little-known chapter in the glorious history of the Jewish contribution to German culture as an intrepid German explorer of the Mosaic persuasion presses forward in the African bush. (*Source: Wir deutschen Juden, 321–1932* [Berlin, 1932?].)

tenth century: "Among the 108 smaller Magyar tribes which were formed by the conquering Magyars, there were Jewish nations."[19]

"Hereness," in this case, at least, meant fervent patriotism. A much favored activity was the compilation of lists of Jews who had fought (and better still, fallen) in defense of their country. Simon Wolf discovered that no less than 7,243 Jewish soldiers had fought in the American Civil War (336 were killed); Wilhelm Filderman, a leader of Romanian Jewry, unearthed the names of 882 Jewish martyrs killed while serving in the Romanian army in World War I.[20] Some Polish Jews made a holy icon of the Jewish officer Bronisław Mansperl, a legionnaire who fought for Polish independence during World War I and fell in 1915, "mort pour la Pologne"[21] (see fig. 5).

The tragicomic hunt for Jewish patriots and martyrs was combined with a rather pathetic effort to claim a kind of spiritual or historical affinity between the Jews and their "hosts." Some Polish Jews liked to speak of the shared history of suffering and martydom that linked together the Polish and the Jewish experience.[22] In 1901 the president of the Central Conference of American Rabbis, a reform organization, proclaimed:

> [In America] the principles, that were first enunciated by Moses and endorsed by Israel at Sinai three thousand years ago, were again proclaimed to the world and ineradicably engrafted upon the then young and already vigorous nation.

Fig. 5: Mort pour la Pologne. The artist Artur Szyk depicts the heroic death of a Jewish officer of the Polish legion, Bronisław Mansperl, who was killed in the struggle for Polish independence during World War I. The Polish eagle spreads its wings in this icon of Jewish martyrdom for the Polish cause. (Artur Szyk, *Statut kaliski,* presented by the Polish government to Nahum Sokilow and to the Hebrew University of Jerusalem in 1933. The National Library, Jerusalem, Israel.)

Here was first sounded the historic bell that announced liberty to all in obedience to the words of scripture, "Proclaim liberty throughout the land, to all the inhabitants thereof" . . . this has ever been the tocsin of Israel and America.[23]

In the concert hall of the Young Men's Hebrew Association in New York City the names of George Washington and Thomas Jefferson are displayed alongside the names of Isaiah and Moses. And in 1954, when American Jewry celebrated three hundred years of prosperous and relatively peaceful residence in the country, a logo was divised that combined Jewish and American symbols into one splendid harmonious whole (see fig. 6).

Those who agreed with the views of the rabbi just cited as well as with the designers of the 1953 symbol of the affinity between Israel and America had little difficulty in selecting their favorite historical figures and their favorite historical epochs. They naturally preferred people who had succeeded in combining loyalty to Judaism with close cultural links to the great outside world. Such a man, so they thought, was the first-century philosopher Philo of Alexandria, after whom the Central-Verein named its publishing house, the Philo-Verlag.[24] Even better was the world-renowned Maimonides, a master of both Jewish and non-Jewish culture, a universal genius who wrote his philosophical works in Arabic, a man of intellect hailed as "the great reformer of those days" by Simon Wolf,[25] and the ideal Jew as portrayed by the American Jewish artist Jack Levine (see fig. 7). But the historical figure who most perfectly fit their needs was Moses Mendelssohn, the German-born eighteenth-century father of the Jewish enlightenment (Haskalah) movement. He was a hero to the small band of Jews preaching Russification and modernization in the czarist empire.[26] In America members of the Mendelssohn Society were among the founders of the Jewish fraternal association B'nai B'rith;[27] and for children the American Jewish Publication Society issued a moving biography of the young Moses Mendelssohn, portraying his heroic struggle to break out of the old, closed Jewish ghetto and to gain secular knowledge

Fig. 6: *Jewishness Is Americanness.* In this logo selected by the American Jewish Tercentenary Committee in 1953, a menorah, the most famous of all Jewish symbols, is topped by eight American (not Jewish) stars. No Hebrew letters were included, much to the disgust of the Jewish nationalists. (*Source: New York Herald Tribune.* March 18, 1953.)

Fig. 7: The Ideal Jew. In this American Jewish artist's depiction of Maimonides, the great medieval Spanish Jewish philosopher and physician, American Jewry's ideal type is represented. (Jack Levine, *Maimonides,* 1952. Courtesy of the Library of the Jewish Theological Seminary of America.)

while remaining loyal to Judaism.[28] It appears that there are no streets named after him in the Zionist and ultra-Orthodox Jewish city of Jerusalem (which does, by the way, contain a street named after the antisemitic Chopin), but he was the patron saint of a large number of modern Jewish organizations that preached acculturation, patriotism, and modernized Judaism.

For such organizations, obviously, the best of all periods of Jewish history was the modern one (post-1789 and pre-1933), which had witnessed, so they believed, the triumph of both enlightenment and emancipation. With regard to ancient Jewish history, when the Jews were an independent nation, the chosen heroes were neither kings nor warriors but rather the prophets, who combined, so it was thought, deep religiosity, a rejection of narrow parochialism, and a universalist outlook. According to an official publication of the leading French Jewish organization, the Alliance israélite universelle, "the grand idea of universal fraternity is the idea of the Jewish prophets."[29] In the 1899 American Reform Rabbi Henry Berkowitz put it this way: "It was the great discovery of the prophets of the eighth century that the God of Israel is the God of mankind, the God of Judea is the God of the universe. This great thought then for the first time broke through the bonds of nationality and announced the Universal religion."[30]

What of non-Jewish allies? The most likely candidates were individuals and organizations that saw in religious pluralism and toleration a highly desirable feature of modern society. This often (but not invariably) ruled out alliances with the political right and pointed to the desirability of linking up with the liberals and the left. Thus in Imperial Germany the Central-Verein looked to the small progressive parties for support.[31] In Romania, where pluralists were in short supply, the Union of Romanian Jews (Uniunea Evreilor Români, or UER), was linked with the Liberal party ("liberal," it might be said, only by Romanian standards). In America, where both political parties believed in pluralism, it was possible to be either pro-Democrat or pro-Republican. Another available option was to join forces with other like-minded minority groups. A fascinating example is the famous alliance between Jews and blacks (then called Negroes) in the United States, an alliance initiated and fostered by the Jews. Louis Marshall of the American Jewish Committee was a supporter of the National Association for the Advancement of Colored People (NAACP) and Jacob Schiff took a serious interest in black education in the South.[32] Jewish support for the black cause (by which was meant most emphatically the cause of integration, not the cause of black nationalism) may have derived in part from disinterested idealism, but it was also based on the perception that American Jews had a real interest in the successful integration of all minority groups into American society. If the blacks, low men on the American totem pole, could make it, so, surely, could the Jews.[33]

In their efforts to achieve their goals, Jewish organizations of the type I have discussed usually preferred low-profile tactics. Not for them the mass rallies and open confrontations favored by others. Rather, they preferred quiet intercession with the authorities. An excellent summary of this position is the statement by Cyrus Adler in a letter to Jacob Schiff:

> The Jewish people, my dear Mr. Schiff, are somewhat to blame, in my opinion, for the attacks [against them]. We have made a noise in the world of recent years in America and England and probably elsewhere, far out of proportion to our numbers. We have demonstrated and shouted and paraded and congressed and waved flags to an extent which was bound to focus upon the Jew the attention of the world and having got this attention, we could hardly expect that it would all be favorable. Now it may be that many persons think this was a wise policy. I do not.[34]

And neither did his colleague Louis Marshall, who back in 1908 had deplored "indiscreet, hot-headed and ill-considered oratory" that would inflict "untold injury upon the Jewish cause."[35]

Finally, the people and organizations belonging to this school of Jewish politics evinced great optimism regarding the future of the Jewish Diaspora. History, they believed, was on their side. Reason would triumph over medieval superstition. The artificial walls separating the Jews from the rest of mankind would, like the walls of ancient Jericho, come tumbling down. When they did, the aims of the Central-Verein, the Alliance, the American Jewish Committee, and their sister organizations would be fulfilled at last. The barriers to advancement would collapse, allowing fully acculturated, patriotic Jews to bring their great talents to bear in the advancement of society for the general good.

It is not easy to find a suitable name for this particular variety of modern Jewish politics. In the eyes of its many enemies, its adherents were "assimilationists," a pejorative word in the vocabulary of modern Jewish politics if there ever was one. But if assimilation means to disappear altogether and to achieve a new identity in place of the old one, it is a completely inappropriate term to describe this group. The Marshalls and Schiffs, the members of the Central-Verein and the Alliance as well as the supporters of Jewish Polonization and Russification did not wish the Jews to disappear. They were survivalists who would never have agreed with Herr Julius Klesmer, the presumably Jewish musician in George Eliot's "Jewish" novel, a man with "cosmopolitan ideas. He looks forward to a fusion of races."[36] Herr Klesmer was a true assimilationist. But the Marshalls and Schiffs rejected "fusion"—they devoutly wished for the preservation and revitilization of the Jews who, as heirs to a great culture, a great history, and above all a great religious tradition had much to offer mankind. The Jewish collective, in their eyes, was something like an important and endangered species in the eyes of a conservationist, a species whose preservation was essential not only to its own members but to the happiness and well-being of the planet.

This school was therefore acculturationist without being assimilationist. It is sometimes called liberal because it usually adhered to liberal Judaism, sought liberal allies, and was usually liberal in its social orientation, but I prefer the term *integrationist*.[37] What its adherents really wanted the Jews to do was to integrate into the majority society without being entirely swallowed up by it. *Integration* in the American context usually refers to the struggle for black civil rights and is not associated with any particular Jewish cause. But the Jews of this political camp and the blacks associated with the NAACP and other integrationist organizations wanted essentially the same thing—to be recognized as being of their countries of residence, not merely in them, and at the same time to retain a strong group identity and cohesiveness—in the black instance based chiefly on the unique historical and cultural traditions associated with their race, in the Jewish instance based chiefly on a unique religious tradition. It will not be the last time that this discussion mentions the interesting parallels between Jewish and black politics.

The Jews Are a Nation

Cyrus Adler, the quintessential integrationist, traveled to Paris in 1919 to attend the international peace conference. There he was not pleased to hear Ozjasz (Yehoshua) Thon, a Polish Zionist leader from Cracow, proclaim: "The Jews are a nation, not a religious sect, and we wish the world to know it."[38] All those who agree with Thon's definition of the Jews belong to the national school of modern Jewish politics. Of course, the definition of the Jews as a nation meant different things to different people. It certainly did not exclude the proposition that the Jews were also a religious group (this was, in fact, the view of Thon himself, who was both a Zionist and a leading rabbi). The point is that for most Jewish nationalists "nation" came first. And this above all—if the Jews were a modern nation, they obviously deserved to possess national rights, which could mean anything from full-fledged statehood to some sort of national autonomy in the lands of their dispersion.

A modern nation requires its own unique national language. This was an article of faith for virtually all nationalists, at least in Eastern Europe, from Albanians to Ukrainians. Therefore, members of the Jewish national political camp, although certainly not opposed to learning and speaking the "language (or languages) of the land"—Thon and his colleagues were fluent in Polish—insisted that the Jews cultivate a Jewish language, teach it to their children, and make it the chief cultural ornament of the organized Jewish community, the jewel in its national crown. To repeat, European Jewry was blessed with at least two languages of its very own, Yiddish and Hebrew (Ladino, or Judeo-Spanish, the language of the Sephardic Jews of the Balkans, was also very much alive in the interwar period, but it was spoken by a relatively small number of people). Jewish nationalists, united in opposing the integrationists' ideological commitment to acculturation, split into Hebraists and Yiddishists. Although it was possible to adopt a two-language policy and favor the cultivation of both Hebrew and Yiddish, fierce enmity between advocates of these two very distinct tongues was common. Extreme Yiddishists, as the passionate advocates of the cause of that often-despised "jargon" were called, sometimes declared Hebrew to be a dead language, the Jewish equivalent of Latin or Sanskrit. If, as was often the case, they were leftists, they were likely to attack the "holy language" (*loshn koydesh*) as a tool of reactionary, obscurantist clerics. The attitude of other Jewish nationalists to Yiddish was reminiscent of the attitude of the integrationists, of which we have already furnished an example. Arthur Koestler, at one time in the course of his ideological odyssey an enthusiastic Jewish nationalist of the Zionist type, had this to say about the language spoken by millions of Jews:

It had no fixed grammar and syntax, no fixed vocabulary, no logical precision. It was not spoken but sung, to the accompaniment of gestures. Nothing said in Yiddish seemed to be a flat statement. . . . I disliked this language, and the mentality which it reflected, from the first time I heard it, and I have never lost my aversion for it.[39]

At least Koestler admits that Yiddish is a language, a concession some of its enemies were unwilling to make. But he and many of his fellow Zionists were surely not pleased by the results of a Jewish cultural conference held in Czernowitz, the capital of Bukovina, in 1908, at which a group of Yiddishists including some celebrated Yiddish writers declared Yiddish to be a *national language* of the Jewish people.[40]

Where should the new, modern national culture be created? The "here versus there" question, like the language question, split the nationalists into two factions. Some believed that the Jewish Question could only be resolved by establishing an autonomous Jewish territory, perhaps even a fully independent state, "there," either in Palestine (the Zionists) or somewhere else (the territorialists). Zionists, the most prominent representatives of this school, were usually Hebraists. Others, known as autonomists, or Diaspora nationalists, believed that the Jewish nation would be able to thrive "here," in the lands of the Diaspora (more specifically the East European Diaspora) and that there was no need for it to be transferred to the Middle East, Alaska, Madagascar, or anywhere else. The social democratic party known as the Bund was probably the most important Jewish organization to take this position, which was shared by the smaller Folkspartey, whose adherents were known as Folkists. These and like-minded organizations were Yiddishist in their cultural orientation. The national advocates of "hereness" believed that their governments, of their own free will or under irresistible political pressure, would grant to the Jews not only equal rights as individuals but also recognition as a national minority with legally defined national minority rights, above all in the realm of culture—for example the right to establish Yiddish-language state-financed schools and other cultural institutions wherever large numbers of Yiddish-speaking, national-minded Jews resided. The teacher Hurvitz in *Three Cities,* Sholem Asch's novel of Jewish life in Eastern Europe, expresses their viewpoint in an argument with the Zionist Zachary Gavrilovich Mirkin: "There's no Jewish nation but this one," says Hurvitz, "and there's no asylum to which it can flee. Our forefathers had enough wandering through the world; we have to stay where we are and do battle for ourselves here!"[41]

In this case, too, as in the case of language, there was room for compromise. There were Jewish nationalists who believed that some Jews should devote themselves to the establishment of the Jewish national home in Palestine, whereas others would be able to maintain a modern Jewish national life in the Diaspora. A dual Hebrew–Yiddish polity could therefore be paralleled by a toleration for both "here" and for "there," a recognition of the legitimacy of the struggle for Jewish national rights in the

Diaspora and for a Jewish state. In many cases, however, hostility between Zionists and Diaspora nationalists ran very deep: The former were accused, among other crimes, of running away from the battle, of promoting a utopian scheme, and of abandoning the Jewish masses fated to remain in Europe; the latter were denounced as blind believers in the continued existence of the doomed Diaspora and as deniers of the deeply rooted historical links of the Jewish people with the Land of Israel.

Jewish integrationists, as we know, were fond of emphasizing their patriotism, their Americanism, Germandom, and so on. For the nationalists things were different. They certainly regarded themselves as loyal citizens of the countries they inhabited, although this was sometimes contested by antisemites, like those Poles who urged them to act on their beliefs with cries of "Żydzi do Palestyny" ("Jews to Palestine"). But they had no compelling reason either to boast of their patriotism or to claim a real or invented affinity to the host nation. The Jewish nation, like all nations, was by definition unique. On the other hand, other nations might well be admired, even emulated. Jewish nationalists, although agreeing with most Polish nationalists that the Jews were not, and could never become Poles, were happy enough to use Polish nationalism as a model and as an inspiration for their own activities. This sort of relationship between Jew and gentile was regarded as more "honorable" than the approach of the integrationists, interpreted in the nationalist camp as smacking of the dread disease of self-hatred, as being both fawning and self-denigrating.

Who were the Jewish heroes of the nationalists, and which eras in Jewish history did they most admire? For the secular Zionists the answers were fairly obvious. They naturally looked with favor on the very distant but not forgotten centuries of Jewish independence in Palestine, and among their heroes were those ancient Jewish warriors who had fought the good fight to conquer their country or to liberate it from foreign oppression—like Bar Kokhba, who led a valiant (but unsuccessful, even disastrous) revolt against Rome, and the more successful Judah Maccabee, who defeated the Hellenized Syrians. Some early Zionist organizations were named after these heroes, for example, the celebrated Bar Kokhba Society in Prague. Other exemplary figures were taken from the modern period of the Jewish national renaissance, and in particular from among the stalwarts of the Jewish rebirth in Palestine—like the members of the pre–World War I defense organization Ha-shomer (The Guard), after which the famous interwar Zionist youth movement Ha-shomer ha-tsair (The Young Guard) was named. The celebrated youth movement Betar (short for Brit Trumpeldor [the Trumpeldor Union]) derived its name both from the Zionist martyr Yosef Trumpeldor, killed in 1920 in defense of a Jewish settlement in northern Palestine, and from the ancient Palestinian Jewish town of Betar, which played a role in the heroic second-century revolt against Rome.[42]

Such heroes were not always suitable for the religious nationalists.

Trumpeldor, for example, was a left-winger, and so were the members of Ha-shomer. These people, presumably, did not worry about eating non-kosher food and traveling on the Sabbath. Much to be preferred were such sages as Rabbi Akiva, also a "Palestinian" and a martyr, killed by the Romans in the second century; several religious Zionist youth movements were named after him. As for the anti-Zionist, antiterritorialist and Yid-dishist Diaspora nationalists, they were not particularly enamored of the Bar Kokhbas of Jewish history, nor did they cherish the periods of Jewish territorial independence. The famous Jewish historian Simon Dubnow, a father of the ideology of Diaspora nationalism, emphasized in his writings the importance of postbiblical Diaspora Jewish autonomous life, when the Jews were organized in legally recognized communities and enjoyed a considerable degree of autonomy—for example, in premodern Poland, which featured Jewish "parliaments" known as the Council of the Four Lands (Va'ad arba aratsot in Hebrew) and the Council of the Land of Lithuania (Va'ad medinat lita).[43] If sixteenth- and seventeenth-century Polish Jewry, led by its most distinguished rabbis and laymen, had its own self-government, so twentieth-century Jewry, at least in Eastern Europe, might develop its own unique national culture within the framework and under the guidance of its still-existing but now secularized and democra-tized *kehiles* (*kehilot* in Hebrew, the government-sanctioned communal organizations).

Now to the question of alliances: Who were perceived to be the na-tionalists' potential supporters among the gentiles? Two interesting alli-ance strategies were particularly attractive to the nationalist school. One was to forge political ties with other oppressed or unhappy national minor-ities with the aim of coercing the host country into making the necessary concessions and granting them national rights. The Zionists of central and eastern Poland, advocates of both the Palestinian solution and national minority rights in the Diaspora, made this the centerpiece of their political strategy in the 1920s when they played a key role in establishing so-called minority blocs. Polish elections in 1922 and again in 1928 featured the participation of a special electoral list comprised of representatives of the Jewish, German, Ukrainian, and Belorussian nationalities, all of whom hoped to compel the stubborn Polish majority to alter what was seen to be an unyielding, chauvinistic policy on the national minorities question. In interwar Czechoslovakia the Jewish national party linked up with represen-tatives of the small Polish minority there. A variation on this theme was represented by the policy of some Russian Jewish nationalists in the imme-diate post–World War I period, who sought a political alliance with the Lithuanians, members of a "weak" nationality in the process of asserting its claims to independence; the latter promised, in return for Jewish support, to recognize Jewish national rights in a free and multinational Lithuanian state. One of Zionism's most celebrated interwar leaders, Vladimir (Zev) Jabotinsky, advocated an alliance between the Jews and the Ukrainians, whose national movement he admired and supported.[44] In contrast to the

American integrationists, whose alliance with blacks (and other local ethnic groups) was designed to promote Americanization and to prove that integration could work in their country, Jewish nationalists sought to work with other powerless or relatively weak nationalities in order to facilitate the establishment in Eastern Europe of a multinational environment in which all nationalities, including the Jews, would be free to develop their national culture. Of course, the Zionists did not believe that the Jewish Question could be solved merely by achieving national rights in the Diaspora—gaining such rights in countries like Poland and Lithuania was obviously very important, but it was perceived by many as a means to an end, namely, the establishment of some kind of "national home" in Palestine. The attainment of extraterritorial national rights in the Diaspora was desirable in that it would enable the Jews to sustain their process of nation building, the logical fulfillment of which was the creation of a Jewish state in Palestine. The attainment of this classic aim of Herzlean, mainstream Zionism suggested another potentially valuable ally, namely, right-wing or even overtly antisemitic forces. After all, antisemites were interested in getting rid of the Jews, and the Zionists were interested in the transfer of Jews to Palestine. There existed, at least in theory, a perfectly natural "community of interest" between them. It would be absurd to argue (as some have) that the Zionists wished to incite pogroms; but given the fact that there were pogroms, that antisemitism was such a powerful force, and that the Zionists believed that only a Jewish state could adequately protect the Jewish people from the dangers of antisemitism, why not come to terms with the antisemites so as to benefit Zionism? It made perfect sense, therefore, for Zionist leaders to negotiate with representatives of antisemitic regimes in Eastern Europe in the 1930s, hoping for support for Zionism's demand to facilitate mass Jewish *aliyah* (the Hebrew term for immigration to Palestine). If Theodor Herzl, the founder of political Zionism, met with the Russian minister of the interior in 1903, directly after the infamous Kishinev pogrom, so Jabotinsky negotiated with Polish politicians in the late 1930s, calling on their government to facilitate large-scale Jewish "evacuation" from Eastern Europe to the Holy Land. This was a very controversial policy and was furiously denounced by Jewish enemies of Zionism—even by many Zionists—as an attempt to make a pact with the devil. Jabotinsky was not very successful—the Poles liked and supported him, but could not open the gates of British Palestine. Nonetheless, one of Zionism's strengths was its ability to find allies among those East European politicians, antisemitic or not, who felt that there were simply too many Jews in their countries and did not know what to do with them as well as those West European and American politicians who feared an influx of East European Jews and much preferred them to travel east rather than west.

If the leaders of the American Jewish Committee and other like-minded organizations advocated low-profile political tactics, the nationalists, divided on so many issues, were united in their support, at least in principle, of open, strident, "proud," and fearless political behavior. They dismayed more cautious Jewish politicians with their demands for the convening of Jewish congresses and national councils. They rejected what they called the politics of *shtadlanut* (*shtadlones* in Yiddish), by which they meant the practice of dispatching Jewish "notables," hat in hand, to negoti-ate with gentile leaders behind closed doors, in smoke-filled rooms. They paraded, demonstrated, shouted, and boycotted—embracing what their enemies called the politics of noise (*tareram*)—and professed, despite their minority status, not to be concerned with what the gentiles might think or say or even do. True, they did not always practice what they preached. But they were the organizers of mass Jewish demonstrations and strikes held in Poland in the late 1930s to protest as loudly as possible against antisemitic violence. They were not afraid to ally themselves with other non-Polish minorities during election campaigns, despite the not unfounded fears of some Jews that such tactics constituted a dangerous anti-Polish provoca-tion, and they did establish self-defense groups of the type that Zangwill's unhappy hero, David Ben Amram, wanted to organize in his Polish shtetl in order to teach the pogromists (*pogromshchiki*) a lesson once and for all.

We already know that Jewish nationalists were split on the question of the ultimate viability of Jewish Diaspora life. Zionists, by definition, were deeply pessimistic—they believed, after all, that antisemitism was endemic to the Diaspora—although even the most fanatic members of this Jewish political persuasion did not really believe that all or even most Jews would, or could, go to Palestine. A Diaspora would therefore continue to exist, but it would be sustained by the existence of a Jewish homeland serving as a cultural and political model and as a magnet for its best and brightest sons and daughters. Without such a territorial center Jewish Diaspora life would inevitably succumb to antisemitism or to the blandishments of assimilation. The Diaspora nationalists would have none of this. They were not all principled enemies of Jewish emigration to Palestine (or to any other place), but they were great believers in the rosy future of Jewish–gentile peaceful coexistence within the framework of the multinational, democratic state. Many clung to this optimism, to this version of *doikeyt*, even in the dark days of the late 1930s. The Yiddish poet Yitshak Katz-enelson, in a famous poem written during the years of mass destruction, depicts the advocates of Diaspora nationalism, the Bundists, and the fol-lowers of the Agudah, as finally waking up to the futility of their position and crying, "To Palestine, let us save ourselves. . . ."[45] But even in those times optimism was not entirely extinguished. Consider the final statement of Shmuel Zygelbojm, the leader of the Jewish Bund, written shortly before his suicide in 1943: "My wish is that those few survivors of the millions of Polish Jews will live to see, along with the Polish population, the realization of the redemption in Poland, in a world of freedom and socialist justice. I believe that such a Poland will arise, and such a world will come."[46] There could be no greater faith than this in the viability of the Jewish Diaspora, a faith based on the belief that the Jewish and Polish nations, inhabiting the same country, could work and even fight together for a better future.

Jewish Jews

Jews who remained faithful to what became known during the nineteenth century as Orthodox Judaism (so long as all Jews were "Orthodox" there was no need for such a term), who spurned the "improvements" introduced by the reformers, and who did their utmost to keep the 613 commandments of Jewish law (while usually rejecting the almost identical number of compositions listed by Ludwig Köchel in his Mozart catalog) could be found in small numbers among the integrationists and in rather greater numbers among the nationalists (they created the special religious Zionist party called the Mizrachi). But a large and politically very potent section within the Orthodox community established its own unique political camp, a "third force" within Jewish politics, which merits a distinct place in our typology. The representative organization here was Agudat Israel (League of Israel), founded in 1912; it is usually referred to simply as the Agudah.

The reply of this Jewish political camp to the first question I asked (see p. 5) lay somewhere in between the responses of the integrationists and the nationalists. The idea that the Jews constituted a "nation" did not frighten the Orthodox, although the preferred term was the more vague Yiddish word *folk* (people: *am* in Hebrew). But they were a religious nation, or no nation at all, a religions-folk in the rather awkward formulation of an early Agudah proclamation dating from 1916.[47] "The Jewish nation," wrote an Agudah leader in 1921, "is the nation of God. . . ."[48] Another favorite formulation had it that the Jews were a *Toyre traye* people (a people loyal to the Torah).

It would be utterly wrong then, indeed sacrilege, to claim that the Jews were a modern nation similar to the Lithuanians or the Albanians or even the Poles. And it followed that to demand modern national rights (as opposed to traditional religious rights) for the Jews was also absurd, as we are told in the following verses from an Agudah youth organization publication in Poland:

> All the peoples of the world, using the sword
> base their existence on land and language.
> But our people dwells alone
> Only God's Torah gives it life.[49]

The notion of "dwelling alone" bore obvious implications for the cultural orientation of the "Torah true" or, as they also referred to themselves, Jewish Jews (*Yidishe yidn*) (see fig. 8). The famous Chinese wall separating Jew from gentile, which the integrationist beavers were so busy chewing away at, was regarded as a blessing. This being the case, one

Fig. 8: Jewish Jews. An artistic portrayal of potential supporters of Agudat Israel at work. (Max Weber, *The Talmudists,* 1934. Jewish Museum/Art Resource, New York City.)

would expect, at least in Eastern Europe, a devotion to Yiddish, not because this language was regarded as a basis of modern secular Jewish nationalism but because its preservation reduced the likelihood of close contacts with the non-Jewish world. In fact the Agudah of Eastern Europe "spoke Yiddish," although it never developed an ideology of Yiddishism. Hebrew, the "holy language," continued to be revered as the language of prayer and of religious learning, but the campaign to make Hebrew a spoken language in the European Diaspora, led as it was by secular nationalists who spread this doctrine in their secular Hebrew schools, was regarded with great suspicion.

There was nothing in the ideology of the Orthodox camp to prevent its adherents from learning and speaking non-Jewish languages. Such things were, after all, necessary. And in Central Europe, particularly in

Germany and Hungary, some Orthodox Jews affiliated with Agudah took a strong stand in favor of the adoption of the language and customs (up to a point) of the land, thereby combining antinational Orthodoxy with acculturation.[50] But the vast majority of Orthodox Jewry, and above all the vast majority of the most conservative section of Orthodox Jewry, the adherents of Hasidism, resided in Eastern Europe. There the Yiddish orientation remained dominant until the end of the interwar period, as did the distinct Jewish dress so despised by the integrationists.

The Land of Israel is, of course, of central importance to every religious Jew. Orthodox Jews of the Agudah variety believed that the Jews would eventually be gathered together in their promised land as the result of the direct intervention of divine forces in human history. It was commonly believed that the Jews would return to the Land of Israel in the Messianic age, whenever that might be. Meanwhile an Orthodox Jewish community was maintained in Palestine, consisting mostly of pious East European Jews who settled generally in the holy cities of Jerusalem, Hebron, Tiberias, and Safed. It is, therefore, not quite right to use the word *doikeyt* to define the attitude of Orthodox Jews to the question of "here versus there." Residence in the land of the gentiles was regarded as "exile" (in Hebrew *galut; goles* in Yiddish) no matter how long it might go on, and it was not the last stop on the Jewish journey, as the integrationists and Diaspora nationalists believed. Nonetheless, the partisans of Agudah were ideologically opposed to Zionist and territorialist schemes. A Jewish national home or state in Palestine/Eretz Yisrael—the work not of God and not of pious Jews but of heretical secularists, of Jewish nationalists who were enemies of Judaism—was regarded as a certain recipe for catastrophe, a revolt against God Himself, and a provocation in the eyes of the gentiles. Cooperation with secularists in the Zionist venture was rejected because nothing good could come of any project dominated by men and women who had jettisoned their glorious Jewish heritage and whose greatest dream was that the Jews establish merely another secular nation-state. True, some Orthodox Jews, organized in the Mizrachi party, favored such cooperation, arguing that in the long run they would succeed in taking over the Zionist movement from within, causing its secular leaders to "return" to Judaism and establishing a Jewish state based on Jewish Orthodox religious law. In the eyes of the Agudah such people were traitors to the Orthodox cause because they were legitimatizing secular Jewish nationalism in the eyes of the pious Jewish masses. In the 1930s, Agudah's principled opposition to the Zionist movement was somewhat muted by the rise of nazism and Polish antisemitism, which made the need for a Jewish refuge in a hostile world so pressing. However, the party never abandoned its ideological enmity to the idea of creating a basically secular Jewish national entity "there," especially "there" in the Holy Land. Most pious Jews would, God willing, remain where they were.

Orthodox Jewry had no difficulty in identifying its Jewish heroes—the great rabbinical authorities of all ages—and its villains—the heretics and, in

the modern period, the Jewish "enlighteners" (*maskilim*), Moses Mendelssohn and his spiritual heirs, whose desire to make Judaism conform to
"the spirit of the times" had opened a Pandora's box of troubles, including
the worst blow of all—conversion to Christianity. For the large Hasidic
community, the pillar of anti-Zionist Orthodox Jewry, whose origins were
in eighteenth-century Poland and Russia, the most important Jewish historical figures were obviously the Rebbes, the charismatic leaders of the
various Hasidic courts to be found all over Eastern Europe (but not in
Central or Western Europe, and not, in the interwar period at least, in the
United States). As for historic periods, what stands out is not so much the
choice of exemplary eras from the past but rather the unanimous feeling
that the modern age was one of extreme danger for the Jewish people. It
was only natural for the Orthodox Jews to look back with longing to the
"golden age" of European Jewry, before the emergence of Mendelssohn
and his ilk, when all were God-fearing and all were under the strict but
benevolent control of the natural leaders of the Jewish people, the rabbis.
Thus, in 1930 when the Polish organization of "Agudah girls" (Bnos
agudah) announced that it intended to fight against the "free spirit" of
modern times, it was also announcing its appreciation of previous, happier
periods in Jewish history.[51]

Unbending, rigid in its devotion to traditional Judaism, this school of
Jewish politics was pragmatic in its alliance systems. Potential gentile allies
included all those political forces that subscribed to religious pluralism
and were willing to allow traditional Jews to practice their religion in peace
and earn a living. As in the case of Zionism, but for different reasons, deals
with right-wingers were possible. In Poland the Agudah made a famous
political alliance with the regime of Marshal Józef Piłsudski—an authoritarian, but no great antisemite, and certainly tolerant of religious (if
not always national) diversity in his country—a leader who preferred the
Orthodox Jews to the socialists, who preached violent revolution, or the
militant national Jews, who wanted to transform Poland from a nation-
state into a "state of nationalities" with national autonomy for all. In Latvia
the Agudah established a good working relationship with the right-
wing regime that took power following the coup of 1934. The socialist left,
regarded correctly enough as antireligious, was usually ruled out
as a possible political partner. Agudah certainly much preferred the politically and culturally conservative environment of interwar Eastern Europe
(at least up until the mid-1930s) to the militantly atheistic and horribly
intolerant Communist regime set up in the Soviet Union, where it could
find no gentile allies at all and where its adherents were fiercely persecuted.

As might be expected the Orthodox camp in general was no champion
of high-profile political tactics. Its philosophy of life counseled against
needlessly provoking the gentiles. The Agudah was an unabashed advocate
of the policy of *shtadlanut,* the very policy so maligned in "proud" nationa-
ist circles. One of its newspapers wrote in 1920 that "the entire Zionist

tareram [noise] over 'struggle,' over the obligation and necessity to struggle, consists only of words and not deeds."[52]

On this issue the Agudah was in basic agreement with the leaders of the American Jewish Committee. In 1936 when the Polish Sejm (parliament) debated legislation to prohibit ritual slaughter of animals (*shkhite*), a matter of life and death for the Orthodox community, a leading rabbinic authority wrote that "it would be fitting to move heaven and earth on this question, but the protest must come from them [presumably Jews abroad] and not from us, for various reasons. . . ."[53] When things became truly intolerable the preferred rabbinic tactic was to call for a public day of fasting—an extreme measure, to be sure, but nonetheless a quiet, passive one.

The Agudah-type Orthodox were natural optimists, at least in the long run. The Messiah would come, and in the meantime the Jews, despite their suffering, would persevere and prevail. In Poland it was noted that the very name Poland (*Polin* in Hebrew) demonstrated that the Jewish connection with this land was divinely inspired and likely to endure (*po* in Hebrew means here; *lin* derives from the verb to dwell).[54] Orthodox optimism, deriving from religious faith, not from the integrationists' faith in enlightenment and liberalism, thus stood in opposition to the fundamental Zionist pessimism with regard to the future of the Jewish Diaspora.

Halfway Houses

The answers to my seven questions were sometimes far from unambiguous. In one particular case, which demands our special attention, they were actually contradictory. When confronted with the "What are the Jews?" issue, it was possible to answer: In the future the Jews shall not be a nation, but at present they are. The Jews of the present might be mostly Yiddish-speaking and the possessors of a distinctive national consciousness; the Jews of the future would most likely acculturate and perhaps even assimilate. It followed that the kinds of organizations they might need *now* would become, in the fullness of time, superfluous: "A better world [was coming] . . . where there will be neither nations, classes, nor religions, but only one united, advancing humanity."[55]

This was a position that even some full-fledged Jewish nationalists might take—Bundists, even Zionist socialists, might believe and hope that in the (probably distant) future nations would merge into one glorious united humanity. But the most notable adherents of this position were the leaders of the "Jewish sections" of various socialist and Communist parties and fronts, semiautonomous organizations that catered to unacculturated, working-class people but at the same time tended to preach the virtues of, or at least accepted the inevitability of, eventual acculturation. It was well expressed by Semen Dimanshtain, one of the leaders of the Jewish section (*Yevsektsiia*) of the Communist party of Soviet Russia), in 1918:

As internationalists, we do not set any special national tasks for ourselves . . . insofar as we speak a different language, we are obligated to make
an effort to have the Jewish masses know their own language, satisfy their
needs in their language. . . . We are not, however, fanatics of the Yiddish
language. There is no "holy Yiddish" for us. . . . It is entirely possible that in
the near future the richer languages of the stronger and more highly developed
peoples will push aside the Yiddish language in every country. We Communists will shed no tears over this, nor will we do anything to obstruct this
development.[56]

Dimanshtain was obviously no Jewish nationalist. Moreover, since he
and his fellow left-wing Jewish section activists, whether socialists or Communists, were total secularists, they could not, in contrast to the integrationists, combine a belief in the necessity for acculturation with a concep-
tion of a Jewish future as a religious sect with a unique, even holy mission.
Their long-term attitude may therefore be considered not merely acculturationist but actually assimilationist. With the disappearance of Yiddish and
other Jewish cultural and religious trappings such as their belief in their
"chosenness" and in the Torah as well as their love, for example, of gefilte
fish, the Jews as a coherent group would disappear, and so would their
special language sections in the various cosmopolitan Socialist and Communist parties. These organizations may therefore be regarded as halfway
houses, positioned between the ultimately doomed ghetto and a future of
universal brotherhood. But temporary though they might have been, they
did regard themselves as the authentic representatives and defenders of the
proletarian, Yiddish-speaking Jewish nation of the present, obliged to be
responsive to its special political and cultural needs. Thus, leaders of the
Yevsektsiia established Yiddish socialist schools for Jewish children,
schools that would presumably be closed down when Yiddish would give
way to Russian, or possibly to Esperanto.

Left, Right, and Center

The answers to our seven questions have yielded three distinct Jewish
political camps—the integrationists, the nationalists, and the Orthodox—
to which must be added the Jewish sections, positioned somewhere between the first two of these factions. Let me now complement this typology by placing the various Jewish political organizations on the left–right
ideological spectrum, just as one might do in the case of French or Lithuanian politics.

The Jewish left consisted of all specifically Jewish organizations that
believed the solution to the Jewish Question must include a thoroughgo-
ing restructuring of Jewish (and perhaps also general) society and the
establishment of a new social order based on justice and the absence of
exploitation. It embraced an almost infinite variety of views, ranging from
hard core bolshevism (the Yevsektsiia, the Jewish bureau of the American

Communist party) through more moderate Marxist social democracy (the Bund and some varieties of the socialist Zionist Poale Zion) to anti-Marxist "reformism" of one kind or another (for example, the labor Zionist Hitahadut party). All claimed to represent a social element variously called the Jewish "proletariat" (whose very existence was denied by some people—most Jewish workers were tailors and shoemakers, not miners or automobile makers) or the Jewish "laboring masses" (whoever they might be) (see fig. 9). All believed that contemporary Jewish society was dominated by the Jewish "bourgeoisie," an element also difficult to define but one that had to be gotten rid of via class warfare or at least weakened in some way. This is the way the leader of the Jewish needle workers' union in a Polish town put it in a novel by Michal Bursztyn: "Our enemies are the master artisans. For us they are the representatives of capitalism in Ployne. They and, of course, . . . the bourgeoisie, whose little sons and daughters fool around, for lack of anything better to do, in the Ha-tikva society."[57]

The Jewish left was divided not only by different interpretations of the essence of socialism but by most of the "Jewish" issues that we have already discussed. Thus it included within its ranks numerous socialist Zionist organizations—all of which wished to create a Jewish socialist or "labor"

Fig. 9: The Jewish Working Class in America. A portrayal by an American pro-Communist artist of the Jewish laboring masses—potential socialists or Communists. (William Gropper, *Biographical Cartoon*, 1925–26. Photograph by Geoffrey Clements. Avery Architectural and Fine Arts Library, Columbia University in the City of New York.)

society on the national soil of Palestine—as well as the fiercely anti-Zionist Bund—a proponent of Diaspora nationalism that wished to transform Poland and the other countries where it was active into socialist societies in which the national cultural rights of all minorities would be guaranteed by law. It also included the socialist-dominated Jewish (or mostly Jewish) trade unions in America and in Eastern Europe—some pro-Bundist, some pro-Zionist, some neither one nor the other—and the various Jewish sections of general socialist and Communist organizations. Nor should we forget the existence of Orthodox proletarian organizations, identified with either the Mizrachi or the Agudah on Jewish issues but leftist in their social orientation; in some cases these organizations felt a strong if uneasy kinship with the secular Jewish left.[58]

The cultural orientation of the Jewish left was primarily pro-Yiddish; this was, after all, the language of the Jewish masses it claimed to represent, and it was closely associated with Yiddish cultural activities. But the strong socialist Zionist component, with only a few exceptions, rejected Yiddishism and labored to create a new Hebrew-speaking Jewish working class in Palestine. In practice many socialist Zionist parties adopted a complicated two-language policy: Yiddish for the Jewish working class of the present East European and American Diaspora, Hebrew for the Jewish working-class-in-the-making in Palestine.

Divided in these highly significant ways, the Jewish left found common ground in its search for a usuable Jewish past. If the integrationists admired the prophets for their universalism and lofty moral standards, so did the socialists, who also regarded them as pioneers in the struggle for social justice, as protosocialists (see fig. 10). Moses the lawgiver was much admired. Barukh Charney Vladeck, a Bundist in the old country and a pillar of the Jewish left in America, in 1920 wrote a play called *Moses Our Teacher* in which the lawgiver is depicted as a heroic fighter against slavery.[59] In general Jewish leftists were proud to point out that the Hebrew Bible, far more than the writings of the other ancient nations, was a source of progressive, even revolutionary, social thought. Thus the scholar Isaac Mendelsohn (who was also a Jewish Communist) claimed in his treatise on slavery in the ancient world that "the first man in the Ancient Near East who raised his voice in a sweeping condemnation of slavery as a cruel and inhuman institution, irrespective of nationality and race, was the philosopher Job."[60] The Jewish artist and left-winger Ben Shahn invoked a famous, if rather obscure, verse from Leviticus in his poster calling for racial equality and cooperation (see fig. 11). And Raphael Soyer cited the prophet Amos as proof of his socialist conviction that all men are created equal (see fig. 12).

Suitable post–old Testament exemplars for the modern Jewish left were more difficult to unearth. Great rabbis would not do, and, unfortunately, there were no Jewish leaders of specifically Jewish social revolutions at hand—no Jewish equivalents to the Russian peasant leaders Stenka Razin or Yemelyan Pugachev. Jesus was a possibility—"my own Reb Yeshua," as the socialist Jewish writer Alfred Kazin calls him—but this link with the founder of Christianity was, for atheistic Jewish socialists, a bit problematic.[61] It was, however, possible to identify with the exploited Jewish masses, sorely oppressed by the Jewish rich—most dramatically during the reign of Nicholas I in Russia, when lower-class Jewish children were rounded up by the "kidnappers" of the Jewish community and drafted into the army (where they were often converted to Christianity and lost forever to the Jewish community). And popular religious movements could also be enlisted, above all early Hasidism, interpreted by some Jewish Marxists as a revolutionary movement directed against the oppressive establishment.[62] Of course, the modern era had provided a large number

Fig. 10: The Prophet as Socialist? This modern Isaiah, as rendered by an American Jewish artist, has the look of a left-wing agitator. (Leonard Baskin, *Isaiah,* 1976.)

לא תעמד על-דם רעך

"THOU SHALT NOT STAND iDLY BY..."

Fig. 11: The Bible Preaches Equality. The Torah is mobilized in support of the ideal of universal brotherhood. (Ben Shahn, *Thou Shalt Not Stand Idly By,* 1965. Philadephia Museum of Art. Given by the Lawyers Constitutional Defense Committee of the American Civil Liberties Union. Estate of Ben Shahn/VAGA, New York, 1992.)

of left-wing heroes and martyrs of Jewish origin—starting with Karl Marx himself, whose blatant and inconvenient antisemitism was ignored or explained away. Their portraits decorated the meeting halls and party offices of Bundists, socialist Zionists, and Jewish Communists.

Thus the Jewish left—whether fully committed to Jewish nationalism or not, whether Zionist or anti-Zionist, whether Yiddishist or Hebraist— established a historical pedigree that enabled its predominantly secular, anti- or nonreligious leaders to claim that modern socialism was not foreign to the Jewish tradition. Its many factions were also agreed on the tremendous importance of linking up with the non-Jewish left in the name of international proletarian solidarity, of the need "to live in brotherhood with their neighbors and to fight shoulder to shoulder with them for a better world. . . ."[63] Alliance building for this Jewish political camp was invested with great importance because the solidarity of Jewish and non-Jewish workers was seen not as a matter of temporary expediency but rather as the supreme test of the ideal of internationalism. It would demonstrate that non-Jews could be brothers, comrades-in-arms, partners in building a new world. This was an especially important matter for the Bund, since its version of the Jewish future was dependent to a very great extent on close cooperation between Jewish and non-Jewish socialists.

The Jewish right is more difficult to define than the Jewish left. If Jewish political parties of the left were proud to declare their ideological sympathy with the general European left, their opponents were usually unwilling to admit any ideological sympathy with the general European right, which in the interwar period was often synonymous with fascism (and, of course, antisemitism). Nonetheless, if we define the right as con-

Fig. 12: *Scriptural Support for the NAACP.* The prophet Amos's message as interpreted by the artist, who includes the following Hebrew text in his picture which can be translated as, "Are you not as the children of the Ethiopians to me, O children of Israel?" (Raphael Soyer, *Amos on Racial Equality,* 1960s? Collection of Rebecca S. Beagle, Oakland, California. Photograph by Lisa Rubens.)

stituting a political camp fiercely opposed to socialism and conservative in its view of how Jewish society should be organized, a Jewish right in the interwar period is definitely discernible. Its main unifying characteristic was its single-minded emphasis on the absolute need for Jewish unity and consequently its deep hostility to all political movements that preached the idea of class war or even class division within the Jewish world. One of the favorite terms in the political vocabulary of the secular right was *monism* (*had-nes* in Hebrew; one flag), implying the supremacy of national unity, a traditional Jewish value, over social division. The Jewish left was attacked for its importing into the Jewish world of dangerous "foreign" ideas that falsely set Jew against Jew and therefore played into the hands of the common enemy, the antisemite.[64]

If the holy principle of Jewish unity was a hallmark (though by no means a monopoly) of the entire Jewish right, on other matters, like the left, it was deeply divided. One of its chief components was Agudat Israel, which was anti-Zionist and antinationalist, at least in the modern sense of the term *nationalist*. This movement's social as well as its religious outlook was very conservative, even reactionary; it held that traditional Jewish elites should continue to dominate the Jewish community and represent it to the gentile community—on this matter its labor organization, Poalei Agudat Israel (workers of Agudat Israel) was not always in agreement with its parent organization.[65] If the left believed that Jewish society was "sick"—class-ridden, priest-ridden, and in urgent need of drastic reform or even revolution—Agudah stood firmly for the domination of the learned and the rich. It was neither by temperament nor by doctrine wedded to democracy, a point made in dramatic fashion by the protagonist of a novel on orthodox life who castigates the secular Zionists as "these enemies of Torah, these heathen-Jews, these swine that peddle away our tremendous spiritual heritage in return for—Democracy!"[66]

Such were not necessarily the views of the major secular component of the Jewish right—the Zionist revisionist movement, established in the mid-1920s and the last of the major Jewish political forces to appear on the stage. It vehemently opposed class struggle on the Jewish street, but despite its socialist enemies' insistence that it possessed fascist characteristics, its mainstream never rejected the democratic way of doing politics. Whereas Agudah was the leading Jewish representative of the traditional, conservative right, the revisionists were dynamic, radical, and militant. As Zionists they were opposed to the status quo in the *galut,* in absolute opposition to the Agudah. Within the Zionist movement, the revisionists were branded as representatives of the right not only because of their hatred of socialism but also because of their emphasis on the need to establish in Palestine a Jewish state (as opposed to something less than that, a "homeland" perhaps) within large, maximalist, "historical" frontiers as well as their insistence on the need for Jewish military action to conquer Palestine. Their youth movement, Betar, was famous (or infamous, as the case may be) for its semimilitary character. Moreover, the revisionists, under the leadership of Jabotinsky, not only wished to make alliances with the East European moderate right but were open admirers of the variety of East European integral nationalism represented by Marshal Piłsudski, the founder of the Polish legionnary movement, the man who, so his admirers believed, had won Polish independence—by means of a military, not a social uprising.[67] The fact that the Jewish right was composed of two such distinct, indeed, mutually hostile elements, made a united front extremely unlikely, just as it was virtually impossible to create a united front of Jewish socialist organizations. It is only in our day, in Israel, that such a front has come into being, featuring an alliance between the Likud party, heir to Polish revisionism, and various Orthodox, non-Zionist factions, including the Israeli version of Agudat Israel.

What was niether the Jewish left nor the Jewish right must by default go under the name of the Jewish center. Those Zionists who were neither socialist nor revisionist sometimes went under the rather strange name of General Zionists (Tsiyonim klaliim in Hebrew). Many of the most celebrated Diaspora Zionist leaders of the interwar period—for example, Chaim Weizmann, Nahum Sokolow, and Louis Brandeis—were members of this group. The Orthodox Zionists, the Mizrachi, also probably belong to the Jewish center—because they were more modern and more progressive in most things than was the Agudah—as do the major integrationist organizations discussed earlier. Also belonging to the center were the Folkists, Diaspora nationalists, but not socialists. The right word for this camp was moderation—a moderation in social views and in religious practice that distinguished them from the more ideological and often more fanatic socialists, nationalists, and religionists of the left and right.

In conclusion, several words of caution are in order. In politics, as in life, theory is one thing, reality another. Political typologies are fun to play with, even helpful (I hope) in trying to understand the subject, but they do not always correspond to real life. I have already said that the answers to the questions I have posed in order to arrive at a typology were sometimes ambiguous. The "frontiers" separating the various camps were not always clearly defined—for example, in the case of the various Jewish socialist "sections" and the members of such Jewish socialist organizations as the Bund. An important complicating factor was the international status of the Jewish people. Since the Jews' situation differed greatly from one country to another, it made perfect sense, and was quite common, for some Jewish organizations to claim that in one country (the United States, for example) the Jews constitute a religious group, but in another country (for example, Poland) the Jews may well be a nation and therefore should have national rights. Jewish socialists in America might well sympathize with the moderate national program of the Polish Bund while believing that this program was not appropriate in the New World, where the Jews evidently did not constitute a national minority in the East European sense of the word. This led to the phenomenon of fellow-traveling, meaning that many Jewish organizations, while clinging to their own ideological views, nonetheless, found it possible to support other Jewish organizations with quite different, even diametrically opposed, positions. For example, American integrationists were often Zionist fellow travelers. They did not convert to the doctrine of Jewish nationalism, but they reasoned that what was good for the fortunate Jews of the "golden land" might not be good for the oppressed Jews of benighted Eastern Europe.

To complicate things further, dramatic events impinging on the Jewish world demanded agonizing reappraisals and changed old attitudes. Jewish organizations in Germany were not likely to preach in 1935 what they had preached in the more hopeful days of, say, 1925 or even 1932.

In short, my typology serves only as a general guide, a kind of scorecard to help identify the main players. The next chapter will discuss the impact of different environments on these "players" and on the different camps of Jewish politics; it will move us away from this academic exercise toward a more realistic, multidimensional picture of interwar Jewish politics.

2

Geography

Having named the main varieties of modern Jewish politics, my next task is to give them a local habitation, that is, to make the connection between politics and geography. Jewish politics was international in character. How was it influenced by the very different surroundings in which it operated? Which environments, both general and Jewish, were most supportive of which sorts of Jewish politics? Where were the ideal environments, the core areas of the major Jewish political camps located? How did the character of a given Jewish political orientation differ from one country to another? Where, for example, is one most likely to find a strong Jewish integrationist movement? What was the core area of Jewish nationalism, of Orthodoxy, of the Jewish left? Why was Polish Zionism so different from American Zionism?

Ideal Environments

According to a famous Yiddish proverb, "As the Christians go, so go the Jews" ("Vy es kristlt zikh, azoy yidlt zikh"). Applying this excellent example of folk wisdom, one should expect that the ideal environment for modern Jewish nationalism would be a region in which nationalism in general was the dominant political force, assuming that this particular type of nationalism was so defined as to exclude the Jews rather than to include them. I have in mind, for example, Poland of the interwar period, a country whose politics was dominated by the kind of nationalism that excluded Jews from "Polishdom," and not Hungary of the pre–World War I period, a time when mainstream Hungarian nationalism was prepared—albeit with some reservations—to embrace the Jews as potential members in good standing of the Magyar nation. All-powerful and exclusivist (therefore usually antisemitic) nationalism is a key ingredient in the ideal environment for Jewish nationalism because it rebuffed individual Jews seeking to merge into the dominant nationality (for example, the Polish nationality in Poland) while serving as a significant model and inspiration for autonomous national Jewish politics. Indeed, it stands to reason that antisemitism in general—whether or not it is linked to nationalism—is a "good thing" for Jewish nationalism, for one thing because it disabuses Jews of the hope that integrationist solutions are possible, for another because it often precludes Jewish economic progress and upward social mobility. When antisemitism is combined with some terrible cataclysm (war, revolution, a combination of the two), Jewish nationalism may do particularly well. Indeed, in some areas of Eastern Europe the rapid rise of Jewish nationalism is at least in part to be explained by the enormous impact of World War I, which led to economic and political collapse, a dramatic rise in nationalist sentiments among the smaller nations of the region, and a sharp decline in Jewish–gentile relations.

It is also more likely that Jewish nationalism will flourish in binational (or multinational) regions inhabited by two or more well-defined national groups whose national status is officially (or informally) recognized by the state rather than in countries that are (or claim to be) mononational and refuse to grant legitimacy to the existence of full-fledged national, as opposed to religious or even ethnic, minorities. Moreover, the national school of Jewish politics is likely to do well in those environments in which the nationalities among whom the Jews live are culturally or socially "unattractive." Peasant or largely peasant nations with national cultures believed by everyone except themselves to be backward or even virtually nonexistent were not likely to tempt Jews to embark on the course of acculturation or integration (at least not at first), even if they attained political power. By the late nineteenth century many Jews wished to transform themselves into Russians and Poles, but hardly any wished to be Belorussians, Lithuanians, Latvians, or Ukrainians, even if they knew that such nations existed.

The cause of Jewish nationalism is also likely to receive a significant boost when a long historical process of Jewish acculturation and integration is brought to a sudden and unexpected halt as the result of some kind of political upheaval—for example, by the rise to political power of previously subjugated nations owing to the collapse of long-standing, once-formidable political–cultural entities. This actually happened after World War I, when the Russian and Austro-Hungarian empires collapsed and a number of totally new states were established. Such an event was, in certain regions, of tremendous benefit to Jewish nationalism.

Finally, I would expect that socially and economically more backward environments have the potential to be conducive to Jewish nationalism because in such places there is likely to be less contact between Jews and non-Jews, less Jewish upward social mobility, no well-established non-

Jewish middle class into which the Jews might aspire to integrate. A backward social structure dominated by remnants of the old aristocracy, the established church, and the peasantry is not one that will facilitate Jewish integration. One has only to compare modern Jewish history in the neighboring lands of Poland, where there was comparatively little Jewish integration, and Germany, where integration was thought by some to be a great success, to be convinced that this is the case.

Now for the Jewish environment. I would argue that modern Jewish nationalism is likely to be especially appealing to Jews who are rooted in traditional cultural and religious life but at the same time are beginning, under the influence of enlightenment ideas, to distance themselves, at least spiritually, from the ghetto. Such a process might, of course, lead not only to rapid acculturation but even to integration; but if this is rendered difficult or ruled out altogether by the general environment (owing to anti-semitism, economic backwardness, or the absence of an "attractive" nation into which to acculturate), many may opt for a Jewish national "solution." Such a solution is particularly attractive because it makes possible an identity both modern and Jewish—thus, the appeal of Thon's statement, "The Jews are a [modern] nation," meaning a community no longer identical with the Orthodox ghetto but still a distinct and well-defined, proud group whose self-identity is not a function of the attitude of the outside world, of the *goyim*.

Where, exactly, is the core area of modern Jewish nationalism to be located? Obviously, in Eastern Europe, home to the largest Jewish communities on the Continent, the most backward part of the Continent and the most antisemitic, a multinational region par excellence whose politics were dominated by competing nationalisms, the place where Jews were far more separated from their non-Jewish neighbors—culturally, demographically, and in every other way—than in the West. But "Eastern Europe" is a rather vague phrase, and a process of elimination may be employed in order to arrive at a more precise geographic definition. The interwar Soviet Union, where nearly three million Jews resided, should have been an excellent environment for the flourishing of Jewish nationalism. It was, after all, in czarist Russia where modern Jewish nationalism and many modern Jewish national movements were invented. But Soviet communism and Jewish nationalism were unable to coexist. During the 1920s the new regime systematically outlawed all prewar Jewish national organizations. True, it was willing to countenance Jewish cultural activities in Yiddish and even promoted a Jewish homeland of sorts, a kind of Soviet Palestine, in far off Birobidzhan. But virtually the only Jewish organizations it was prepared to sanction were firmly under the control of the Communist party and its "Jewish sections." And even these sections were abolished in 1930. Jewish nationalism of both the Zionist-Hebraic and autonomist, Bundist-Yiddish varieties came to be strictly forbidden.

One must, therefore, turn to anti-Communist Eastern Europe, or East Central Europe, as it is sometimes called. Here political and cultural pluralism if not always Western-style democracy prevailed, despite a sharp turn in the 1930s to the authoritarian political right in most of the countries of the region. Jewish nationalism did not fare especially well in the westernmost outposts of this area—Hungary and Czechoslovakia. The Hungarian case, of considerable interest, will be considered later. Czechoslovakia was certainly a reasonably favorable region for Jewish nationalism. It was officially a multinational state in which the Jewish nationality enjoyed official recognition. Its Jewish inhabitants, prewar subjects of the Austro-Hungarian Empire and traditionally strongly attracted to German culture (in the Czech lands) and Hungarian culture (in Slovakia and Subcarpathian Rus'), suddenly found themselves living in a new political–cultural reality dominated by the previously subservient and oppressed Czechs and Slovaks. But Czech acculturation had made deep inroads into the basically middle-class Jewish society of Bohemia and Moravia even before World War I, and the relative absence of virulent antisemitism in this part of the world, where liberalism and democracy reigned until 1938, also played a role in making Jewish nationalism in Czechoslovakia a significant but not very impressive force.[1]

This leaves us with the Balkans (Yugoslavia, Bulgaria, Romania), the Baltic states (Lithuania, Latvia, Estonia), and, of course, Poland. From a simple numerical standpoint, by far the most important Jewish centers here were in Poland (over 3 million Jews, some 10 percent of the total population) and Romania (around 800,000 Jews if we are to believe Romanian statistics). The other countries were home to very small Jewish populations—about 150,000 in Lithuania (where the Jews constituted 7 percent of the total population), 100,000 in Latvia, no more than a few thousand in tiny Estonia.

If one keeps in mind the factors enumerated in my discussion of what constitutes an "ideal environment" for Jewish nationalism, it will be obvious that the Baltic region represented precisely such an environment. Both Lithuania and Latvia were new political creations (the former had been an independent state long ago, in the Middle Ages, before being swallowed up by Poland; the latter had been politically and culturally dominated for nearly a thousand years by an endless succession of Germans, Swedes, Poles, and Russians). Their politics was dominated by nationalism. Both the Lithuanians and the Latvians presided over multinational populations and granted a degree of cultural autonomy to their officially recognized national minorities. Antisemitism was certainly present, though it was not, by East European standards, too oppressive. Above all, the idea of a Jew actually becoming a Latvian or a Lithuanian *by nationality,* that is, a Latvian or Lithuanian "of the Mosaic persuasion," was exceedingly farfetched, almost comic. The new Lithuanian and Latvian ruling cultures were both utterly foreign to, and looked down on by, the Jewish population, whose educated elite had, in the old czarist Russian days, gravitated to either Russian or German culture (the latter was historically important in mostly Protestant Latvia). The stormy events of 1917–

18, which led to the wholly unexpected, almost undreamed independence of these two countries from Russian rule, created a cultural vacuum for the Jews—the old cultural orientations were no longer acceptable, whereas the new ones were as yet unknown and clearly undesirable. Consider the plight of Moyshe Halpern, an imaginary but representative Jew, born, say, in Kaunas (Kovno in Russian) in 1895. The son of well-to-do, somewhat enlightened Yiddish-speaking parents, he attended Russian-language schools and came to identify strongly with the politically dominant Russian culture. The establishment of an independent Lithuanian state in 1918 (itself a certain indication of the tremendous appeal of nationalism) found him totally ignorant of the new reigning language and national culture— and contemptuous of it as well: Where were the Lithuanian Pushkins and Tolstoys? With Russian now regarded as the language of the vanquished but still-dangerous enemy and Lithuanian a totally foreign language, might not Moyshe's process of Russification be brought to an end, to be replaced not by Lithuanian acculturation but by a new appreciation for, and a new readiness to, embrace a modern Jewish national identity? If it was no longer expedient for Halpern to identify with Russian culture and if he could not imagine himself to be a Lithuanian, what could he do? It was precisely the logic of this situation that led some Zionist leaders to favor with great enthusiasm the establishment of an independent Lithuanian state where, so they correctly predicted, there would be no pressure to acculturate, let alone assimilate, and every chance for their political ideology to capture the hearts and minds of the Jewish population.

The character of the Jewish Baltic communities, shaped by centuries of Polish and Russian rule, was also conducive to the flourishing of Jewish nationalism. These were to a large extent working-class and lower-middle-class Jewries, mostly Yiddish-speaking, rooted in Orthodox Judaism but strongly affected by the Jewish enlightenment movement (historically strong in the Lithuanian lands). Most were not adherents of Hasidism, the most conservative and closed of Jewish Orthodox sects. Such communities could be expected to provide support for Jewish nationalism in all its varieties.

In fact the connection between modern Jewish nationalism and the region of Lithuania (encompassing those areas that were part of "historical Lithuania," or to be more precise "Lithuania-Belorussia"—but not included in the interwar independent state) antedated World War I (see fig. 13). The Lithuanian lands in the nineteenth century acted as a kind of buffer zone between Polish culture, with its capital in Warsaw, and Russian culture emanating from St. Petersburg and Moscow. The inhabitants were mostly non-Russians and non-Poles. A "modern" Jew in Warsaw or Łódź, the heartland of ethnic Poland, might aspire to true integration into the Polish nation, and a Jew in some southern Russian city, say Odessa, might hope to integrate into the Russian nation. However the Jews of Kovno and Vilna lived neither in ethnic Poland nor in ethnic Russia but rather in a classic multinational region dominated by "weak" nationalities

Fig. 13: *The Russian Empire Province-by-Province.* The Lithuanian–Belorussian lands comprise the provinces of Kovno, Grodno, Vilna, Vitebsk, Minsk, and Mogilev. (Map by Carta, Jerusalem, Israel.)

and far from the Polish and Russian capitals. Our imaginary Moyshe Halpern may have been Russified, but he almost certainly did not regard himself as a Russian by nationality and was not so regarded by the Russians themselves.

The Jewish inhabitants of this area were known as Litvaks or Lithuanians (*Litvakes* in Yiddish); in the Jewish world of Eastern Europe these Litvaks were celebrated—or damned—for their well-known tendencies toward modernization, secularization, radicalism, and the logical extension of all this, namely, modern nationalism. The Litvak as an agent of change is a staple of Jewish fiction and memoirs. Israel Joshua Singer (Isaac Bashevis Singer's brother) recalls in his memoirs of pre–World War I Jewish life how he, a Polish Jew visiting in Warsaw, encountered "Lithuanian Jews wearing modern dress that was strange to me. . . ."[2] It was from a Jew who hailed from Grodno, an important Lithuanian town, that Singer "learned about Zionism, Socialism, about strikes and revolutions, about the assassination of policemen, officers, generals and even emperors."[3] And in his novel of Jewish life in Łódź Singer tells us of the famous "invasion" of Lithuanian Jews into that great metropolis in the Polish heartland that began in the 1890s. The "invaders," we are told, brought with them "their secular Hebrew and general spirit of enlightenment."[4]

If individual Lithuanian Jews brought with them, wherever they traveled, the idea that the Jews constituted a modern nation, Jews who traveled to Lithuania from other regions in the Russian Empire were well aware of the fact that they were entering the very heartland of modern Jewish nationalism. Some were converted. In Sholem Asch's novel *Three Cities,* Mirkin, a Russified Jew quite estranged from Jewish life, travels to the old Lithuanian capital of Vilna. There he is transformed:

> Like every exiled Jew who has spent his whole life in a foreign environment and has neither seen nor known Jews, Zachary Gavrilovich Mirkin was profoundly impressed by the Jewish national tradition when he encountered it for the first time, and succumbed to this national Zionist atmosphere which stilled the longings of his hungry soul. Like everyone who first comes into contact with Jewish national feeling he, too, was wildly enthusiastic and even entertained vague projects of going to Palestine and doing pioneer work of some kind![5]

The Jewish socialist Bund, which combined nationalism and socialism, was founded in pre–World War I Vilna, as was the Orthodox Zionist organization, the Mizrachi. In the interwar period the link between Jewish nationalism and Lithuania became truly dramatic. In the 1920s and 1930s independent Lithuania functioned as a kind of paradise for this modern Jewish political camp (see fig. 14). National schools, the most important institutions of national cultural autonomy, flourished, in particular Zionist-inspired Hebrew schools of the Tarbut network (*tarbut* means culture in Hebrew). It was possible for Jews in this country to receive their entire education, from kindergarten through high school, in these institutions. Jewish politics in the 1920s and 1930s was dominated by Zionism; nowhere else in the Diaspora did such a high percentage of Jews purchase the shekel, signifying their support for the Zionist venture, and a significant number of Lithuanian Jews actually went to Palestine.[6] For Zionist emissaries Lithuania appeared to be an oasis of "Palestinianism," whose Jewish communities supported Tarbut schools and Zionist youth movements and where the youth, imbued with the right sort of national consciousness, were busily engaged in preparations for aliyah to Palestine.

If independent Lithuania was a mecca of Jewish nationalism in the interwar period, adjacent areas, some actually part of historic Lithuania and now separated by "artificial" post–World War I frontiers from the Lithuanian state, also qualified as core areas of Jewish nationalism. This was true of Latvia, particularly southern Latvia, known as Latgallia, whose capital city was Dvinsk (Daugavpils in Latvian). It was also true of large parts of Poland, the eastern borderlands, known in Polish as the *kresy* (see

Fig. 14: Independent Lithuania. (Reproduced from Ezra Mendelsohn, *The Jews of East Central Europe Between the Two World Wars* [Bloomington: Indiana University Press, 1983].)

fig. 15). The Jews of this region (which included the city of Vilna), many of whom were no less *Litvakes* than their neighbors in independent Lithuania, maintained in the interwar period the national traditions of their immediate forebears, all the more so since the new Polish ascendency brought a halt to the previous process of Russification and made a Jewish national orientation even more probable. Within the context of interwar Polish Jewish history it was probably this region that was the most imbued with modern Jewish nationalism, more so than Central (Congress) Poland and Galicia, where Jews were much more Polonized (and where antinational Jewish Orthodoxy was much stronger). The modern, national Hebrew-language Tarbut schools flourished in the *kresy* as nowhere else in the Polish state (see fig. 16). Here, in the words of one Zionist observer, was the "crucible (*kur*) of national Judaism."[7]

Modern Jewish nationalism also flourished in the Romanian province of Bessarabia, and for similar reasons. For one hundred years Bessarabia had been a backwater of the Russian Empire, a multinational region, a capital of antisemitism (recall the Kishinev pogrom of 1903), whose largely Yiddish-speaking Jewish population was gradually exposed to Russian culture. Then, suddenly and unexpectedly, Bessarabia became a part of the much-expanded Romanian state. Jews who went to bed as "Russians" woke up to find themselves "Romanians." Once again a Jewish national orientation seemed the logical course of action for a Jewish community now cut off from Russia and largely ignorant and probably contemptuous of Romanian. During the interwar period Bessarabia was a great center of Zionism, of Hebrew and Yiddish secular schools, and of the national Jewish political party, which was Zionist-dominated. If Vilna was the Jerusalem of Lithuania, Bessarabia was the Jerusalem of Romania. It was rivaled in this regard only by the once-Austrian and now brand-new Ro-

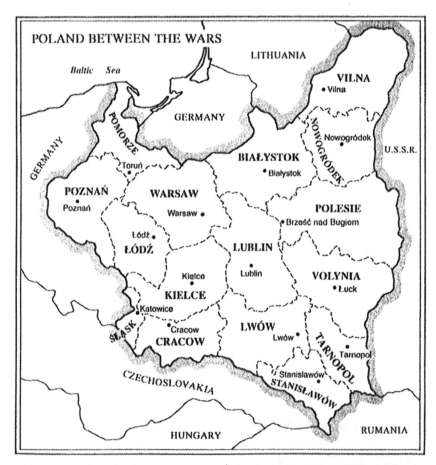

Fig. 15: Interwar Poland. The eastern borderlands (*kresy*): Vilna (Wilno in Polish), Nowogródek, Polesie, Volynia, and the eastern part of Białystok; Western Galicia: Cracow; Eastern Galicia: Lwów, Tarnopol, Stanisławów; Congress Poland: Łódź, Kielce, Warsaw, Lublin, and the western part of Białystok. (Map reproduced from Israel Gutman, Ezra Mendelsohn, Jehuda Reinharz, and Chone Shmeruk, eds., *The Jews of Poland Between Two World Wars,* copyright 1989 by the Trustees of Brandeis University, [Hanover, N.H.: University Press of New England, 1989].)

Fig. 16: *Tarbut High Schools in Poland, 1929.* Asterisks indicate the existence of a Tarbut high school. Note that they are virtually all located in the eastern regions (*kresy*). (*Source: Ha-va'ad ha-merkazi le-ha-histadrut ha-tsiyonit be-folaniyah* [Warsaw, 1929]. Map by Carta, Jerusalem, Israel.)

manian province of Bukovina, where speakers of German, Yiddish, Romanian, and Ukrainian mingled and where, as in the Lithuanian lands, the Jews were ignorant of the language of the land and no single nationality dominated the scene (see fig. 17).

Core areas of Jewish nationalism were typically peripheral areas so far as the majority nationality was concerned; indeed, from the Jewish national point of view it was often the case that the more peripheral, the better. This was certainly true in Poland, Romania, and Czechoslovakia. In the ethnic heartlands of these countries—Central Poland and Western Galicia, Wallachia and Moldavia, Bohemia and Moravia—Jews were more subject to acculturationist pressures and more likely to identify with the cultural orientation of the dominant nationality than in the multinational, economically backward borderlands, where Polish, Romanian, and Czech culture were so much weaker. The Lithuanian-Belorussian lands were also, after all, peripheral areas within the context of the pre–World War I Russian Empire.

Another region where Jewish nationalism flourished was Bulgaria. The very small community of largely Sephardic Jewry in this Balkan country was not subjected to strong acculturating influences during the period of Ottoman rule when, like other minorities, the Jews were treated as a distinct religious-national group and enjoyed considerable autonomy. Neither Turkish nor the local Slavic language made much impression during the preindependence period (up to 1878); the non-Jewish language with the highest prestige was French, which was taught in the schools of the Alliance israélite universelle. Modern Bulgarian nationalism, like its Lithuanian and Latvian equivalents, was a rather late bloomer, and Bulgarian culture was certainly not very attractive to the Jews. After the attainment of independence by the largely peasant Bulgarian nation, a process of acculturation began, but generally speaking Bulgarian Jewry made the transition from a prenational religious Jewish identity under the Ottomans not to an integrationist-type identity as "Bulgarians of the Jewish faith," but rather to a modern Jewish national, Zionist identity. As a historian of

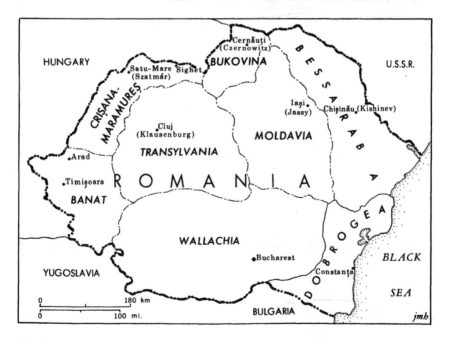

Fig. 17: Interwar Romania. (Map reproduced from Joseph Rothschild, *East Central Europe Between the World Wars* [Seattle: University of Washington Press, 1974].)

Bulgaria puts it, "Lacking meaningful identification with the national and nationalistic aspirations of the Bulgarian majority, the Jews of Bulgaria identified more closely with the ideals of modern Jewish nationalism, of which political Zionism became the dominant expression."[8]

Outside Europe, in the East European Diaspora beyond the sea, an additional core area developed in a rather unlikely place—South Africa. Like the Baltic states, Romania, and Poland, South Africa was (and still is) a multinational state. Jews could not really become Boers, who constituted a peculiar national-religious entity reminiscent in some ways of the Jews themselves. They adopted English culture, but they did not come to see themselves and were not seen by others, in this unusual semicolonial setting, as Englishmen of the Jewish persuasion. Their leading historian has commented, "Owing to the Afrikaner-English duality, the pull of acculturation towards the English, with attendant erosion of Jewish distinctiveness, was bound to be considerably weaker than was the case in Britain itself, where English culture was both indigenous and supreme." The unique South African context endowed the Jewish identity with "an ethnic-national dimension of its own, which . . . found expression in Zionism."[9] It probably helped that many Jewish immigrants in South Africa hailed from the great center of European Jewish nationalism, Lithuania.

It would be logical to assume that the ideal environment for Jewish integrationism must be in most ways the very opposite of the ideal environment for Jewish nationalism. That would mean, among other things, a country or region that was either mononational (in fact or claimed to be so) and that refused to recognize the legitimate existence of minority nationalities; a country dominated by a culturally "attractive" nation into which the Jews would be all-too-happy to integrate; and a country liberal enough to accept Jews into the national fold and to support the proposition that talent, not nationality, race or religion, determines one's economic success or failure. Far from being a backwater, one would expect this region to be characterized by economic dynamism and a growing urban sector.

As in the case of Jewish nationalism, Jewish integrationism requires the existence of a substantial number of Jews prepared to distance themselves from the spiritual ghetto. But in economically dynamic, culturally attractive, and above all politically liberal countries—in particular in their glittering urban centers—such Jews would be likely to reject not only old-style religious orthodoxy (in favor of some sort of modernized Judaism) but also modern Jewish nationalism. All ideologies of separatism would be repellent to them.

Was the United States such a country? It was certainly characterized by exceptional economic dynamism, and its high culture was extremely attractive. It also possessed a liberal tradition of integrating all minorities—or at least all white minorities—into the American nation. And in the long run most of its Jews certainly came to reject both Yiddish and East European

Orthodoxy. On the other hand this country, if not binational like the province of Quebec (a good place for Jewish nationalism, by the way), was very definitely and very dramatically multiethnic. Moreover, in the interwar period its Jewish community was dominated by fairly recent arrivals from the European heartland of Jewish nationalism and Jewish Orthodoxy. For both these reasons America, at least in the short run, was an environment less hostile to a certain variety of Jewish nationalism than one might assume.

A truly ideal environment for Jewish integration was France, the very model of a highly centralized nation-state with a brilliant high culture. Its capital acted as a magnet for ambitious Jews from the provinces, who usually discarded, soon after arrival, any vestiges of their old Yiddish language and their religious orthodoxy. The great majority of native Jews in this country did, indeed, define themselves as Frenchmen of the Mosaic faith and identified with the secular, pluralistic revolutionary tradition that had made possible their emancipation and their uniquely successful absorbtion (so they believed) into the French nation. If Jewish nationalism had any foothold in this country, it was in the more traditional communities of nationally mixed Alsace-Lorraine and among the new immigrants from Eastern Europe.[10]

But in general Zionism was notoriously weak among the "real French Jews," whose most famous organization, the Alliance israélite universelle, developed into a formidable enemy of Jewish political nationalism. The Dreyfus affair may have pushed Herzl, a Hungarian, in the direction of Palestine, but it did not have that effect on the French Jews.[11] It is difficult to come up with the name of a single distinguished or famous French Zionist leader in the interwar period. Moreover, as France refused to recognize the existence on French soil of national minorities and as all "real" French Jews spoke French, no Diaspora nationalism based on Yiddish could possibly develop.

Another splendid environment for Jewish integrationism was Italy. The equivalent in this country to the French Jews' passionate identification with at least certain aspects of the French revolutionary legacy was the Italian Jews' identification with the Risorgimento, the nineteenth-century secular, anti-clerical movement for Italian unification. An acute observer of Italian Jewish history has written that "the success of the House of Savoy in uniting the peninsula, and the unlimited support that the Jews gave to this nationalist, unitarian Italian policy, allowed them to integrate into the Gentile society more quickly and more deeply than in any other country, including the United States, and to believe in the existence of unique historical conditions."[12] Italian nationalism was perfectly happy to include Jews within its definition of Italians, and Jews were perfectly happy to be so defined. As King Victor Emmanuel III put it to Herzl in 1904, "Jews, for us, are full-blown Italians."[13] Even Mussolini seems to have shared this view, at least during the early years of his reign.

In Central or East Central Europe the most interesting example of a highly favorable environment for Jewish integration was Hungary. During the second half of the nineteenth century the Hungarians—more fortunate than the Poles—were able to establish their own virtually independent state within the context of the Austro-Hungarian Empire. In their multinational part of this multinational empire they promoted with great vigor Hungarian national cultural hegemony. A great success of this campaign was the rapid development of a dynamic Hungarian political and cultural center in Budapest (which became a united city in 1873). It is particularly important to emphasize that Hungarian nationalism during the so-called liberal era (up to World War I) was inclusive, not exclusive, and delighted to absorb non-Hungarians. Thus Slovaks, Romanians, Germans, Serbs, and even Jews were invited to become Hungarians by adopting the Magyar language and otherwise identifying themselves with the Hungarian national cause.

Many Hungarian Jews, particularly in the heartland of the Hungarian nation (which became the fully independent Hungarian state in the interwar period) did so. True, Hungarian was not as attractive a culture as French or German, but thanks to the rise of Hungarian political power and the rapid development of its capital city it became ever more compelling. Many Jews not only became Hungarian speakers but they adopted Hungarian names and professed Hungarian nationalism. The Hungarian national composer Márk Rózsavölgyi's original name was Rosenthal; the famous Hungarian violinist Eduard Reményi was originally called Hoffmann; the philosopher György Lukács's family name was Löwinger. Numerous Jews left their small towns for Budapest, which became the home of a large Magyarized Jewish middle class that mostly adhered to a variety of Reform Judaism. True, this city produced the founder of political Zionism (Herzl left Budapest for Vienna at the age of eighteen) but integrationism, not nationalism, was the political credo of its Jewish community. By the interwar period Hungarian Jewry had been speaking Hungarian and identifying with the Magyar nation for half a century. For most of this period Hungarian Zionism, not to mention any other kind of Jewish nationalism, was virtually nonexistent.[14]

What would constitute an ideal environment for antinational and anti-integrationist Orthodox Jewish politics? As both orthodoxy and nationalism, in contrast to integrationism, were based on the fundamental idea that Jews should be to one degree or another segregated from the gentile world, both should do well in the types of communities where such segregation was traditionally part of the social order. Economic backwardness certainly helped to preserve traditional Jewish religious life. One would also expect, keeping in mind the Yiddish proverb quoted earlier (p. 37), that the more secular the society the less likely a powerful Jewish Orthodox presence. David Levinsky, the hero of Abraham Cahan's novel, came to America as an Orthodox Jew, but his Orthodoxy could not survive the economic and social dynamism and aggressive secularism of New York: "If you are a Jew of the type to which I belonged when I came to New York and you attempt to bend your religion to the spirit of your new surroundings, it breaks. It falls to pieces. . . . It was inevitable that, sooner or later, I should let a barber shave my sprouting beard."[15]

This shaving off of beards was rather less likely to happen in the backward, traditional, highly religious and priest-ridden regions of Eastern Europe (though, of course, it happened there too). The celebrated Hebrew poet Chaim Nahman Bialik spoke of "abandoned corners of our Exile" where the flame of pure Orthodoxy still burned.[16] Such corners were in fact not so abandoned—they were still inhabited by hundreds and thousands of Jews who resisted both the almost indecently rapid escape from traditional Judaism that Cahan describes as taking place in New York and the intense interest in gentile culture and politics that, as I. J. Singer tells us, was evinced by so many Litvaks.

Even in these places, however, Orthodox Jewish politics could take root only if the local Orthodox leaders were prepared to enter the modern political arena, a step many regarded with great trepidation. The core area of Orthodox Jewish politics, therefore, was located in those regions of Eastern Europe where the traditional Jewish Orthodox elite was prepared to co-opt the ways of modern politics and to organize the God-fearing masses in order to combat the Jewish heretics—nationalists and integrationists—and all their works.

In his novel of Lithuanian Jewish life in the late 1860s and early 1870s, which takes place in a town whose Jewish inhabitants live "such a life as no European could imagine," a place "all of whose [Jewish] inhabitants are pious and God-fearing," Reuven Asher Braudes describes the establishment of such an organization, an early version of Agudat Israel called Mahazikei ha-dat (The Upholders of the Faith). "The Society was dedicated to the defense of the holy Talmud and the *Shulkhan Arukh,* and opposed to all those who slandered it, so that the wicked heretics might be answered as they deserve, so that the mouths of the transgressors against religion and its defenders might be stopped up."[17]

Lithuania, as already noted was particularly hospitable to modern Jewish national doctrines, but if it was crowded with *Litvakes* spreading the doctrines of nationalism and socialism, it was also a potential base of Orthodox Jewish politics because plenty of Jews in this backward part of the world still remained faithful to the world of their fathers and mothers. However, the main core area of modern Orthodox Jewish politics was not in Lithuania, but in Central Poland, also known as Congress Poland or the Kingdom of Poland. This area was heavily Hasidic, and its dominant Hasidic "dynasty," located in the town of Góra Kalwaria (near Warsaw) and led by the Gerer rebbe, took the lead in the early twentieth century in organizing the Orthodox masses around the Agudat Israel party in order to have some chance of defeating the very same enemies, now much increased, that Braudes's Orthodox forces had identified half a century before. As other Hasidic leaders did not care to engage in this kind of activity and also resented the hegemony of the Gerer rebbe within Agudah, Cen-

tral Poland became the heartland of Agudah activity. Polish Galicia was
also a heavily Hasidic region, but the religious leadership there had little
desire to get involved in the modern political game. They had, according to
one historian, an "abhorrence of politics," meaning politics of the modern
type.[18] Subcarpathian Rus' (sometimes called Ruthenia, part of Czechoslovakia in the interwar period—an abandoned corner if there ever was
one) was a bastion of Jewish Orthodoxy of the strictest kind where the
Hasidic leaders were also not friendly to Agudah, which was regarded as
too "modern," as an organization likely to contaminate the religious youth
by its participation in elections, its publication of newspapers, its establishment of too-modern Jewish religious schools, and so forth.

Another important base of Agudah activity was, amazingly enough,
Germany. True, in this country most Jews had abandoned strict forms of
Judaism in favor of some form of reform; true, most, as we would expect,
were supporters of integrationism (the largest single German Jewish organization in the interwar period was the Central-Verein). But a stubborn,
small minority was able to combine an openness to the outside world with
an absolute devotion to Orthodoxy. This minority provided the Agudah
with some of its most notable leaders and cooperated with the Polish
Hasidic rebbes in one of the strangest internal alliances of modern Jewish
politics.[19]

If Jewish nationalism was naturally stimulated by the existence of a
general nationalist atmosphere, if Jewish Orthodoxy was encouraged by a
general spirit of strict religiosity and a lack of secularism, and if integrationism was stimulated by a prevailing liberal concept of the melting pot—even
if there was no real melting—one should then expect the Jewish left to do
well in areas where socialism was very much part of the general political
culture. One would also expect core areas of the specifically Jewish left to
be those regions where the "Jewish laboring masses," so beloved of Jewish
socialist leaders, were an important part of the Jewish community and
where they still possessed certain attributes of nationality—above all their
Yiddish speech. Without these Yiddish-speaking masses one might have
many Jews in the general left, but hardly a *Jewish* left.

Such conditions obviously existed in much of Eastern Europe: in the
Soviet Union (where, however, an independent Jewish left was not possible), Poland, the Baltic region, and parts of Romania. The Bund, the most
famous of all Jewish socialist organizations, was founded in Vilna and was,
at least at the beginning, very much a Lithuanian party.[20] But Central
(Congress) Poland, with its large industrial cities and huddled Jewish
masses employed in the factories and workshops as well as its strong general socialist tradition dating back to the czarist period was probably the
chief core area of the Jewish left in interwar Europe. One thinks in particular of Łódź, the Polish Manchester, whose textile factories and countless
shops were manned by tens of thousands of Jewish workers and of Warsaw, less industrialized than Łódź but the city where the various Polish
Jewish socialist parties of the interwar years had their headquarters. Thus

the narrator of Isaac Bashevis Singer's novel *Shosha* describes the streets in
the Jewish quarter of the largest Polish city:

> "On Karmelicka Street I passed the 'Workers' Home,' the club of the left-wing
> Poale Zion. In there, they espoused both Communism and Zionism, believing
> that only when the proletariat seized power would the Jews be able to have
> their own homeland in Palestine and become a socialistic nation. In No. 36
> Leszno Street was the Grosser library of the Jewish Bund, as well as a coopera-
> tive store for workers and their families. The Bund totally rejected Zionism.
> Their program was cultural autonomy and common socialist struggle against
> capitalism."[21]

Other strongholds of the Jewish left were in the great Jewish working-
class centers created by the mass immigration from Eastern Europe—
above all New York, to a lesser extent some other east coast American
cities, and London. Jewish immigrants to these cities occasionally brought
with them—along with their other belongings—some socialist baggage
from the old home. Others, petty businessmen or *luftmentshn* (people who
lived from nothing) in the *shtetl* became workers for the first time in the
New World and joined unions in the garment trades that were often led by
former Russian Jewish revolutionaries (see fig. 18).

Finally, the Jewish secular national right: The non-Jewish model for
this variety of modern Jewish politics was the kind of nationalism that
characterized, indeed, dominated the politics of interwar Poland, Romania, and the Baltic states, among other places. And one should therefore
expect that revisionist Zionism, the representative organization of the secular right in Jewish politics, should do well in all these East Central European countries. Poland, and again in particular Central Poland, was its
main base—here the dominant political tone was set by Piłsudski, a strong
nationalist but no antisemite and therefore a legitimate inspiration and
guide for Jewish politics—as nazism in Germany most emphatically was
not. Singer's narrator continues his description of Jewish politics on Kar-
melicka Street by noting: "In another courtyard was the club of the Revisionists, the followers of Jabotinsky, extreme Zionists. They encouraged
the Jews to learn to use firearms and contended that only acts of terror
against the English, who held the Mandate, could restore Palestine to the
Jews."[22]

Right-wing Zionism was strong in countries like Poland, but it was
obliged to contend there with a no less powerful socialist tradition. This
was not the case in another, distant part of the Jewish world where the
Zionist right flourished, namely, South Africa. In this peculiar country,
socialism of any kind was almost entirely lacking, indeed, virtually illegitimate, and it was only natural that Jewish nationalism, so dominant there,
would take on a right-wing coloring. In 1938 Jabotinsky went so far as to
say, "South Africa is our main field."[23] What he meant by this, presumably,
was that his movement encountered less Jewish hostility there than anywhere else.

***Fig. 18:** The Formation of the American Jewish Proletariat.* Off the boat and into the sweatshop. (Larry Rivers, *History of Matsah: The Story of the Jews,* Part III, 1984. Collection of Sivia and Jeffrey Loria, New York City.)

I have suggested various recipes for the flourishing of various kinds of Jewish politics, but it must be conceded that these do not always work. There are surprises: I have already noted the presence of Agudat Israel in Germany—and Germany in general represented a special, complicated, "mixed" case. It should have been—and was—a center of integrationism, but Zionism, too, had deep roots and a fairly strong presence in Germany. In the prewar period the World Zionist Organization was located in Berlin, and the movement was especially strong (as one would expect) in the eastern, binational region of Posen (in German; Poznań in Polish); in the interwar period it remained a force, thanks among other things to the rising strength of antisemitism.[24] There were, too, some Zionists in France and Hungary, some Jewish socialists in South Africa, and if one looks hard enough one can find integrationists in Lithuania and Bulgaria.

Moreover, as I have noted on several occasions, the environment, both Jewish and general, was liable to change, sometimes rather suddenly. The establishment of the Soviet regime in Russia transformed a great center of Jewish nationalism and Orthodoxy into a cemetery of both these Jewish political camps. There were no similar revolutions in the other countries of

Eastern Europe, but there were dramatic changes in regions that, according to my criteria, were ideally suited to Jewish integrationism. The rise in the number of Jewish immigrants from Eastern Europe (Ostjuden) in Germany and France in the interwar period gave Zionism and Jewish socialism a boost in countries where liberal integrationism was the most natural and predictable Jewish political stance. In America the established German Jewish aristocracy, integrationist to the core, was challenged by the arrival, from the 1880s up to 1924, of hundreds of thousands, eventually millions of Ostjuden. Finally, in much of Central and Western Europe the history of the interwar period was marked by the defeat of the nineteenth-century tradition of liberalism and pluralism, which had fostered Jewish integrationism and without which integrationism as an article of Jewish political faith could hardly survive.

One last point needs to be made. During my discussion of the geography of Jewish politics special claims have been made for one particular country. Poland has been named as a core area for a number of conflicting Jewish political tendencies—Jewish nationalism in general (in particular in Polish Lithuania), the Jewish left and Agudat Israel (in particular in Congress Poland), and the Jewish national secular right (also in Congress Poland). Interwar Poland, the home of over three million Jews, the heartland of East European Jewry, inevitably became the most important and dramatic of all the arenas in which the internal Jewish political struggle over the future of the Jewish people was waged.

Regional Variations on a Theme

Contrasting conditions in the various Jewish Diasporas had a considerable impact on the way Jewish political organizations functioned. Suffice it to point out that full-fledged Jewish *political parties* that participated in general elections and sought to elect representatives to national Parliaments and local city councils emerged almost exclusively in those countries that recognized and tolerated the existence and autonomous political activities of national minorities, and only in those countries where a sizable number of Jews identified themselves as members of a modern national minority. It never occured to American Zionists to establish a political party in order to elect their leaders to the U.S. Senate or the House of Representatives, just as American Poles never considered such a step. Such political behavior was clearly illegitimate in America, where the various religious and ethnic groups were expected to make their way in politics through integration into the two-party system. But in Poland the Zionists did what seemed to almost everyone to be the natural thing when they formed their own national Jewish political party (or rather parties) and entered with great enthusiasm into the electoral campaigns for the Polish Sejm and Senate. In that country the most prominent Zionist leaders—Yitshak Grünbaum, Leon Reich, Yehoshua Thon—sat in Parliament as elected representatives of the Jewish national minority, and so did leaders of the Agudah and other Jewish political parties. This was considered perfectly normal in a multinational state in which not only Jews but Ukrainians, Germans, Belorussians, and other minorities formed their own political parties and contested seats for the Parliament in order to further their special national interests. Jewish politicians in other multinational East European countries—Lithuania, Latvia, Romania, and even Czechoslovakia—emulated their Polish Jewish colleagues by establishing specifically Jewish national political parties. But German, French, and English Zionists, living in more or less homogeneous nation-states, did not.

In Poland the Jewish Bund was organized as a full-fledged political party, like all other socialist parties. It attempted, in vain, to elect its leaders to the Polish parliament, and did succeed in sending its representatives to Polish city councils. In Latvia, of all places, this organization managed to elect a delegate to the national parliament. In America, where there were plenty of Bundists, or former Bundists, almost all of whom had come to the New World from the Russian Empire, the Bund did not function as a political party. Its sympathizers were active in various Jewish left-wing organizations and established progressive Yiddish schools for their children. Rather than run their own candidates for office, they joined the American Socialist party (usually as members of its Jewish section) and transformed themselves into American socialists. The essential difference was noted by the celebrated Old World Bundist leader Vladimir Medem, who in 1921 addressed a convention of the Bundist-dominated Jewish fraternal society Arbeter Ring (Workmen's Circle) in New York:

> The Arbeter ring and the [Polish] Bund are two different organizations in two different countries, with different tasks. . . .
> We [in Poland] are a political party, you are a fraternal association. But still we have much in common . . . we both are characterized by the fact that we serve as a kind of home for the [Jewish] workers.[25]

What was true of the Bund was also true of the Zionist socialists. The American leader of the Zionist socialist organization Poale Zion (Workers of Zion), Baruch Zuckerman, echoed Medem's words in 1934 in a discussion with members of the organization's youth movement:

> Our Party in Eastern Europe in particular does play a political role in the Jewish kehila [communal organization] and in the minority struggle of the Jews with the ruling powers; our party in America has no specific political physiognomy and does not engage in any political struggle save as an auxiliary to the American Socialist Party or within the American Jewish Congress.[26]

I have no similar quotations from Agudah rabbis, or rebbes, but surely no Orthodox religious leader in the interwar years ever dreamed of sitting in the U.S. Congress as the representative of a special political party of "Jewish Jews." After all, the relatively weak pro-Agudah forces in America realized that the American Congress was not the Polish Sejm.

If the nature of the general environment often governed the *form* of

Jewish politics, it also played a role in determining the *content* of these politics. Indeed, form and content were closely related, as the Zionist case will illustrate.

There were, as Zangwill's wretched hero David Ben Amram discovered, a bewildering number of Zionisms—religious Zionism and secular Zionism, cultural Zionism and political Zionism, socialist Zionism, general Zionism, and right-wing revisionist Zionism. But the movement was also divided by geography. It is impossible to understand the history of modern Zionism without making the necessary distinction between "western" and "eastern" varieties of the movement, "east" meaning Eastern Europe, "west" meaning Central and Western Europe and the New World. Generally speaking, East European Zionism was Palestinocentric and Hebraic, meaning that it possessed a strong commitment to aliyah (that is, sending its supporters to the Holy Land) and to cultural work aimed at the revival of Hebrew as the spoken language of the Jewish community. It expended much energy and funds on training young people for productive lives in the Jewish-state-in-the-making and on establishing Hebrew elementary and high schools based on Palestinian models. But the majority of its mainstream leaders regarded themselves as representatives not only of Zionism in this narrow, "classical," Palestinian and Hebraic way but of the entire East European, Yiddish-speaking Jewish nation, a nation living in a hostile environment and involved in a life-and-death struggle for civil and national rights—the latter regarded as an absolutely necessary stage in the all-important process of Jewish nation building. Their effort to lead this struggle obliged the Zionists to abandon a purely Hebraic orientation in favor of a bilingual (Hebrew-Yiddish) or even trilingual (Hebrew-Yiddish-Polish) strategy in their Jewish education policy; more important, this struggle obliged them to become deeply involved in what was called in the Zionist lexicon *Landespolitik* (local politics) or *Gegenwartsarbeit* (lit. "present work"). As was stated earlier, Polish Zionist leaders were, as leaders of political parties, bona fide Polish politicians. Yitshak Grünbaum, head of the Polish General Zionists in the 1920s, was a fervent advocate of aliyah, a propagandist in favor of the Hebrew-Zionist Tarbut school system, and a fund-raiser for Palestine. But he was also a Sejm delegate, a mover and shaker on the local political scene, a man who wished to play (and for a time in the early 1920s did in fact play) a great role in general Polish politics as a leader of those forces fighting against Polish chauvinism and for a more democratic, pluralistic, tolerant Polish "state of nationalities" (rather than "nation-state") in which all citizens, irrespective of nationality or religion, would receive equal treatment and equal opportunity. The dual commitment to classic Zionist aims (for example, aliyah and the revival of Hebrew) and to the local political struggle for Jewish civil and national rights in Poland (implying a commitment to the struggle for Polish democracy) was a serious source of tension within East European Zionism. But its leaders had little choice; after all, they could hardly abandon the arena of local Polish politics to their opponents—the advocates of *doikeyt,* the Agudah, the Folkists, the Bund- ists, and even the integrationists—and concentrate only on transferring Jews to Palestine. Such a policy might well have resulted in completely marginalizing the Zionist movement, in losing the support of the Jewish masses whose main concern (in the short run at least) was with the diffi- cult, even threatening situation in Poland (and in Romania, Czech- oslovakia, and the Baltic states). Theirs was, by necessity, a broad, all- inclusive, catholic variety of Zionism, as required in the new era of mass democratic politics in the multinational East European states.

In the West things were entirely different. Here there was no Jewish national minority in the East European sense of the word and it followed that no one, including the Zionists, was interested in fighting for the implementation of Jewish national autonomy—an outlandish notion in France, England, Germany, Hungary, or the United States. *Gegenwartsar- beit* was not much of an issue because there were no Jewish political parties active in the local political arena. Individual American Zionists might be Democrats (like Stephen Wise) or Republicans (like Abba Hillel Silver), but the Zionist Organization of America (ZOA), in sharp contrast to the Polish Zionist Federation, wished to play no official role in local politics. There was no equivalent in Washington, D.C., or Berlin to Yitshak Grün- baum of Warsaw or Leon Reich of Lwów.

In theory Western Zionists were pro-Hebrew, but they entertained no fantasies about "Herbraizing" the Jewish communities in their countries and, in contrast to their Polish and Lithuanian colleagues, they made no serious efforts to create national alternatives—in either of the two Jewish languages—to the local state-run school system. The situation was similar with regard to aliyah, the cardinal Zionist activity without which all the rest was useless. If it was impossible to persuade American Jews to speak Hebrew, it was equally impossible to persuade them to leave the "golden land." True, by no means all East European Zionists packed their bags and went off to Palestine. The Hebrew novelist Shmuel Yosef Agnon makes note of this when, in his novel of interwar Poland, he has one of his characters remark, "If we make a reckoning we will find that more of us died for Poland's freedom than in draining the swamps [of Palestine]."[27] Still, East European Zionism was able to boast of a fair number of dy- namic, truly Palestinocentric movements whose only purpose was to send its people to the Zionist paradise—for example, the various pioneering youth movements and, above all, the Halutz (Pioneer) organization. West of the Polish border such organizations also existed, but only in pale imitation of Eastern Europe. A few American Zionists actually did go to Palestine—for example, Henrietta Szold, the celebrated founder of the women's Zionist organization Hadassah. But even she wrote in 1932 of her urgent desire "to 'devolute' here and return to America for the remain- der of my days."[28] In one of his ironic stories of Anglo-Jewish life Israel Zangwill captured the terror that descended upon Jews of the West when contemplating removal to Palestine. Mabel, one of his characters, remarks that many Christians harbor pro-Zionist sentiments, "Zionism's all very well for Christians," she thinks, since "they're in no danger of having to go to Palestine."[29]

West European and American Zionism was therefore much more narrowly conceived than its East European counterpart. In fact fund-raising was often its most significant activity. This was true even in South Africa, where Zionism may have been very much in the ascendency but where it was very definitely of the Western variety. In that bastion of Jewish nationalism fund-raising "was the axis around which revolved the practical commitments of Jews who considered themselves to be Zionists. For many it was, to all intents and purposes, synonymous with Zionism."[30] True, South African, American, and other Western Zionists lobbied their governments to promote the Zionist cause and did their best to persuade the Jewish community to support the idea of transforming Palestine into a Jewish homeland or state. Their Jewish nationalism, however, was basically that of acculturated or acculturating Jews who were fighting for the national rights of Russian and Polish and Romanian Jews. It was far removed from the nationalism of their counterparts in Poland where, as the English gentile Zionist Wyndham Deedes put it (with a measure of exaggeration), "The Jews . . . are for the greater part ardent Zionists. No 'lipservice' Zionists; but men and women who have already done great things for and in Palestine."[31]

The contrast between the Eastern and Western models of Zionism sometimes led to clashes within the World Zionist Organization—thus the struggle immediately after World War I between Russian-born Chaim Weizmann and the American Louis Brandeis is sometimes represented as a conflict between the little town of Pinsk (where Weizmann grew up) and the capital city of Washington.[32] It is but one of many examples of how different environments produced variations on a particular Jewish political theme. As was noted earlier, in Poland the Agudah was antiacculturationist, devoted to Yiddish, medieval headgear, and *peyes* (long sidelocks worn by men). In Germany, however, a modern nation-state with an acculturated Jewish community, the Agudah spoke German and its leaders were rabbis learned in secular subjects and sometimes even enthusiastic about European culture. The tension in world Zionism between Zionist Pinsk and Zionist Washington was paralleled in the antinational Orthodox world by the tension between Hasidic Warsaw and acculturationist Frankfurt a/M. The ideological twists and turns of the Jewish left were also much affected by the general environment. Thus Poale Zion split in 1920 into left and right factions—the former pro-Communist, opposed to any cooperation with the "bourgeois" Jewish world, and strongly Yiddishist; the latter less enchanted with Soviet Russia, more inclined to cooperate with mainstream Zionism, and more favorable to Hebrew. The left dominated in countries like Poland, so exposed to radical influences emanating from the East, whereas the right did better in the more moderate socialist atmosphere of Central and Western Europe and the United States.

Particularly instructive, I believe, is the example of the integrationist school of modern Jewish politics. There were integrationists everywhere in Europe, but it was usually the case that the further east one went, the more integrationists were willing to abandon what might be called the classical integrationist position in favor of compromise with the nationalist position. Consider the case of interwar Romania. In that country the leading integrationist organization was the Union of Romanian Jews (UER) whole leader, Wilhelm Filderman, was considered by some to be the Louis Marshall of Romanian Jewry. The UER was committed to the principle of the political integration of Jews into the Romanian state and therefore opposed the establishment, by the Zionists, of a national Jewish party. But in the extremely unfriendly, antisemitic atmosphere of this multinational state par excellence, many Jews (especially those of the new territories of Transylvania, Bukovina, and above all Bessarabia) clearly regarded themselves—and were regarded by others—as a national, not merely a religious minority. Thus the UER found it difficult to maintain a pure integrationist position. It held long, inconclusive debates on the question of whether the Jews might or might not be a national group, and included within its ranks people who were certainly not prepared to accept the formula that defined the Jews as merely "Romanians of the Mosaic persuasion."[33]

In pre–World War I Russia, too, integrationist-type organizations and leaders flirted with definitions of the Jewish people that sound rather different from those of Louis Marshall and Jacob Schiff. The famous Russian Jewish lawyer G. B. Sliozberg—a liberal and fighter for Jewish emancipation, as well as a leader of both the "defense bureau" established to protect Jewish rights and of the Union for the Equal Rights of Russian Jews—was a great admirer of Marshall's and certainly no Zionist. The Jews, he believed, were fated to become an integral part of Russia, where they had resided since the very beginnings of Russian history. Nevertheless, Sliozberg was operating within the context of an officially antisemitic empire in which resided a huge, mostly nonacculturated proletarian and lower-middle-class Jewish population in the multinational Pale of Settlement. This was not France or even the United States. It is not surprising, then, that Sliozberg and his colleagues believed in the existence of a "Jewish national culture," a Jewish people (*narod*), and a Jewish "cultural-historical unity" in Russia.[34] For him and many of his colleagues the idea that Jews might be "Russians of the Mosaic faith," members of the Russian nationality, was alien, probably impossible.[35]

Such notions were not completely alien in regions of Polish ethnic domination—in Galicia, for example and especially in Central (Congress) Poland. I have suggested that this latter region was a core area of Jewish nationalism and of Agudat Israel, but it also spawned, remarkably enough, a relatively small but influential group of Jews who during the nineteenth century did in fact subscribe to a classic integrationist position. Congress Poland, after all, was a kind of Polish nation-state within the Russian Empire, totally dominated culturally, if not politically, by the Polish nationality; its Jewish population included a small number of secularly educated, wealthy people who wished to adopt Polish culture—a "high culture" in the East European context—and (if possible) integrate into the Polish nation.

In interwar Poland, now an independent state, several Jewish organizations—student groups, associations of Jewish war veterans, and so forth—held up the banner of Polish patriotism and extolled the tradition of Polish Jewish cooperation symbolized by Jewish participation in the struggle for Polish independence. They fought against such avowedly separatist forces in Jewish life as Zionism, Diaspora nationalism, and Orthodoxy. Even in the ranks of these organizations, however, a certain amount of rethinking took place in the 1920s and 1930s, the result, no doubt, of the fact that Polish antisemitism refused to disappear. In 1937 when anti-Jewish feelings were running high and were being promoted by the state, the third conference of the Society of Jewish Veterans of Poland's Wars of Independence heard one of its leaders declare, "We do not ask to what nationality [our members] belong," thus allowing for the existence of "Jews by nationality" as well as "Poles of the Mosaic persuasion" in the ranks of this superpatriotic, so-called (by its enemies) assimilationist organization.[36]

The lot of Polish Jewish integrationists was not a happy one, especially in the late 1930s. Something similar happened in Germany. In contrast to Russia, Romania, and Poland this country was long a stronghold of integrationist sentiments and the home of the powerful Central-Verein, which certainly boasted of far more members than did the Zionist movement. In the Weimer period—when Jewish optimism in the future had been somewhat shaken by World War I, the increase in anti-Jewish feeling and the rise of extreme "Volkist," exclusivist German nationalism—some integrationists began to emphasize that a purely religious definition was not sufficient. The idea that the Jews constituted a tribe (*Stamm*) gained greater currency. Thus in 1929 Ludwig Holländer of the Central-Verein emphasized that German Jewry was a "Schicksals—und Stammesgemeinschaft" (community of common fate and common origin). This did not, however, imply that the German Jews were a political nation that required national rights in Germany.[37]

The search on the part of the integrationists for a proper formula to express the essence of their Jewishness points to the particular vulnerability of this Jewish political camp. Jewish nationalists (at least of the Zionist persuasion) usually gained from growing antisemitism, which their doctrine predicted; the Orthodox were also more or less immune to gentile hostility, which they expected. But the integrationists, as Max Mandelstamm put it in 1897, wanted to "hug and kiss" their gentile compatriots.[38] When the latter responded by saying, "What's the hurry?" or by outright rejection, long-standing ideological positions had to be reconsidered. In short, both in multinational settings where many Jews defined themselves as a nationality (as in czarist Russia and interwar Romania) and in nation-states where antisemitism was strong and getting stronger (as in

Germany), the line between Jewish integrationism and Jewish nationalism was likely to be rather blurred.

The aim of this chapter has been to demonstrate the obvious—the vital importance of regionalism in Jewish politics. My next task is to concentrate on several of these regions and consider the results of the struggle among the various Jewish political forces for hegemony on the local "Jewish street." Who won and who lost—and why?

3

Dynamics

One way to study the balance of power among the various schools of Jewish politics is to employ the case study method. I propose in this chapter to consider the dynamics of Jewish politics in the two largest and most important Jewish communities in what was once called the "free world," those in Poland and the United States.

Poland

Enough has already been said about the Jewish community of the interwar Polish Republic to indicate that it was unique. It was huge—by far the largest in non-Communist Europe. Most Polish Jews were rooted in Orthodox Judaism, although many were in the process of abandoning it; most were Yiddish-speaking, although during the interwar years many of those who did not know Polish learned it; most declared themselves, on official census forms, to be "Jews by nationality," not only "Jews by religion." Most were lower-middle and working class, although the relatively small number of Jewish professionals and intellectuals played a great role in Polish cultural life. Many lived in little "Jewish" towns (*shtetlakh*), but Jews also constituted around one-third of the population of the great Polish cities of the central and eastern regions of the state. In all essentials the Jews of Poland were very different from the more acculturated, less religious, less numerous, and richer Jews of Central and Western Europe, though in some ways rather similar to the much smaller Jewish communities of the Baltic states and Romania.

The general environment in which the Jews of Poland lived was also

special. In sharp contrast to the other great East European Jewish community, that of Soviet Russia, Polish Jewry enjoyed a great deal of freedom.
Poland, first a democracy and then a semidemocracy, remained until 1939 a
country where political and cultural pluralism was tolerated; therefore
Polish Jews could practice their religion without fear, and they could also
practice whatever variety of politics they wished, from the extreme right to
socialism (everything save communism was permitted). Poland was also a
multinational state, in which more than one-third of the population was
non-Polish (Ukrainians, Belorussians, and Germans, along with Jews, constituted the main non-Polish elements). As noted earlier, the inhabitants
lived in an environment in which nationalism, above all, but also socialism
and traditional religious piety were extremely strong. Although the Jews
were emancipated, they lived in a state that tolerated antisemitism and even
embraced it as official doctrine. The degree to which Poland was, or became an officially antisemitic country is controversial, but by the late
1930s, a time of rising Polish exclusivist nationalism and great economic
misery, some Jews became convinced that their community had no future.
This is the view expressed by the narrator of Isaac Bashevis Singer's novel
Shosha: "The Jews in Poland are trapped. . . . The Poles want to get rid
of us. They consider us a nation within a nation, a strange and malignant
body. They lack the courage to finish us off themselves, but they wouldn't
shed tears if Hitler did it for them."[1]

Singer's personal conclusion was, "My only chance to survive was to
escape from Poland."[2] But he also remarked on the existence of other
options. "There was no lack of demagogues and plain fools who promised
the Jewish masses that they would fight alongside the Polish gentiles on the
barricades and that, following the victory over fascism, the Jews and gentiles in Poland would evolve into brothers forever after."[3] And then there
were those who prayed and waited patiently for the Messiah, having been
promised by their leaders that "if the Jews studied the Torah and sent their
children to cheders [religious elementary schools] and yeshivas, the Almighty would perform miracles in their behalf."[4]

Medieval Poland was said to have been a paradise for Jews. Interwar
Poland was surely not, but it was a paradise for modern Jewish politics. In
this connection we must bear in mind that mass Jewish emigration from
Eastern Europe was no longer possible in the interwar years, thanks mainly
to the new American immigration laws of the early 1920s. This fateful
development, the importance of which is hard to exaggerate, dramatically
raised the stakes of Jewish politics. I. B. Singer and some others may have
succeeded in escaping, but the great majority of Polish Jews were indeed
trapped. Prior to World War I hundreds and thousands of Polish Jews—
then living in the czarist and Austro-Hungarian empires—had voted with
their feet by leaving en masse for greener pastures. Now, no longer able to
find refuge from economic misery and persecution in the New World, or in
Western Europe, they looked perforce to the various Jewish political organizations to offer a way out.

[left margin, handwritten:] 1 Interwar - no emigration to America

I have said in chapter 2 that Poland's eastern provinces (the *kresy*) provided an ideal environment for Jewish nationalism and that Central Poland was an important center for the Agudah, the Jewish left, and the Jewish secular right. The existence on Polish soil of integrationists has also been noted, but in fact these people, the local equivalents of the Western adherents of the American Jewish Committee, the Central-Verein, or the Alliance—active as they were in the major cities of Central Poland and Galicia—were only bit players on the Jewish political stage. The Polonization they favored did come to pass, but it was not accompanied by a widespread acceptance of the integrationist ideology—Polish antisemitism saw to that. In Poland, Jewish politics was national, socialist, and Orthodox politics. This country's Jewish community represented the great hope: of world Zionism, which saw in Polish Jewry the single most important source of aliyah; of the organized Jewish left, which was based on the hundreds of thousands of Yiddish-speaking Jewish "proletarians"; and of antinational Orthodoxy—for Poland was home to the largest "Torah true" community in the Jewish world. To win the allegiance of the Polish Jewish masses was to win the most glittering prize that Jewish Diaspora politics had to offer.

Nahum Sokolow, the famous leader of the world Zionist movement, stated on a visit to his Polish homeland in 1933 that only a talmudist could possibly understand Polish Jewish politics.[5] There were endless numbers of political parties and youth movements (for example, in the 1920s there were no less than six socialist Zionist parties). Virtually every secular organization had its orthodox double: if there was a secular pioneer (Hehalutz) movement, there must needs be an Orthodox one as well. And various socialist Yiddishist organizations, like Poale Zion-left and the Bund, had their Hebraist equivalents, like the Hitahadut party. A further complicating factor was that the Polish state was divided, for some Jewish political movements, into three and sometimes even four separate "countries"—Poland (meaning Congress Poland), the *kresy* (the eastern borderlands), Eastern Galicia, and Western Galicia. Thus the so-called General Zionists were the proud possessors of three distinct organizations, with their capitals in Warsaw, Lwów, and Cracow, respectively, and there was little love lost between Polish and Galician Zionists. Generally speaking, Galician Jewish politics, heir to the Austrian tradition, was more moderate than Polish Jewish politics, whose practitioners had begun their careers in the harsh conditions of the prewar Russian Empire. But such regional subtleties will be of interest here much less than the general picture. In this mad scramble who came out on top?

It all depends when. In the beginning, in the immediate postwar period, the moderate Zionists, by which I mean both the General Zionists and their Orthodox allies, the Mizrachi, were undoubtedly the dominant force. Their star had begun to rise during the German occupation of 1915–18 when the terrible suffering of the Jewish population, the dramatic rise of nationalism among Poles and the other nationalities of the region, and the issuing of the Balfour Declaration (in 1917) combined to galvanize support for Zionism. In 1917 a highly successful Polish Zionist conference (dominated by General Zionists) was held, at which leaders of the movement predicted with some accuracy that their variety of Jewish nationalism was fated to rule the roost in the Polish lands. In late 1918 these Zionists, attempting to prove that they were the authentic leaders of Polish Jewry, took the lead in establishing a number of national Jewish councils that both claimed to speak for all Polish Jewry and to represent this large national minority to the leadership of the brand new Polish state. In fact these councils, in particular the council set up in Warsaw, did not speak for all Jews, but they were more active and more representative than anything the enemies of Zionism could manage. At a time of political chaos—the collapse of Germany, the wars between Poland and her Ukrainian, Lithuanian, German, and Russian enemies—these councils seized the political initiative within the Jewish community, and their leaders could claim with some plausibility to be authentic leaders, if not *the* leaders, of Polish Jewry.

There were other important signs of Zionist strength in these early years. Observers of the Polish Jewish scene in 1917 detected a general enthusiasm (*Stimmung*) for Palestine on the "Jewish street." This former backwater of the Ottoman Empire had, after all, been promised to the Jews by Great Britain, which was now in the process of "liberating" it from the Turkish yoke. In a novel of Jewish life in immediate postwar Poland, one encounters a veteran Zionist named Levi, who after years of lonely struggle now felt "he was no longer alone in Ployne. England and the League of Nations were on his side!"[6] Indeed, in 1920 the great powers, meeting in San Remo, Italy, approved British rule in Palestine, an event that caused much rejoicing in Polish Zionist circles. Headlines in the Zionist press announced, among other things, that "the trumpet of salvation is blowing."[7] Some were convinced that a Jewish state was at hand, an event seen as perhaps more miraculous but not wholly unlike the remarkable establishment of the new states of Eastern Europe, like Poland itself. The "pull" of newly liberated Palestine and the rather strong "push" from Poland, where a number of awful pogroms and anti-Jewish excesses had occurred during the years 1918 to 1920, resulted in a wave of interest in aliyah. True, more Jews wanted to go to the land of Columbus than to the Land of Israel, but America's gates, wide open up to 1914, were now being closed. America's new immigration laws were an obvious blessing for the Zionist movement, which fervently hoped that Tel-Aviv and Jerusalem would replace New York as the major target for East European Jewish migration. In Poland in 1919–20 there was so much interest in travel to the Middle East that the world Zionist movement took fright, fearing that newly liberated Palestine was hardly in a position to absorb large-scale Jewish settlement.

A highly auspicious sign for Zionism in the early days of the new Polish state was its strong appeal to young people. When Margolin, the hero of Yehuda Varshaviak's novel *Lights from the Darkness,* returns to his hometown after the war, his Zionist friend says to him, "Well, and you, . . . which organization will you join? Are you still being stubborn, do you still not grasp what Antoni the drummer boy, with his simple but clear mind, understands, that all the Jews must join our organization?"[8]

Margolin resists, but many young Polish Jews did not. This was the period in which a number of Zionist youth movements were being established, the most famous being Ha-shomer ha-tsair (The Young Guard). These organizations (to which I shall return) catered to boys and girls up to the age of eighteen and usually combined "harmless" nonpolitical scouting activities based on the techniques of General Robert S. Smyth Baden-Powell with a commitment to secular Hebrew culture and eventual aliyah. Their graduates (*bogrim*) were supposed to join another Zionist movement that got started around this time—the Pioneer (He-halutz in Hebrew). The young members of the Pioneer were all supposed to go to Palestine. While still in Poland they studied Hebrew and engaged in vocational training (*hakhsharah* in Hebrew)—farming, working in stone quarries, or in the building trades. They were often the subjects of ridicule. When first spied in Ployne, Bursztyn's fictional Polish Jewish town, Jews identified them as "a camp of gypsies who look like Jews."[9] "They plough, plant and reap like gentiles [*goyim*]" is the way the Hebrew novelist Agnon puts it in his novel of Galician Jewish life in the 1930s.[10] But they and their younger associates in the youth movements became, in the early 1920s, an important part of the Zionist movement—representing Palestinian activism and Hebraism in its purest and most fanatic form.

In the first major electoral test of Jewish politics in Poland, the elections to the constituent Sejm in early 1919, the Zionists did very well. In Central Poland and Western Galicia they set up electoral lists and campaigned vigorously for Jewish support. As things turned out the majority of Sejm delegates representing specifically Jewish lists were Zionists of one kind or another, and in Western Galicia (in the disputed regions of Eastern Galicia and the *kresy* no elections were held) the Zionists did particularly well. Famous Zionist leaders—Yitshak Grünbaum of Warsaw and Yehoshua Thon of Cracow—took their seats in the Sejm as the best known and most popular spokesmen of the Polish Jewish population.

In the general elections of 1922 an even more famous victory was won. This time the Polish General Zionists set up their controversial minorities' bloc together with representatives of other national minorities. In Galicia, where such tactics were regarded as needlessly provocative, no such bloc was established, but this did not prevent the General Zionists there from entering the Sejm in significant numbers. The large Jewish delegation that sat in the Polish Parliament from 1922 to 1928 was again dominated by moderate Zionists. Yitshak Grünbaum, the chief Jewish architect of the electoral victory, reached the apex of his popularity among Polish Jewry, of whom he now became a kind of uncrowned, secular national king. Indeed, 1922 came to be regarded as the greatest of all victories of General Zionist *Gegenwartsarbeit*, which aimed at altering, even transforming, Polish policy toward the various minorities and at "conquering" Polish Jewry in the process.[11]

Around the same time as these exciting electoral victories, the Zionists were distributing a great many shekels, whose purchase signified agreement with the program of the World Zionist Organization. In the early 1920s hundreds of thousands of Polish Jews are reported to have bought (for a derisory sum) the shekel; although these figures should be regarded with some suspicion, they seem to fit a general picture of Zionist success. True, there was one major cloud on the horizon. It soon became perfectly clear that despite the ecstasy and near-messianic fervor that accompanied the Balfour Declaration, the British conquest of Palestine, and the establishment of the British Mandatory government under the leadership of a Jewish High Commissioner, relatively few Jews could, or would, actually go to Palestine. British policy, worked out in cooperation with the World Zionist Organization, limited immigration largely to Jewish "capitalists," who had to prove that they possessed a significant amount of liquid capital, and to "productive" workers, who were granted "certificates" enabling them to enter the country. As the situation in Poland normalized after the chaos of 1918–20 interest in Palestine waned; it turned out that few "capitalists" were interested in going, and the number of certificates was kept small. As a result, in the early 1920s only several thousand a year made the journey from Poland to the Holy Land, many of them young, single pioneers—a tiny number given the size of Polish Jewry.

Even in this regard, however, things changed radically, and in a pro-Zionist direction. In 1924—a fateful year in modern Jewish history—the last in a series of new American immigration laws was passed that put an end to large-scale Jewish immigration from Eastern Europe. At the same time the economic situation in Poland worsened as a result of a new fiscal policy, particularly hard on the middle and lower-middle classes, and new opportunities began to open up in Palestine. The result was a relatively large wave of aliyah, this time including not only pioneers but also so-called bourgeois Jews; this episode is known in Zionist history as the Fourth Aliyah or as the Grabski Aliyah (ironically named in honor of Władysław Grabski, the Polish finance and prime minister responsible for the economic reforms). In 1925 an unprecedently large number of Polish Jews went to Palestine, some 17,000. Even on the aliyah front, then, things were looking up. The two faces of Zionism—its work in Poland and its work for Palestine—were apparently succeeding. Zionists, mostly General Zionists, were leading the way both in the parliament and in the effort to create a Jewish majority in Palestine, the essential precondition to the creation of a Jewish state. And if these two sides of Zionist policy were potentially contradictory, no one seemed to mind. Had the Zionists really succeeded in radically improving the Jewish lot in Poland, how many Jews would have wished to go to Palestine? We shall never know.

It was a heady, heroic time. During these years David Svirsky, the protagonist of a short story by Isaac Bashevis Singer, left for the Holy Land:

> Off he went, a twenty-one-year-old young fellow, the head of a platoon of the Tsivkever *shomrim,* a merry person, in love with all the girls, well read in novels and travel books, an actor in a dramatic circle to benefit the national fund, the leading Zionist in town, a good friend to all the children of the well-to-do.[12]

Zionist success in the early years of Polish independence was partly the result of confusion among the anti-Zionists and the non-Zionists. Agudat Israel, which was just getting organized during the war, made a respectable showing in the 1919 elections; but it was practically nonexistent outside Congress Poland, and its leaders (including some venerable rabbis) were much less effective in playing the democratic political game than were the more modern, better-educated Zionists. In 1922 Agudah actually joined the minorities' bloc under the leadership of the much-disliked secularist Grünbaum, an admission of its feelings of inferiority in the political though certainly not in the cultural arena.[13] The Jewish socialist left was temporarily derailed by the civil wars of the early 1920s between the adherents of socialism and communism. In 1920 Poale Zion, the Zionist socialist party, split into pro-Communist and anti-Communist factions, a disaster for socialist Zionism from which it took some time to recover. The Bund also went through hard times, losing some of its members to communism, seriously divided on the issue of the Soviet Union, and deprived of its historic Russian base by Bolshevik totalitarianism. It made a respectable showing in the 1922 elections but failed to dispatch a single representative to the Sejm. It, too, like Agudah, enjoyed little strength in Galicia, where it had not been very active in the prewar period. The integrationists were no factor in electoral Jewish politics: How could they be at a time of widespread anti-Jewish pogroms and "excesses?" A rather new anti-Zionist force did emerge—the Folkists, middle-of-the-road, Yiddish-oriented Diaspora nationalists who claimed that Zionism should stick to Palestine and not meddle in the daily struggle of the Polish Jewish masses. But its appeal was short-lived.

I intend to analyze some of the reasons for Zionist success in chapter 4. But I must mention at this point that by the early 1920s Zionism had already demonstrated a number of unique strengths. Acting according to the dictum that nothing Jewish was alien to it, its range of activities was remarkable. It prosecuted the struggle for Jewish national and civil rights in Poland and sent idealistic pioneers to Palestine. It established Hebrew schools, controlled mass-circulation Yiddish dailies (for example, the famous Warsaw *Haynt,* read by Jews everywhere in the country), and established a Polish-language press as well (particularly in Lwów and Cracow, the two capitals of Polonized Galician Jewry). Moreover, it alone of all Jewish political forces could attract, at least potentially and sometimes actually, every type of Jew—Orthodox and secular, socialists of every stripe, and antisocialists. In highly nationalistic and obviously antisemitic Poland, it best fit the zeitgeist and the general Jewish mood. Indeed, everything that had happened in Poland during the years 1918 to 1920 seemed to point to the correctness of the Zionist ideology—the rebirth of Poland was a model that the Zionists wished to emulate, and Polish antisemitism seemed to prove their gloomy prognosis regarding the future of the East European Diaspora.

But the Zionist success of the early and mid-1920s did not endure. One disaster was the collapse of the Fourth Aliyah in 1926, the result of economic crisis in Palestine. Many of the Polish immigrants to Palestine (*olim*) had a hard time; some even returned to Poland. Of those who returned (known in the Zionist lexicon as *yordim* [singular *yored*]—an unpleasant appellation, meaning those who go down), some bitterly denounced Zionism and all its works, whereas others, filled with shame and hopelessness, sunk into despair. This was the fate of I. B. Singer's hero Svirsky, who became a *yored* and is told by his uncle: "It is the almighty's desire that Jews should be in exile, this is why a Jew can make a living even in the most miserable countries. The only land where a Jew has no hope is the Land of Israel."[14]

In the late 1920s aliyah declined to a trickle, the result not only of the crisis in Palestine but of the improved economic climate in Poland. The pioneering movement faded away, and the hope evaporated that a mass removal of Jews from Poland to Palestine might both contribute to the solution of the Polish Jewish Question and effect a demographic revolution in Palestine. As the Polish socialist leader Ignacy Daszyński said to the Hebrew poet Leib Jaffe in 1928, many more Jews were being born each year in Poland than were going off to the Holy Land. Was this not proof of the movement's impotence?[15] Daszyński's views are repeated by a Polish officer in a novel by I. B. Singer, who tells a downcast Zionist named Hertz Yanovar: "I don't want to hurt you, but Zionism is a failure. Palestine cannot absorb the Jewish overpopulation in Poland. And I won't even mention the Jews of other countries."[16]

If this were not bad enough, Zionist work in the Diaspora also began to falter. The startling success of the minorities' bloc in 1922, which was interpreted by many Polish nationalists as an effort by non-Poles and anti-Poles—led by the Jews—to wield excessive influence in the Polish state, did not translate into real political power. What had Grünbaum and his colleagues in the Sejm achieved? The struggle for Jewish national rights in Poland in the wake of the electoral victory was hardly successful—the Polish state continued to ignore Jewish demands to fund Jewish cultural institutions—and if anti-Jewish violence declined, systematic economic discrimination against Jews continued. General Zionism was rocked with bitter internal feuds between advocates of confrontation with the authorities (mostly "Poles") and those who favored accommodation with the government (mostly "Galicians"). In 1925 the "Galicians" of Lwów and Cracow, who had disliked the minorities' bloc as a needless provocation, entered into semisecret negotiations with the government in order to "regularize" Polish Jewish relations. These negotiations, strongly denounced by the Warsaw Zionists as a typical example of *shtadlanut* worthy only of cowardly "assimilationists," were, in the end, no more successful than the tactics of the minorities' bloc. And, to make things even worse, in Congress Poland the Zionist Federation split into warring factions over a rather arcane dispute as to whether non-Zionists should be allowed to play an influential role in building Palestine.

Then came the 1926 coup d'état engineered by the war hero Marshal Piłsudski, an event that changed the course of Polish politics. Piłsudski, a former socialist, was supported and liked by most Jews; it is also true, as has already been noted, that economic conditions improved in the years immediately following the coup. But his semiautocratic rule, although not destroying Polish democracy, rendered it less effective. As a result, the decline in Zionism's Palestinian activities, as reflected in the crisis in aliyah, was paralleled by a decline in Jewish political influence in internal Polish politics. In the elections of 1928, dominated as they were by the government through its newly formed official government party, the number of representatives of specifically Jewish political parties returned to the Sejm dropped significantly. It was never to return to the dizzying heights achieved in the glory days of 1922. This was a serious blow to Zionism's program of *Gegenwartsarbeit*.

The marked decline in popular enthusiasm for Zionism and in its political clout created something of a political vacuum in the Jewish world. Did the anti-Zionists fill it? To a certain extent, yes. Not the integrationists, who even now failed to establish themselves as a serious political force. But the Agudah, which had definitely placed itself on the Jewish political map in 1919 and again in 1922, was definitely on the rise. This was apparent even before the decline of Zionism. It was, for example, triumphant in elections to the local Jewish organs of self-rule, the *kehilot* (*kehiles* in Yiddish). These institutions, long a part of East European Jewish life, were officially recognized by the state and had as their task the supervision of Jewish religious life in the numerous cities and towns of the country. They controlled funds raised through taxation and their leaders enjoyed a certain amount of patronage. The governing boards of these *kehilot* were chosen in democratic elections (only men could vote however), and the elections were contested by the major Jewish political parties. The leading historian of the Polish Agudah has calculated that in the elections of 1924 in some one hundred *kehilot*, almost all in the Agudah stronghold of Congress Poland, the Orthodox Jewish party and those groups that cooperated with it received about 40 percent of the mandates. Other Orthodox and anti-Zionist groups that were not allied with Agudah, such as the Hasidic followers of the Aleksanderer rebbe, also did well. In both the Warsaw and the Łódź *kehilot*, Agudah emerged as the single strongest party.[17]

Recall that 1924 was a year of Zionist successes, and these electoral results reveal a very important aspect of Polish Jewish politics—namely, a readiness to switch from party to party according to the type of elections and the issues at stake. Jews who identified with Zionist ambitions in Palestine, and who might have voted for Zionist-led blocs in Sejm elections, may well have voted for the anti-Zionist Orthodox leaders in local Jewish elections. They obviously saw no contradiction between voting for university-trained, secular, Polish-speaking Jewish nationalists to represent them in the Parliament and voting for bearded traditionalists to run the *kehilot,* perceived as religious bodies. They were prepared, in other words, to support Zionist efforts to encourage Jewish settlement in Palestine and at the same time to place their religious affairs in the hands of people who strongly denounced the Zionist enterprise.

Agudah enjoyed other triumphs in the 1920s. Under its watchful eye there emerged the largest of all Jewish private school systems, larger than both the Zionist-inspired Tarbut Hebrew system and the left-wing Yiddish secular schools. These schools provided thousands of boys and even girls with an Orthodox education and proved that the death of Jewish Orthodoxy, long predicted, was greatly exaggerated. Successes on the educational front were, of course, of tremendous moment to Agudah, whose very raison d'être was the war against the rising tide of secularism. The party also made a useful political agreement with Piłsudski's government. In 1928 it abandoned the secular Zionists and their minorities' bloc and ran some of its candidates for Parliament on the official Piłsudski-inspired government list. It was roundly denounced for such tactics by the Zionists and the Jewish left, by now disillusioned with the great Polish general, but the Orthodox camp was now able to claim friends in high places. Its alliance with the forces of the moderate Polish right lasted until well into the 1930s and brought it considerable benefits.

I have noted the weakness of the Bund in the 1920s, but this Marxist organization that claimed to represent the Jewish proletariat (meaning mostly craftsmen) and championed Jewish national cultural autonomy (based on Yiddish) survived the early 1920s—factionalized, but intact. It proceeded to build a solid base in the Jewish trade union movement that it dominated. It also got into the business of Jewish education, helping to establish a network of Yiddish-language secular schools known as Tsisho (a Yiddish acronym for Central Jewish School Organization), smaller than the Orthodox and Tarbut systems but significant nonetheless. The Bund received only some eighty thousand votes in elections in 1922, not enough to send a representative to the Sejm, but it performed more successfully in city council elections.[18] By the late 1920s it was very definitely a force in Jewish political life in Poland, as it had been in czarist Russia.

The 1930s witnessed a revolution in Jewish Polish politics, the causes of which are to be found both in developments in Poland and in the Jewish world. The economic depression, which hit Poland very hard, combined with already existing economic discrimination against Jews to make their economic situation worse than ever. Polish politics moved to the right, and in the late 1930s, following the death of Marshal Piłsudski in 1935, the country was ruled by a clique of antidemocratic extreme nationalists; for the first time the government, through its official political organization, openly preached antisemitism, and its anti-Jewish bias was strongly supported by the Catholic church. The triumph of nazism had a considerable impact in neighboring Poland, as it did in other countries of the region that were also adopting extreme right-wing policies, like Hungary and Romania. The Polish left—both the Socialist and Communist parties— were a serious factor in Poland's politics, and they resisted what they referred to as the fascist menace, but to little effect. No anti-Jewish laws were passed (in this respect Poland was a more tolerant place than Hungary), but in the late 1930s "low-level pogroms" broke out again, as in the years 1918 to 1920; Jewish students were terrorized in universities; and Jewish merchants were terrorized in the marketplace.

One might well expect that this environment of economic misery, growing right-wing extremism, and mounting violent antisemitism would have a serious impact on Jewish politics. Also keep in mind that a new generation of Jews was reaching maturity in the 1930s, a generation that had grown up in independent Poland and was therefore more Polonized, more secular, and thus more likely to be influenced by the various types of Polish nationalism and socialism than its parents. The youth was, of course, particularly hard hit by the awful situation. "What should the Jewish youth do?" we read in a Jewish novel of the times, "No one will give them a job."[19] For some, at least, political radicalism was the answer. As the novelist Leib Hazan puts it, the old generation sat around and prayed, waiting for the Messiah to relieve them of their woes, but the youth "were hoping for a redemption brought about by their own deeds and by their own heroism."[20] In short, in Poland of the 1930s conditions were ripe for a more radical style of Jewish politics.

Developments within the Zionist movement illustrate this very well. In the 1920s the dominant Zionist figure was the General Zionist Sejm deputy who claimed to represent all of Polish Jewry and who devoted himself to parliamentary activities aimed at improving the lot of Polish Jewry (and, in those more optimistic times, at changing Poland as well). By the 1930s such people and activities had been marginalized by the decline of Polish democracy, and the prestige of General Zionism quite naturally suffered as a result of its leaders' failure to arrest the decline in the Jews' condition. Fortunately for the movement, the 1930s also saw a revival of interest in Palestine and in aliyah because Palestine had by now recovered from the economic crisis of the late 1920s and was able to absorb new immigrants. With *Landespolitik* discredited and Palestine opening her gates once more, Polish Zionism now became, for the first time, a truly Palestinocentric movement. The "bourgeois" General Zionist Sejm deputy, typically a liberal lawyer or engineer, departed from center stage and was replaced by the *halutz* (the pioneer) who had little interest in local politics and contempt for Zionism's parliamentary maneuvers. During the early and mid-1930s the pioneering movement enjoyed its greatest success, as tens of thousands of young people spread over the country, "conquering" new areas and devoting themselves to *hakhsharah* (vocational training) in expectation of their imminent removal to Palestine. An important reason for its success in mobilizing mass support was that its members, having successfully passed through the various stages of training, were particularly well situated to receive those now highly valued certificates that enabled "productive elements" to enter Palestine. It was widely perceived as the only organization capable of offering a way out to Polish Jewish youth. Mendel and Hannah, the heroes of Mordecai Halter's novel *We Are Preparing*, two *kibushnikes* (lit. conquerers), arrive at a little town and are told by the local Hebrew teacher that only they can save the local youth, "You must stay here. . . . Your mission is to save the youth, to give them new meaning. In my opinion that is the significance of your conquest!"[21]

Activist Palestinian Zionism, as opposed to "bourgeois" *Sejmzionismus* (a contemptuous expression meaning Zionism of the Sejm) was to a great extent socialist Zionism. The secular Pioneer organization itself identified with a kind of moderate Zionist socialism (the religious pioneers were also left-wing, though reluctant to call themselves socialists). Most of the Zionist youth movements (whose graduates went on to the Pioneer) were also supporters of socialism of one kind or another. These organizations believed in the need to transform their members into productive laboring people (farmers and workers) so their left-wing sympathies were natural enough. They were committed to the establishment of communal societies in Palestine, and they were affiliated with the Palestinian Jewish labor movement, whose ranks they automatically entered on arrival in the Jewish state-in-the-making. They were not particularly concerned with politics in Poland, but their natural preference was for the political left, both Polish and Jewish, the only force actively engaged in fighting Polish fascism. The Jewish political party that best represented their interests was Poale Zion-right, which had traditionally combined an interest in the struggle to improve the condition of the Jewish working class in Poland with support for pioneering and active Palestinianism. By the 1930s it had combined with other Zionist socialist parties to form a united Zionist socialist front, the equivalent in Poland to Mapai, the mainstream Jewish socialist party in Palestine established in 1930.

This united socialist Zionist front, usually known as labor Palestine (Eretz Yisrael ha-ovedet), became in the last decade of the interwar period the leading force within Polish Zionism. In elections held in Poland to select delegates to the biennial Zionist congresses, elections in which those who had purchased the shekel were entitled to participate, it did far better than the once-mighty General Zionists. Symbolic of this growing strength was the tremendous enthusiasm with which David Ben-Gurion, the leader of Mapai, was acclaimed when he came to Poland in 1933. It was this version of Zionism—labor Zionism, allied with the European left and dedicated to pioneering, to the kibbutz, to the idea of Jewish productivization—that seemed to be taking over Polish Zionism.

I say "seemed," because just as Palestinocentric labor Zionism was rising to ascendency, it was challenged by a new variety of Zionism known as revisionism. Revisionism was a true creature of the hothouse atmosphere of the 1930s, a time when the enemies of the Jews were growing ever stronger, and it called for a new, creative approach to the deepening Jewish crisis. It despised labor Zionism—in fact, hatred of the left was the cornerstone of its ideology—but it shared some of its characteristics. It also stood for radical Palestinianism, and it had contempt for the poor General Zionists—not only because of their preoccupation with local politics but also because of their alleged timidity, their exaggerated and unmanly fear of the *goyim*, which rendered them incapable of making the necessary effort to convince the British and the leaders of other countries of the absolute necessity to take drastic action to save the doomed Jews of Eastern Europe. As against the radical left-wing slogans of *halutsiyut* (pioneering), it promoted its own radical slogans calling for Jewish military preparation and for "evacuation," meaning the organized mass transfer (voluntary, of course) of millions of mostly East European Jews to Palestine—a transfer to be arranged through international agreements and with the assistance of the antisemitic but pro-Zionist East European countries. Only such a transfer would save European Jewry and win the life-and-death demographic struggle for Palestine.

In 1935 the revisionists quit the World Zionist Organization and established their own rival New Zionist Organization. Immediately before this act of secession it had done well in elections to the Zionist congresses, although never as well as the left. Betar (the revisionist youth movement) became a serious rival to the socialist Zionist youth movements. Zev Jabotinsky had always believed that Poland would provide him with his mass political base (South Africa, after all, contained only some ninety thousand Jews, not 3 million). He said this in 1927, when his movement was in its initial stages.[22] In 1939, after the destruction of Poland, he told the Labor Zionist leader Berl Katznelson, "You have won. You have America; a rich Jewry. I only had poor Polish Jewry. I have lost the game."[23] In fact Jabotinsky never really "had" Polish Jewry, but there is no doubt that his movement together with socialist Zionism ruled the Zionist roost in the 1930s, providing as they did more dramatic, more dynamic, more rousing, and therefore more attractive models of political behavior than did the by now rather discredited General Zionists and their Mizrachi allies.

I have said that in the 1920s the representative Polish Jewish political leader was the General Zionist—speaking out against antisemitism in the Sejm; working out joint electoral lists with German, Ukrainian, and Belorussian nationalists; negotiating with the government. In the early and mid-1930s the General Zionists were replaced by *halutzim* hacking away in the stone quarries of Poland and the revisionists planning "evacuation" and engaging in military training in preparation for the heroic conquest of Palestine. All were Zionists. But in 1936 the tragic vulnerability of Zionism was again exposed, this time more dramatically than in 1926. Once again, now in the wake of the Arab uprising in Palestine, aliyah was much reduced; indeed, the British came under intense Arab pressure to halt it altogether. This was a terrible blow for a movement that had become so Palestinocentric as a result of the decline of Polish democracy and of the ever-worsening condition of Polish Jewry. Zionist activities shrunk, and activists disappeared. The Halutz found itself in crisis. The Zionist prediction that the Jewish condition in the Diaspora would become ever worse had been vindicated, but the Zionist solution—aliyah to Palestine—once again appeared to be bankrupt.

The Zionist misfortune represented a new opportunity for the anti-Zionists. The traditional, conservative Agudat Israel, whose alliance with the regime now lay in tatters, was not well placed to exploit it. Much better placed was another radical party, the anti-Zionist Bund. An observer of the Jewish political scene, say in 1920 or even 1930, might well have concluded that the thirty-year-old dispute between Bundists and Zionists had been decided (in Poland at least) in favor of the latter. The Bund was still a force, but its well-known claim to be "the sole representative of the Jewish proletariat" and a leading factor within Polish Jewry was much ridiculed and hardly tenable.

And yet, in the 1930s, this party rose again (for the last time, I might add). This was an extremely unexpected development and seemed to fly in the face of all logic. The Bund was the great apostle of *doikeyt* on the "Jewish street"—its slogan, "We remain here." In a novel of Polish Jewish life in the 1930s, the Polish mayor of a little town asks Hersh when he will be leaving for Palestine with all the other Jews. Hersh may not have been a Bundist, but his reply was in keeping with that party's most fervently held position: "It's no use, Wojtusz. We Jews must live here together with you in Smolin. This is the way it has always been."[24]

Such stubborn optimism may have been admirable, but why should it have appealed to the Jewish masses at a time of growing economic misery and rising antisemitism. The Bund was also the great advocate of cooperation with the Polish left despite its disapproval of what it regarded as the too-nationalistic line of the main Polish socialist party. But there had been little proof of love between the Jewish and Polish working classes, and some proof of the opposite. Moreover, prospects for revolution in Poland looked exceedingly dim in the late 1930s as the semifascist colonels strengthened their grip on the country. Finally, the party was a leading advocate of cultural national autonomy for the Jews in Poland, a policy that had always been something of a nonstarter and now looked to be totally dead.

Nonetheless, the Bund had some great successes in the late 1930s—in elections to city councils and even to *kehilot,* traditional preserves of the Orthodox right—elections that took place in the great cities of Congress Poland like Warsaw and Łódź and even in Galicia, where the party had always been weak. Indeed, by the late 1930s the Bundists could, and did, claim—without appearing ridiculous—that they had become the single strongest Jewish political party in Poland.[25]

As I have said, the Bund owed much of its new-found popularity to the Zionist debacle: The sharp decline in aliyah and the absolute failure of the revisionists to implement their grandiose transfer schemes seemed to indicate that the Bund had been right when it argued against the pos-sibility—on practical grounds—of a Zionist solution to the Polish Jewish problem. Optimism in a solution "here" might have been difficult to sus-tain, but what choice was there to *doikeyt* in the dark years of 1937, 1938, and 1939? Even if the Bund had not forged a particularly close alliance with the Polish Socialist party, at least there was some potential here for cooperation with the only important Polish political force fighting against fascism. And then there was the role of the Bund in standing up to the onslaught of the Polish violent antisemitic right. Its cadres of dedicated socialists—bearers of the oldest continuous revolutionary tradition on the "Jewish street" and well versed in underground, antigovernment activity—organized demonstrations against Polish antisemitism. Paradoxically, this class-oriented party, which ever since its founding in 1897 had preached the doctrine of class struggle within the Jewish community, became a leading force in the general Jewish struggle against antisemitism.

The support the Bund received during the last years of Polish indepen-dence almost certainly did not signify a large-scale conversion of Polish Jews to Bundist ideology, to Marxism, to class struggle on the "Jewish street," or to Yiddish-based secular national autonomy. Rather, it reflects this militant socialist party's success in filling a political vacuum no other Jewish organization—not the Orthodox and certainly not the inte-grationists—could fill. Had Poland not been dismembered in 1939, and had aliyah-centered Zionism picked up again, the Bundist ascendency would probably have been of short duration. This will never be known.

To sum up, in the contest for the support of the Polish Jewish masses, the school of Jewish nationalism proved by far the strongest. Within the national camp the Zionists, taken all together, were certainly the most influential, but as Zionism became more and more dependent on aliyah, this camp proved terribly vulnerable to the vagaries of British immigration policy and economic conditions in Palestine. As for the contest among left, right, and center, in the 1930s the Jewish left, embracing both the Zionist socialists and Bundists, was definitely on the rise (the number of Jewish Communists was also rising, but not all of them were active in Jewish politics). Jewish politics in Poland suffered from what might be called the yo-yo effect—various movements went up and down in response to exter-nal events over which they had little, if any, control. But the general trend seems clear. In a country dominated by nationalism and, from 1926 on, veering sharply to the political right, the most potent Jewish political response was a combination of nationalism and socialism, the former in conformity with the majority political culture, the latter resulting at least in part from a feeling that the left was the only political force willing to combat the rise of (antisemitic) right-wing extremism. Here is one "model" of the dynamics of Jewish politics: the non-Communist East European model. I now go on to consider the dynamics of Jewish politics in an entirely different context, that of the United States.

America

By the interwar period the majority of American Jews were of "Polish" (or "Polish-Russian" origin); of course, America was nothing like Poland and Jewish politics in that country was nothing like Polish Jewish politics. American Jewry in 1918 was an immigrant community consisting mostly of men and women who had fled from economically depressed and anti-semitic Eastern Europe not to further any of the "Jewish futures" envisioned by the various schools of Jewish politics but merely to make a better life for themselves and particularly for their children in the golden (but also *treyf* [unclean]) land. As Delmore Schwartz, the American Jewish poet, put it:

> "O Nicholas! Alas! Alas!
> My grandfather coughed in your army,
>
> Hid in a wine-stinking barrel,
> For three days in Bucharest,
>
> Then left for America
> To become a king himself."[26]

Not all Jews succeeded in making kings of themselves in America, but most were certainly transformed by the economic dynamism and political liberalism they encountered in the New World. I have already quoted Abraham Cahan's views on the inevitability of the decline of Judaism in the face of unrestrained capitalism and limitless opportunity. Prophets of gloom were numerous, and many shared the view of the *melamed* (religious schoolteacher) in Henry Roth's classic novel of American Jewish life, *Call It Sleep*:

> What was going to become of Yiddish youth? What would become of this new breed? These Americans? This sidewalk-and-gutter generation? He knew them all, and they were all alike—brazen, selfish, unbridled. Where was piety and observance? Where was learning, veneration of parents, deference to the old? In the earth! Deep in the earth! On ball playing their minds dwelt, on skates, on kites, on marbles, on gambling for the cardboard pictures, and the older ones, on dancing, or the ferocious jangle of horns and strings and jiggling with their feet. And God? Forgotten, wholly. Ask one who Mendel Beilis is? Ask one, did he shed goyish blood for the Passover? Would they know? Could they answer? Vagabonds! Snipes! Jiggers with their feet! Corrupt generation![27]

Would America, a paradise for Jews as individuals, become the grave-yard of Judaism and of the Jewish collective? Actually, the new environment, in which both religion and ethnicity flourished, was much less threatening to Jewish survival than Roth's *melamed* believed. It was, however, an environment to which Jewish politics of the Polish variety might be imported but could not be sustained for long.

To identify the major forces in American Jewish politics is to highlight the differences between the situation in the United States and in the old country. The camp of integration, allied to religious reform, enjoyed great prestige. Its flagship organizations were the American Jewish Committee, presided over by the most important Jewish leader of his times, Louis Marshall, and the Reform movement, whose great leader, Isaac Mayer Wise, had died in 1900, yet it continued to represent a large number of American Jews. The immigrant masses were not necessarily attracted by Reform Judaism or by the elitist American Jewish Committee, whose founders were of wealthy German Jewish stock, but they did appear to be extremely receptive to the integrationist message. Thus Harry in Michael Gold's famous novel of Jewish life in New York: "America is a wonderful country. One can make much money here, but first one must learn to speak English. . . . That is what I am always preaching to our Jews; learn English, become an American."[28] And the Jews listened to such preaching. Consider the words of Abraham Cahan's hero, David Levinsky, when queried as to his nationality:

> "I used to be [a Russian]," I answered with a smile.
> "I am an American now."
> "That's right."[29]

Despite all this evidence of rapid Americanization, most Jews did not give up their traditional religious practices the very moment they set foot on the soil of the New World. Orthodoxy continued to exist, but its political arm, Agudat Israel, was extremely weak in America, perhaps because the Hasidic leaders who organized it in interwar Warsaw and other Polish, Lithuanian, and Latvian cities had few followers in the New World.[30] On the other hand, Jewish nationalism—above all the Zionist variety—was very much in evidence in the New World. To some extent it was an import from Eastern Europe, but it also attracted many "native Americans." American Zionism was essentially different from Polish Zionism because it did not regard American Jewry as a "national minority" and therefore did not propose to struggle for the national rights of American Jewry; not only did it not urge American Jews to speak Hebrew, it also did not encourage them to go on aliyah. In all this it was similar, I believe, to other varieties of ethnic nationalism in America—for example, Irish nationalism, black nationalism, or Polish nationalism—movements concerned with helping compatriots in Europe (or Africa) and in raising the prestige of constituents, but not in gaining for them the status of a full-fledged national group in the United States or in persuading them to "return" to Poland, Ireland, or anywhere else (I shall have more to say on this subject in chapter 6).

If the emergence of Zionism as a force in American Jewish life may be regarded as something of a surprise in this fabled land of the melting pot, less surprising was the existence of a strong American Jewish left. True, socialism in the New World was never the political factor that it was in the Old World. No socialist organization in interwar America could compare in influence to the Polish Socialist party in interwar Poland. Nonetheless, on the eve of World War I American socialism was definitely picking up steam. The year 1912 was a high-water mark, the time when socialist presidential candidate Eugene Debs received nearly a million votes. That same year *Forverts,* the great Yiddish socialist daily celebrated its fifteenth anniversary and its editor, Abraham Cahan, probably the most important figure on the American Jewish left, expressed his joy in the fact that "this temple of ours, the socialist movement, is growing. And it continues to grow! It is spreading, it is conquering and winning. These are our most precious moments. Such are the times in which we are living."[31]

The most prominent leaders of American Zionism were "natives," the best example of whom was Louis Brandeis, whereas the Jewish left was led by former East European radicals of one type or another. A minority were socialist Zionists, the radical fringe of American Zionism. Some were of the Bundist persuasion, others one-time Russian socialists who in America entered the specifically Jewish movement. They did not establish full-fledged political parties in America, but many were active in Yiddish-language Jewish sections of the Socialist and Communist parties. Others became trade unionists, leaders of the so-called Jewish unions in the garment industry, above all the ILGWU, founded in 1900, and the Amalgamated Clothing Workers of America, founded in 1914. Also important were the socialist fraternal orders, such as the Arbeter Ring (Workmen's Circle) and the Yiddish-language section of the Communist-dominated International Workers Order (IWO).

The specifically Jewish left in America was based on the Jewish working class, whose economic and cultural interests it wished to serve. This meant a commitment to work "in Yiddish" and strong opposition to the middle class and wealthy Jewish "assimilationists" who opposed the "language of the masses." The Jewish left played a great role in the promotion of Yiddish culture in America—many notable Yiddish writers, for example, were closely identified with the left and published in its Yiddish newspapers and magazines (see fig. 19). But all this did not necessarily imply a commitment to a national Jewish future à la the interwar Polish Jewish socialist movement, whose activists, whether Bundists or Zionists, saw themselves as the leaders of a national minority in a multinational state. The "Jewish sections" of the Socialist and Communist parties were on the whole anti-Zionist, as were their equivalents in Eastern Europe. The most prominent leaders of the Jewish left—Abraham Cahan, editor of the *Forverts;* David Dubinsky of the ILGWU; and Sidney Hillman of the Amalgamated—may have been sympathetic at times to the cause of East European Jewish socialism (Dubinsky and Hillman had been Bundists in

Fig 19: Jewish Socialism in Action. The Yiddish sign reads: "Nature has given everyone an appetite, but our bosses have stolen the key. (Perhaps the artist meant to write "bowl" [*shisel*] and not "key" [*shlisel*].) (Ben Shahn, *East Side Soap Box,* 1936. Private collection. Estate of Ben Shahn/VAGA, New York, 1992.)

Russia) and were certainly willing to aid it from afar, but they were not really Jewish nationalists of the East European type. They and other Jewish socialists in America, despite their national Jewish "past," tended to be skeptical regarding the future of the Jewish Yiddish-speaking nation in America, and some took a position similar to that of the Russian *Yevsektsiia* activists (see pp. 27–28). A socialist press in Yiddish was necessary so long as the Jewish masses required it, but when it was no longer necessary, when

American Jews had made the inevitable transition from Yiddish to English, it might well die a natural death. Jewish activists in the Yiddish section of the pro-Communist IWO favored the establishment of Yiddish-language socialist schools for their members' children, but they could not help asking whether such schools were really necessary "when the children, when they grow up, will at any rate no longer read Yiddish newspapers and books."[32] This skepticism was well summed up by Barukh Charney Vladeck, a Bundist in the old country and a hero of the Jewish left, who wrote the following in 1911: "If life every place, and in America especially, should come to this: that Jews should stop existing as a nation and in about 100 years, there won't be in America any Jewish newspapers, any Jewish schools, nor any Jewish writers, it would not bother me."[33]

If one of the characteristics of Polish Jewish politics was a polarization between right and left, in America the right-wing component was virtually nonexistent. There were Orthodox Jews but virtually no political religious right (the leading institution of American Orthodoxy, Yeshiva College, was staffed and led mostly by religious Zionists). The militant nationalism of revisionist Zionism, so close to the models of Polish, Romanian, Lithuanian, and Boer integral nationalism, made practically no impression in the Zionist movement of a country foreign to the intense national conflicts of Eastern Europe and so dominated by liberal and pluralist politics. American Zionism was more or less identical with General Zionism, and the leaders of the integrationist organizations were also political centrists— some Democrats, some Republicans. American Jewish politics was therefore at the outset "center-left," or liberal-left. What made it stand out in the nonideological, liberal American political context was its strong socialist component. This was, however, to change during the interwar period.

During the 1920s and 1930s Jewish politics in America was characterized by two major developments: the growing rapprochement between the Zionists and the integrationists and the decline of the specifically Jewish left (though emphatically not of Jewish participation in the general left). The roots of the first development went back into the pre–World War I period when some integrationist-type Jews—without abandoning their strong ideological distaste for Jewish nationalism—had proved willing to assist in the struggle to build a modern Jewish society in Palestine and in this way to extend a helping hand to the persecuted Jews of Eastern Europe who might wish to settle there. Cyrus Adler, an arch anti-Zionist who was to become the president of the American Jewish Committee, wrote a letter to Herzl in 1897 offering to help the founder of political Zionism in his attempts to solve the Jewish Question on a territorial basis, although Adler preferred Mesopotamia to Palestine.[34] In 1908 the banker and philanthropist Jacob Schiff, no less an opponent of the idea that the Jews constituted a modern nation, gave a large sum of money to help establish the Technikum, an engineering school, in Haifa, Palestine.[35]

Support for the Palestinian venture on the part of Jewish anti-nationalists—let us call it Zionist fellow traveling—gained impetus during World War I. This was to be expected, given the dramatic increase in Jewish suffering in the East European war zone, the no less dramatic English conquest of Palestine, and the issuance of the Balfour Declaration. In addition there was the new antiimmigration legislation in the United States, which signified that Jewish migration to the New World could no longer be regarded as a potential solution to the East European Jewish Question. At the very beginning of World War I American Zionists conceived the idea of convening a democratically elected "Jewish Congress" that would, among other things, press Jewish demands for Palestine and for national minority rights in Eastern Europe as well as represent American Jewry at the peace conference. Such a congress was abhorrent to the integrationists on ideological and tactical grounds; it was regarded by them as an effort by the nationalists to take over American Jewry. Adler wrote to Marshall:

> the Congress was conceived in sin and born in iniquity; . . . it is a struggle to overthrow the existing Jewish institutions and substitute a new regime in their stead, this new regime to create the Jews all over the world including America into a nationality. The purpose has been openly avowed by the leaders and if successful will endanger the whole future of the Jews in America.[36]

Nevertheless, after a bewildering series of twists and turns, Marshall and his followers did in fact agree to participate in democratic elections to such a congress.[37] In 1919 Louis Marshall went off to Paris to represent the congress, and through it American Jewry, at the peace conference. Not only did he and his committee support "with profound appreciation" the Balfour Declaration—Zionism's greatest diplomatic achievement—but he actually went so far as to make the case for Jewish national minority rights, not for American Jews, of course, but for the Jews of Eastern Europe. Thus in the matter of Eastern Galicia—a former Hapsburg region fiercely contested by the Poles and the Ukrainians (it was eventually absorbed by Poland)—Marshall argued that the Jews there, caught between two bitterly hostile nationalities, must be accorded the status of a national minority with a separate electoral college of their own.[38] In the end the Poles did not allow this to come to pass. Marshall and his allies were, however, successful in persuading the victorious powers, above all the United States, to coerce Poland and a number of other East European countries into signing the so-called minorities treaty that guaranteed to the Jews and other groups not only equality before the law but a modest measure of group rights.

Having danced to the tune of the Zionists in 1919, the leading American integrationists during the 1920s carried on negotiations with the Zionists that were aimed at concluding a formal alliance. In the year of Marshall's death (1929), he and his colleagues agreed to join in the work of the Jewish Agency for Palestine, officially recognized by the British as the organization in charge of directing the transformation of Palestine into a national home for the Jews. The cementing of this Zionist-integrationist alliance was naturally aided during the 1930s by the growing crisis of European Jewry—the rise to power of Hitler in Germany and the mounting distress of Polish Jewry in that period. From the Zionist point of view the alliance was crucial because it seemed to hold out the promise of great things in the realm of fund-raising and political support. The term *non-Zionists,* as opposed to *anti-Zionists,* was now invented to define the new ideological position of what I would call the fellow-traveling integrationists.[39]

Particularly interesting and characteristic was the evolution of the position of American Reform Judaism, a Jewish "church" quite unknown in most of Eastern Europe, certainly unknown in Poland. Reform Judaism, whose founders were mostly German Jews, may be said to have represented the American Jewish Committee at prayer. Among the non-Orthodox American Jewish denominations the conservatives were traditionally pro-Zionist, the reformed anti-Zionist. I have already quoted Isaac Mayer Wise, the great founding father of American reform, to the effect that Judaism was no "tribal" religion. "Whatever Judaism may or may not be, it is a religion; whatever the Jew may or may not be, he is primarily a member of a religious community." Thus wrote reform Rabbi David Philipson in 1909, expressing a view that in its emphasis on the need for Jews to be loyal to Judaism and in its implied hostility to any type of secular Jewishness was reminiscent of the position of reform's greatest enemy, Orthodox Judaism.[40] Among the most dearly held tenets of this movement was the belief that the Jews had a mission to spread the benefits of Judaism, the "universal religion"—now denationalized and free of various outdated practices—all over the civilized world. It followed that the dispersion of Jewry among the nations was not unfortunate, but actually providential.

True, there had been dissenting voices in the pre-World War I years, and some Reform Jews, even Reform rabbis, did in fact become Zionists—most famous was Judah Leon Magnes, for a brief time Rabbi at the citadel of American Reform Judaism, Temple Emanu-El in New York City. (Magnes, untypically even for a Zionist, settled in Palestine and became the first chancellor of The Hebrew University of Jerusalem.) During the war itself debates on the question of Palestine intensified. In 1917 the majority report of the committee on the president's message to the movement's annual conference declared, "We look with disfavor upon the new doctrine of political Jewish nationalism, which finds the criterion of Jewish loyalty in anything other than loyalty to Israel's God and Israel's religious mission."[41] Nonetheless, during these difficult years the Reform movement began to buckle—to move with the "spirit of the times." It ceased to be anti-Zionist and became "non-Zionist."[42] The importance of the *yishuv* (the Jewish community of Palestine) was acknowledged, as was the crucial fact that "Zionism has aroused interest and enthusiasm among many who had been indifferent to, and even alienated from, their fathers' faith."[43] In other words, in the face of the growing estrangement of American Jews from all forms of Jewishness, hostility to secular Zionism as an illegitimate form of Jewishness was now tempered by an awareness that any form of Jewishness was preferable to no Jewishness at all. In 1930 the Zionist national anthem *"Ha-tikvah"* ("The Hope") was introduced into the Reform hymnal after a lengthy debate, during which the Zionist leader (and Reform rabbi) Stephen Wise said: "If you omit the *Hatikvah,* it is as though you are saying to the Jewish people: 'We are a church and nothing more.' You are saying to the world: 'We have nothing to do with the collective life of the Jewish people; we have broken with their dreams, we are done with their hopes, we stand alone, a Jewish Church.'"[44]

In 1936 the commission in charge of drafting the "guiding principles of Reform Judaism" declared that it was "the obligation of all Jewry to aid in the upbuilding of Palestine as a Jewish homeland, in making it not only a haven for the oppressed but also a center of Jewish culture and spiritual life."[45] In 1937 this formulation was adopted. Reform Judaism was now firmly in the camp of the Zionist fellow travelers.

The alliance between integrationists and Zionists was the result of the former's sensitivity to the needs of the threatened Jewish communities of Europe. It was also made possible because American Zionism was essentially different from East European Zionism—it did not, after all, stand for the nationalization of American Jewry, and it did not demand national rights for American Jews, something that Marshall and his colleagues would never have countenanced. The alliance was a very important historical phenomenon, prefiguring as it did today's nearly united Jewish stand, in America and in Europe, behind Israel. However, it did not mean that Zionism in America became a great mass movement. Support for Zionism went up sharply during and directly after World War I, as it did in Poland (and virtually everywhere else). After that, enthusiasm waned. Membership declined.[46] Integrationists, despite their Zionist fellow-traveling, spent large sums of money on trying to solve the Jewish problem in the Soviet Union not by transporting those Jews to Palestine, which was deemed impossible, but rather by transforming them into farmers in the Crimea and the Ukraine. The movement continued to be promoted by some noted intellectuals and many Conservative rabbis, mostly spiritual Zionists, who downplayed the idea of establishing a Jewish state and emphasized the need to create in Palestine an ideal society imbued with the ideals of the prophets—a second United States or something even better (in the words of Zionist writer Ludwig Lewisohn, "[an island of] justice and goodness [in a mad world]).")[47] But the masses, busy making it in the New World, rapidly acculturating, faded away. In Isaac Rosenfeld's novel of Jewish life in America, the young hero's stepmother is a Zionist who used to "dance the Hora and sing Hebrew songs and take courses in farming." None of this, however, interests the youngster.[48] Perhaps the dire predictions of Abraham Cahan and Henry Roth were really coming true. Perhaps it was Sammy Glick—Budd Schulberg's famous antihero, who grew up "no different from the little wops and micks who cursed and fought and cheated"—who best represented this new generation far removed from the East European Jewish nation.[49] This was not really the case. In fact, in the 1930s Zionist activity began to pick up again. Recall that in Poland Zionism's credibility was greatly harmed by the precipitous decline of aliyah from 1936 on, this the result of British policy over which the Zionists had little influence. In America, on the other hand, where Zionism had never been aliyah centered, the virtual closing down of Palestine to Jewish immigration did not have the same impact. Indeed, restrictions on aliyah at the very time that the Jewish crisis in Eastern and Central Europe was escalating so dramatically incensed many American Jews and gave the Zionist movement in the United States a shot in the arm. By 1939 membership in the ZOA was on the rise again, as it was in the womens' Zionist organization, Hadassah, and in other organizations.[50]

In Poland Zionism was sorely challenged and perhaps even momentarily overcome in the late 1930s by an old, formidable enemy—the Jewish Bund. In America things were different. Above all, the history of the Jewish left in that country in the interwar period was the history of a movement in decline.

This did not appear to be the case during and immediately after World War I. In 1914 the socialist Meyer London was elected to the U.S. Congress with the support of Jewish workers from the lower East Side of Manhattan—he was not running as a candidate of a Jewish party, of course, but he was identified with the specifically Jewish left through his work as a lawyer for the Jewish unions and as a Bundist sympathizer. His election was regarded as a triumph for Jewish socialism.[51] The great Jewish trade unions were finally placed on a secure footing. Moreover, while people like Brandeis and Marshall rejoiced over the Balfour Declaration of 1917, another event of that year, the Russian Revolution, galvanized the Jewish socialists. If Russia, the capital of world antisemitism and home of the largest of all Jewish communities, was now free, and if the revolution would spread all over Europe, then who needed Zionism.

The future looked bright indeed. But it was not. For one thing the general American left declined dramatically in the 1920s, the result of the great schism caused by communism, government persecution, and economic prosperity. But there were several ills that afflicted the Jewish movement in particular.[52] The first has to do with sociological trends. The American Jewish working class was formed by the great East European Jewish immigration. Jews, not necessarily workers in the old country, came off the boats and marched into the sweatshops and factories of the lower East Side. This is what happened to the family described by Sholem Aleichem in his last novel: In Russia its members had been rabbis and cantors, in the New World they became garment workers. "That's America," they say in resignation.[53] But after World War I there was much less immigration, and the Jewish working class was not replenished by fresh arrivals from the East. Moreover, there was a lot more social mobility in the

United States than in economically depressed and antisemitic Poland. In the book written and illustrated by the radical American Jewish artist William Gropper, *The Little Tailor,* a Russian Jewish tailor, freshly arrived in the land of Columbus, was told that in America he could look forward to opening "a fine salon of his own on Fifth Avenue"[54] (see fig. 20). The reader is left with the clear impression that he would achieve this all-American aim. And even if he remained forever a prisoner of the sweat-shop, his children at least would have every chance of rising above their working-class parents. Indeed, the "Jewish unions" did become progressively less Jewish as the years passed, although their leadership remained firmly in the hands of immigrant Jewish socialists.[55]

Moreover, the Yiddish secular culture—so assiduously nurtured by the Jewish left—also began to decline, much faster in dynamic America than in backward Poland. By the 1930s Barukh Vladeck's prognosis was coming true. And without its national cultural base, without Yiddish, how could a specifically Jewish left continue to exist? How could it be justified? The well-known Jewish predeliction for the left continued, but now, in the 1930s, when the Great Depression gave the radical movement, especially communism, a new lease on life, young Jews were more likely to join or support the American left rather than its specifically Jewish, Yiddish-speaking component. The biography of Joseph Freeman, a Communist intellectual stalwart, is instructive. He was born in a Ukrainian shtetl but grew up in America, eventually attending Columbia College. As he puts it, "By the time we were leaving the university we were no longer, culturally, Jews." By then "I had long ago ceased to think of men as being divided into Jew and gentile, black and white, American and European."[56] In his youth a Zionist sympathizer, Freeman moved into the radical left after World War I, but he was not attracted to the Jewish socialist or Communist movement. Rather, he became an editor of the pro-Communist *New Masses* magazine, the organ of cosmopolitan Communists and their fellow travelers.

Freeman's sentiments were shared by American-born playwright Arthur Miller, who recalled that in the 1930s "I was struggling to identify myself with mankind rather than with one small tribal faction of it." (Like Isaac Mayer Wise, Miller did not like the idea of belonging to a "tribe.") In those days, he tells us, he believed that "we were leaving behind parochial narrowness of mind, prejudices, racism, and the irrational, which were having their ultimate triumph, it seemed to us, in the fascist and Nazi movements that were everywhere growing in strength."[57] And Alfred Kazin writes in his memoirs of those years that he and his wife "were both in a terrible rush to get away from everything we had grown up with"—for which we may read Judaism and Jewishness of every sort.[58]

The 1930s were the heyday of the formation of the radical Jewish cosmopolitan (or universalist) intelligentsia, whose politics were left-wing but whose language and culture were Anglo-Saxon, American. Whatever it was, this important group was emphatically not interested in "ethnic" or

He was going to create new designs for clothes starting right here in this small room. Some day he would have a fine salon of his own on Fifth Avenue. His would be the garments of people with a future—the people of America.

Fig. 20: The End of the Jewish Labor Movement in America. From Old World tailor to New World entrepreneur. (*Source:* William Gropper, *The Little Tailor* [New York: Dodd, Mead 1955]. Courtesy of the Tamiment Institute Library, New York University.)

national Jewish politics, nor did it wish to work in Yiddish, in contrast to the previous generation of American Jewish left-wingers led by such figures as Cahan, Vladeck, and Dubinsky.[59]

The numerical decline of the Jewish working class and the Americanization of the new Jewish left-wing intelligentsia, which led inevitably to a lack of interest in specifically Jewish politics and culture, was bound to harm the Jewish left. But sociology was not the only factor at work. The emergence of communism as a force on the American left also had a role to play in this process. True, the rise of American communism signified the organization of a distinct Jewish Communist movement, with its own language section within the Communist party, its own press (led by the *Frayheyt*), its fraternal society, its cultural work, and so forth. Many Jewish Communists were former Bundists swept off their feet by the successes of bolshevism, just as some of their comrades had been in Poland and Russia. Communism also made serious inroads in the Jewish unions in the 1920s and 1930s. But Jewish communism was ultimately controlled by dictates from above, by Moscow and by the Communist International (Comintern); however, Moscow's policy sometimes clashed disastrously with the views and interests of most Jews. In 1929, for example, *Frayheyt,* after first condemning the Arab attacks on defenseless Jews in Palestine that occurred in that year, quickly changed its line in accord with Comintern policy and applauded the pogroms as a legitimate expression of Arab self-defense against Jewish encroachments. This disgusted many Jews, including many left-wingers on the fringe of the movement.[60] Even worse was the party's approbation of the Soviet–Nazi pact of 1939. Many Jews with impeccable left-wing views could not stomach that. The events of 1941 saved the situation, for a while at least, as the Soviet Union once again stood in the forefront of the anti-Fascist campaign. But much damage had been done.

Finally, and most important of all, the anti-Communist Jewish social democrats of the unions, of the Arbeter Ring, and of the *Forverts* were being drawn, slowly but surely, into mainstream (and I emphasize the word *mainstream*) American politics. This was an event of great significance without parallel in the Jewish radical political experience in Poland. As early as 1928 David Dubinsky, head of the ILGWU and once a loyal socialist, refused to back the socialist candidacy of Norman Thomas in the presidential election. One reason for the willingness of some old socialists to abandon the movement was their disgust in the face of Communist inroads into its institutions. But the great breakthrough came during Franklin D. Roosevelt's (FDR's) New Deal. Both the president and the mayor of New York, Fiorello La Guardia (a Republican), were pro union and were taking strong action to alleviate the Depression. Both welcomed Jewish support and took Jews into their administrations. La Guardia— himself half-Jewish, but identified as Italian—appointed the famous Jewish socialist Barukh Charney Vladeck, an old Bundist who had done his time in czarist prisons, to his New York City Housing Authority (in 1934). Consider the career of Sidney Hillman. He had been a revolutionary in Lithuania, a Bundist, and a Russian social democrat. He, too, had spent time in prisons. In America he was a trade unionist, in time becoming the undisputed leader of the Amalgamated Clothing Workers of America. And in the 1930s he established a "strong political friendship" with FDR, eventually becoming the president's most influential advisor on labor.[61]

The organizational framework in which the old Jewish socialist trade unionists—the Dubinskys and Hillmans—cemented their alliance with the New Deal was the American Labor party, founded in 1936. "The thought," Josephson explains, "was to channel the 'regular' Socialists into the Roosevelt camp."[62] Dubinsky writes, "It gave us a way to break down the resistance of old-line Socialists—me among them—who would not vote for any candidates on the Democratic line."[63] The new party, active only in New York State, was a considerable success. Through it the once socialist Jewish trade union movement was Americanized, domesticated. It was during the 1930s, in fact, that many Jews became supporters of the left-wing (that is, liberal-wing) of the Democratic party, where many remain to this day. A fitting graphic symbol of this development was the mural painted in 1937–38 by the American Jewish artist Ben Shahn for the community center of Jersey Homesteads (later renamed Roosevelt) in New Jersey, a cooperative settlement of New York garment workers. Shahn's political views were far to the left of center, but in this painting he celebrates the triumph of the New Deal. "In the last panel, under a poster of FDR, whom Shahn revered, appears the ground plan of Jersey Homesteads itself, and seated around a drafting board are the figures of John Brophy, Sidney Hillman, David Dubinsky, Senator Robert F. Wagner, and that remarkable apostle of social progress, Heywood Broun"[64] (see fig. 21).

Just as some leaders and organizations of the old Jewish left were now finding it possible to support the Democratic party as led by FDR, so we may discern a certain softening in their traditional hostility or indifference toward Zionism. In 1920 the ILGWU adopted a resolution expressing its gratitude to the British Labour party for having supported the Balfour Declaration. In 1921 a delegation of Zionist socialists from Palestine came to America to raise money and seek friends for the Jewish labor movement in Palestine and a few conquests among Jewish American labor leaders were made—most notably Joseph Schlossberg of the Amalgamated Clothing Workers union.[65] A few years later Abraham Cahan himself, editor of the daily socialist newspaper the *Forverts*, traveled to Palestine and recorded his strongly positive impressions of the Jewish community there.[66] Cahan and his powerful newspaper were furious when the Jewish Communists approved of the Arab-instigated pogrom of 1929 in the Holy Land. Interesting, too, is the attitude of Morris Hillquit, a celebrated leader of American Marxism. Hillquit had never been closely associated with the specifically Jewish left, but he had played a role in the Jewish trade union movement (for a time he was the lawyer of the ILGWU). He had never been a Jewish nationalist of any kind—quite the contrary—but in 1926 he confessed, "Zionism makes a strong sentimental appeal to me, chiefly as a manifestation of awakening national self respect of the Jewish people." He quickly added that Zionism, like all other national movements, must guard itself against the dangers of degeneration into jingoism—"If it ever develops in that direction, it will forfeit all claims to Socialist sympathy."[67]

A certain sympathy for the Jewish labor movement in Palestine does not mean that the Jewish moderate (non-Communist) left was converted during the interwar period to Zionism. But this trend toward a degree of support for the (hopefully) socialist society being built by socialist Jews in Palestine is reminiscent of the integrationists coming to terms with the Palestinian venture. If the Jewish labor movement's alliance with the New Deal was a reflection of its Americanization, it was also the case that its soft underbelly vis-à-vis Zionism was an important further step toward joining the American and the American Jewish mainstream.

Comparing the Jewish political experience in Poland and in America is a bit like comparing apples and oranges. By the late 1930s, at the very time when so many American Jewish political leaders were finding a home in the incumbent Democratic party, the ruling Polish political party—established by Piłsudski's epigone in 1936–37 and antisemitic to the core—explicitly forbade Jewish membership. If Jewish politics in America gravitated to-

Fig. 21: *The Americanization of the American Jewish Labor Movement.* Jewish labor leaders identify with the New Deal. (Ben Shahn, *Fresco Mural,* 1937–38, Roosevelt, N.J. Estate of Ben Shahn/VAGA, New York, 1992.)

ward the center, in Poland the center did not hold, and by the 1930s the Jewish left and right were setting the tone. Although American Jewish politics were characterized by fellow-traveling and by a growing irrelevance of old ideological positions, the Polish Jewish political community (rent in 1935 as it had been in 1905 by the old, classic internal ideological splits) exhibited no such tendency. True, even in Poland there was some erosion: Agudah, for example, did become more favorable to the idea of settling in Palestine in the 1930s and, as already pointed out, the integrationists in Eastern Europe were more national than elsewhere. But, taken as a whole, Polish Jewish politics remained highly ideological. Hebraists remained Hebraists and Yiddishists remained Yiddishists, Bundists refused to support Zionism and vice versa; even the Agudah—although it did countenance the vocational training of some of its youth in preparation for aliyah—remained in principle bitterly opposed to all secular Jewish doctrines.

If Polish Jewish politics was hard, in America it was soft, presaging the happy days of post-World War II unanimity with regard to Israel. This is another way of saying that Jewish Polish politics was East European and American Jewish politics was American. "As the gentiles go, so go the Jews."

4

Appeal

Chapter 3 has charted the fortunes of the various Jewish political movements in two radically different countries. The first, Poland, was home to a typical East European Jewish community similar in many ways to the neighboring communities of Lithuania, Latvia, eastern Czechoslovakia, and Romania. The second, America, witnessed during the interwar period the coming of age of a Western-type Jewry, in many ways reminiscent of those in Western and Central Europe. It is surely paradoxical that in this Western-type, rapidly acculturating community Zionism—albeit of a rather peculiar type—encountered much less organized opposition than in the heartland of Jewish nationalism, Poland, where it was severely challenged by antinational Orthodoxy and especially by the anti-Zionist Jewish left, above all the Bund.

In this chapter I propose to look more closely at the underlying sources of appeal of several of the Jewish political camps, in particular of the Jewish left and of the varieties of Jewish nationalism.

The Left

In his novel *The Ordeal of Gilbert Pinfold* Evelyn Waugh records the following conversation concerning his eponymous antihero, who is mistaken for a Jew:

> "I don't say he's an actual card-carrying member of the Communist party, but he's certainly mixed up with them."
> "Most Jews are."
> "Exactly."[1]

Along the same lines, a Polish barber in a novel by Isaac Bashevis Singer maintains, "Every one of them [the Jews of Poland] is a secret Communist and a Soviet spy. They have one aim—to root out us Christians and hand over the power to the Bolsheviks, the Masons, and the radicals."[2] In yet another I. B. Singer novel a concerned Pole says to a Jewish acquaintance, "Mr. Yanovar, the percentage of Jewish Communists is astonishingly large. The proportion is simply fantastic . . . the situation is unbearable. Today the Jews are the spreaders of Bolshevism throughout the face of the earth. I'm not exaggerating. This puts the very existence of the Jewish race in danger."[3]

Of course, our Polish friend, or rather Isaac Bashevis Singer, is guilty of hyperbole. And yet there is something, even quite a lot, in what he says. I have already observed the strength of the Jewish left (consisting of socialist Zionists, Bundists, and activists in the Jewish bureau of the Communist party) in Poland. Taken together these forces dominated Jewish politics in the last years of independent Poland. In America the specifically Jewish left may have fallen victim to sociological trends, but the attraction of socialism remained extremely strong for many individual Jews. In the generally "reformist," nonpolitical American trade union movement, the Jewish garment trades were conspicuous for their political radicalism, and American communism was more successful among the Jews than among any other ethnic group, with the possible exception of the Finns.[4] In a book by R. Zaltsman on the IWO, the American pro-Communist fraternal and cultural association, a remarkable ethnic breakdown of the organization is presented (see fig. 22). It demonstrates that in the 1930s the Yiddish-language section of the IWO constituted no less than 31.4 percent of the total membership; the next largest language section, the English-speaking one, accounted for a mere 8.9 percent, followed by the Ukrainian, Hungarian, Slovak, and Russian sections (of course, there were probably many Jews in these non-Jewish sections as well).[5] A highly disproportionate number of Jews fought as foreign volunteers in the Spanish civil war, some as members of a special Jewish Polish Communist company.[6] Jews did, indeed, make up a very high percentage of members of the Polish Communist party—even in independent Lithuania, where there was so little acculturation, the same phenomenon may be observed. Nor should one forget to mention the amazing case of Hungary, whose short-lived Communist regime of 1919 really was almost totally dominated by "Hungarians of Jewish origin."[7]

In fact, for some Jews growing up in the 1930s Jewishness was synonymous with political radicalism. Alfred Kazin tells us that socialism was an integral part of his culture and that he was a socialist, "like everyone else I knew."[8] Grace Paley doubtless speaks for many when she writes, "I also really felt that to be Jewish was to be a socialist. I mean that was my idea as a kid—that's what it meant to be Jewish."[9]

How to explain the tremendous attraction (perhaps one should call it

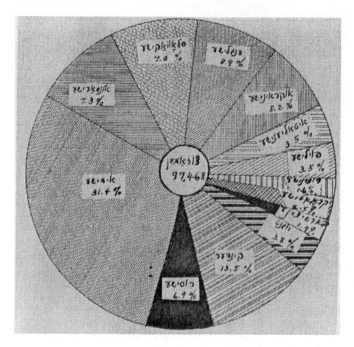

Fig. 22: The Jews Dominate the Left. According to this pie chart, the Yiddish-language section of IWO accounted for 31.4 percent of all members. Next came the English-language section, with 8.9 percent; the Ukrainian section, with 8.2 percent; the Hungarian section, with 7.3 percent; the Slovak section, with 7 percent; the Russian section, with 6.9 percent; and the Polish section, with 3.5 percent. (*Source:* R. Zaltsman, *Tsu der geshikhte fun der fraternaler bavegung* [New York, 1936], p. 239.)

the fatal attraction) of the left? Much ink has been spilled on this question and many hypotheses offered.[10] On the face of it the answer seems fairly obvious. Would not a people confronting discrimination, hatred, and humiliation (in Eastern Europe in particular but in the West as well), a people blessed, or cursed, with a large, poverty-stricken working class and lower middle class—would not many members of such a group inevitably gravitate toward the only political force dedicated to revolutionary change? This in many countries was the left, the only group that firmly and bravely opposed nazism, fascism, and other antisemitic movements. The poet W. H. Auden is reported to have said, "I simply can't understand why every Negro isn't a Communist. It's the only system that holds out any hope for them."[11] He might well have said Jew instead of Negro. "I hate injustice," said the American Jewish artist Ben Shahn, "I guess that's about the only thing I really do hate."[12] Such an eminently Jewish sentiment naturally led him to identify with the left. Irving Kristol has said, "It would be hard for Jews, most of us coming from poor, working-class families, not to be radical. So we wanted to be radical."[13] In one of his autobiographical sketches Philip Roth tells us that as a child he often experienced antisemitism, "Small wonder that at twelve, when I was advised to begin thinking seriously about what I would do when I grew up, I decided to oppose the injustices wreaked by the violent and the privileged by becoming a lawyer for the underdog."[14] Sigmund Freud, in his famous 1926 letter to the B'nai B'rith lodge in Vienna, observed, "As a Jew, I was prepared to be in the opposition."[15] In his case "opposition" did not translate into socialism, but for those with a greater interest in politics than Freud possessed it usually did.

Not only did the left stand, or at least appear to stand, in opposition to the organized forces of antisemitism, but it also seemed to represent that much-longed-for neutral ground, a place where Jew and gentile could meet as absolute equals, sharing the same ideals of brotherhood and universalism. True, this was not invariably the case. For one thing the left possessed an antisemitic tradition of its own, ostensibly based on the perception that the capitalist class was strongly permeated by Jews. Moreover, the influx of Jews into the various Communist parties after World War I was not always welcomed—not so much because of antisemitism but because of the perfectly natural desire of these organizations not to be identified by the public as too Jewish. Even in America the Communists tried desperately to recruit blacks and other non-Jews because "the most decided disproportion . . . was the Jewish presence in the Party."[16]

Nonetheless, Jews of a certain kind felt at home in the subcultures created by socialism and communism. They believed that they were welcome there and that they could pursue their political ambitions there. For Howard Fast, the American writer and Communist, a man who had experienced his share of antisemitism while growing up in New York City, the party was one of the few places "where I sensed no smell or whisper of anti-Semitism."[17] This perception of the left as a subculture free of all prejudices was an essential aspect of its unique attraction.

Moreover, socialism and communism were largely urban creeds, oriented toward the factory worker or artisan and the intellectual, and in modern times Jews have always been overrepresented in cities and within the intelligentsia. This was particularly the case in Eastern Europe where the Jews were by far the most urban (and most literate) of all the nations. One should, therefore, not be too surprised if in Poland, for example, proportionately many more Jews than the mostly peasant Poles, Ukrainians, or Belorussians were attracted to Marxism and the other socialist systems.

I now come to a paradox in the story of the nexus between Jews and the left. Many have argued for a link between the attraction to the left and the heritage of Judaism—messianism, the traditional hope for *tikun* (mending [the world], the name, not coincidentally, of a contemporary left-wing Jewish magazine) and above all the teachings of the prophets. I have already pointed out that for many Jews of the left the prophets were the true heroes of Jewish history. For many observers it was precisely this heritage that explained why so many modern Jews gravitated to the left. In a well-known Hebrew novel of the Russian Revolution one is told that the radical hero, Soroke, had studied the Bible in his youth before turning to the Haskalah and to Russian literature, "His mind was filled with enthusiastic opinions and dreams of *tikun olam* [mending the world] and similar things that tempt Jewish youths."[18] Morris Winchevsky, a founding father of Jewish socialism, is on record as saying, "For almost everything I write I have to thank [Isaiah], that poet-preacher who entered my mind and my heart with his love for orphans and widows and other defenseless and dispossessed people."[19] In his novel of Jewish life on the East Side of Manhattan Sholem Asch explains why so many Jewish workers were attracted to socialism:

> The Jewish masses brought with them [to America] the entire heritage of their prophetic forefathers, the entire baggage of a lofty ethical and moral teaching, which they had employed in the revolutionary struggle against czarist slavery. The revolutionary spirit which lives within the Jewish masses has been wondrously effective here in America.[20]

And Asch's young hero, Nathan, pressed into service as a socialist agitator, explains to the Jewish workers how Marxism is nothing but a continuation of the ethical teachings of Judaism as exemplified by Moses, the prophets, and Jesus.[21]

The prophetic heritage argument, which explains the influx of Jews into the left by emphasizing the close links between its social ideals and the Jewish religious-ethical tradition, is easily joined to the idea that for many Jews socialism was in fact a new religion. Marxism, with its certainties, its inexorable laws of history, has been often regarded as having much in common with talmudic Judaism, this despite the undoubted antisemitic bias of Marx himself. Sidney Hook, who should know, writes that communism "provided a mode of life every whit as integrated and sustaining as the religion they [the Jews] had abandoned. They could feel themselves once more, even if persecuted, a chosen people not of God but of history, a vanguard, liberated from the exclusionist and chauvinistic prejudices of their forefathers, preaching a salvation open to all mankind."[22] Like Maxim in Lionel Trilling's novel of American communism, the Jewish socialists could boast of an "extreme commitment to the future," just like their rabbinic ancestors.[23]

By the same token, one might well argue that the fanatic Jewish Marxist of the American or Polish Communist party was nothing more than a newly minted, secularized version of the old religious fanatic and martyr who, armed only with his religious texts and his unshakable faith, had heroically and successfully defied the world. Thus the Russian Jewish nov-

elist Vasily Grossman's description of the Jewish Bolshevik true believer
Lev Mekler. Did the *Communist Manifesto* convert him to communism,
Grossman asks,

> or was it that the smoldering coals were buried deep within his thousand-year
> inheritance, ready to burst into flame—to do battle with Ceasar's Roman
> soldiers, to confront the bonfires of the Spanish Inquisition, to join in the
> starving frenzy of the Talmudists, to emerge in the shtetl organization for self-
> defense during the pogroms?[24]

According to Grossman's vision the very logic of Jewish history appears to
lead, inexorably, to an identification between the modern secularized Jew
and communism.

But if the Jews' influx into the left can be plausibly explained by
referring to Jewish historical continuity, it is also the case that the left
attracted Jews because it appeared to them to be the very opposite of the
traditional Jewish world, the much-despised ghetto. After all, many Jews
on the left had reacted violently against the Orthodox Jewish world in
which they or their parents had grown up. These people, some of whom
possessed a general education and saw themselves as intellectuals, detested
what they saw as the horribly restrictive, oppressive, bigoted, and stifling
world of East European Orthodoxy, whether in the ghettos of the old
country or in New York City and other centers of the East European
Jewish dispersion. They wished both to escape from it and to play a part in
hastening its historically determined, inevitable demise. There may have
been an element of self-hatred here, a well-known malady among all minorities, but one should keep in mind that many Jews who so despised
everything the ghetto stood for became Zionist socialists or Bundists—
whatever they may have suffered from, they can hardly be charged with
hating the Jewish people.

A famous literary expression of radical Jewry's violent rejection of the
traditional Jewish world is *Jews Without Money* by the American Jewish
Communist Michael Gold. Reb Moisha, the religious schoolteacher
(*melamed*), is described as "a walking, belching symbol of the decay of
orthodox Judaism. . . . He was a foul smelling, emaciated beggar who
had never read anything, or seen anything, who knew absolutely nothing
but this sterile memory course in dead Hebrew which he whipped into the
heads and backsides of little boys."[25]

The society that produced such a man, a society whose incredible
restrictiveness had no real parallel in the Christian world, must obviously
be destroyed; and only the left, in Gold's estimation, was capable of destroying it. He concludes, "O workers' Revolution, you brought hope to
me, a lonely, suicidal boy. You are the true Messiah. You will destroy the
East Side when you come, and build there a garden for the human
spirit."[26]

Perhaps the worst aspect of traditional Judaism in the eyes of the
Jewish socialist intellectuals was its exclusivism and chauvinism. Thus the

Jewish Communist Peysakh Novik, describing Jerusalem in the early 1930s, writes, "The air is thick with religion, thick with hatred—the product of religion."[27]

Hatred in this context means, among other things, hatred of the gentile, the drunken and violent *goy* of the Jewish imagination. Judaism, at least the Judaism as shaped by the rabbis, meant despising the non-Jew, whereas socialism signified a breaking down of all religious and national barriers. Searching as they were for the obverse of Judaism, it is hardly surprising that many in the Jewish left, and many Jews in the general left, were obsessed with the need to forge close ties with the non-Jewish world. Here, I believe, was one of the most profound sources of the attraction of the left for those who had abandoned the God and the rabbis (but not the prophets) of Israel. The old idea of the chosenness of the Jewish people, *"atah bahartanu"* ("You [God] have chosen us"), a common refrain in the Jewish liturgy, was rejected with contempt in favor of what only the left could provide—brotherhood with the gentiles. How else to understand the importance of the theme "black and white together," so dear to the hearts of Jewish leftists in America and so often depicted by left-wing American Jewish artists (see fig. 23). Alfred Kazin informs us that the Jewish Communists in America in the 1930s rebuked the Jewish socialists because "we had no *Negro comrades* of our own"[28]—a strange rebuke, indeed, explicable only if one realizes that the notion of Jewish proletarian unity with the most despised group in American society possessed great symbolic power, prefiguring as it did the coming universal brotherhood of man. In the early 1920s, a Polish Bundist declared, "The greatest task which remains, from an organizatinal standpoint, is to unite the Jewish and Polish trade union movement."[29] Such unity was obviously desirable for tactical reasons, but this comment may also be read as a fervent Jewish wish to achieve true comradeship with the Polish gentiles, a comradeship condemned in the old Jewish world and attainable only within the framework of socialism. The joys of this comradeship are well expressed by Joseph Freeman, who worked on the radical journal *The Liberator* after World War I:

> Most of the editors were native, Nordic Americans . . . yet no racial or national distinctiveness ever appeared between them and the Jewish poet Michael Gold, the Negro poet Claude McKay, or the Italian poet Arturo Giovannitti. Traditional racial barriers were transcended not only in the common work of the publication and in personal friendship, but even in the more intimate relations of love and marriage. I felt that on a small scale the *Liberator* group represented that ideal society which we all wanted, that society in which no racial barriers could possibly exist.[30]

In short, my argument is that the left's message of solidarity among the various groups into which humanity was at least temporarily divided was extraordinarily attractive to those Jews who regarded the Jewish ghetto with horror and disgust. They had, in effect, traded off the Jewish God and

Fig. 23: Black and White Together. Martin Luther King's vision as interpreted by the American Jewish pro-Communist artist William Gropper. (William Gropper, *I Have a Dream,* 1963. Collection of Bill Cosby.)

the Jewish ghetto for this comradeship which, I believe, they took far more seriously and believed in far more fervently than did most non-Jewish socialists.

The alliance with the gentiles signified not only comradeship but also power. It is said that the leaders of the tiny Montenegran people were fond of boasting that they, together with their allies the Russians, numbered over one hundred million people. For Jews on the left the longed-for alliance with the international working class signified their transformation from a despised and powerless minority into an integral part of a mighty force, potentially the majority of mankind. This must have been, from a psychological point of view, an extremely satisfying compensation for the loss of old certainties, of God and Torah.

I. J. Singer has given us a splendid literary account of this state of mind in his novel *Comrade Nahman,* a cautionary tale of a wretchedly poor Polish Jewish baker, Nahman, who, like so many of his generation, found his way from the traditional Jewish elementary school (*heyder*) to the Jewish left. On entering a library run by Jewish socialists in Warsaw he is told, "Have a look, comrade, and everything will become clear to you."[31] It does. In due course he becomes a loyal Communist, suffers for his ideals, is imprisoned, and eventually makes his way to the Soviet Union, where he takes part in May Day celebrations in Red Square. This is the greatest moment of his poverty-stricken, tortured life: "For the first time in his life he felt truly happy; all his suffering and pain had been worth-

while . . . Among the hundreds and thousands of marching proletarians goes Nahman the baker from Warsaw, marching by the great red
square."[32]

There is no happy end to this story, for Nahman is betrayed and
abandoned by those he imagined to be his allies. But the point is clear. For
Nahman, who has left behind him the rabbinical world his father hoped he
would make his own, the left has provided him with power, with strength,
with hope; it has transformed him from an isolated, powerless Jew in a
hostile, antisemitic world into a man with a powerful ally—the Soviet
Union and the world proletariat. The same feeling was expressed by a
young Polish Jew whose Zionist socialist organization was participating in
a May Day parade: "Today is not a holiday only for Jews, it is an international holiday for all nations. It is a workers' holiday . . . we are a power
[*Mir zenen a koyekh*]."[33] And a young man who in the 1920s joined the
Bundist youth organization *Tsukunft* (Future) reports that at that moment
"my fate, my hopes, my dreams were bound up with the aspirations and
aims of millions of proletarians of the entire world."[34]

One may conclude that the connection between the Jews and the left
made good sense on both political and psychological grounds. But it has
often been regarded as a Jewish tragedy, a great disaster, and not only
because it weakened religious Judaism and led to increased antisemitism.
Many have bewailed the inability of thousands of young Jewish idealists to
withstand the false temptations of socialism and have accused them of self-
hatred, of abandoning their people, of serving foreign gods, of "dancing at
someone else's wedding."[35] Typical is the well-known Israeli historian
David Vital, who writes of "The brilliant regiments of high-spirited, de-
cent, altruistic young men and women who rallied to Marxism in the wake
of the movement's own eponymous founder, only to be destroyed by it and
within it."[36] These brilliant regiments stand accused not so much of du-
plicity as of naïveté, of acting in the name of lofty ideals not fully shared, or
not shared at all, by their gentile allies. In Raphael Soyer's drawing (see p.
33) a white woman cradles a black child, but did any black artists depict
black women holding white babies in their arms? In a novel by Yehudah
Varshaviak the hero, Margolin, fights for Polish independence as a soldier
in a special Polish socialist legion. He witnesses the death of a Jewish
soldier from this legion whose last words are: "[W]hat have we to do with
all this?"[37] When Margolin returns home after the Polish victory, he meets
Jewish women who had been raped by the victorious Polish soldiers and
imagines the screams of terror of innocent Jews caught up in the horrors of
war: "These were the voices of Jewish men and women tortured by the
rampaging soldiers after their sudden victory, who in the frenzy of triumph
completely forgot about the lofty proclamations they heard so often and
which some of them could recite with such sincerity."[38] To fight side by
side with potential participants in pogroms (*pogromshchiki*) in the name of
socialist brotherhood in which the gentiles do not, in their heart of hearts,
believe—this is truly the stuff of Jewish tragedy. The undeniable existence

of antisemitism among the gentile workers was a standing reproof to the ideals of the Jewish left and to Jews in the general left, whose international slogans were sometimes nothing more than, as the novelist Leib Hazan puts it, "a voice crying in the wilderness, with no real meaning."[39]

Serving foreign gods, entering into alliances based on idealistic slogans rejected by one's allies—what better and more terrible example of this than the support given by so many Jews on the left, and by some Jewish left-wing organizations, to the Soviet Union? Jewish support for bolshevism certainly helped to fan the fires of antisemitism, especially in Eastern and Central Europe, and from our perspective this may well have been the most tragic aspect of the nexus between the Jews and the left. But one should not lose sight of the fact that it was also, in the eyes of many Jewish left-wingers, the embodiment of their great expectations from socialism, the jewel in the crown, so they thought, of the Jewish–socialist alliance. To be linked with a mighty power, a power that had set about to uproot the hated ancien régime in antisemitic Russia and the hated shtetl along with it; a power that, at least in the 1920s supported Jewish secular, Yiddish-based culture; a power that outlawed antisemitism at home and fulminated against fascism abroad—what could be better than this?

Little wonder that I. J. Singer's fictional character Nahman the baker, parading happily in Red Square, had plenty of real-life parallels. Joe Rapoport, an American Jewish Communist of Russian origins, described his impressions of Moscow in 1934: "In my youth, in the Tsarist days, a Jew could not enter Moscow without special privileges. But there I was walking on the cobblestones of Red Square, once the parade grounds for the Tsar's troops."[40]

How strange it was that Jewish radicals, who have been described—and who sometimes saw themselves—as the inheritors of the spiritual legacy of Isaiah and Micah, served as loyal supporters and apologists for Stalinism and were able to describe a brutal tyrant as a "beloved figure"[41] and his country as "the hope of the world—the only large nation run by men of reason."[42] The most charitable interpretation that can be put on this sad alliance between Jewish radicals who would not harm a fly and a wicked regime that murdered millions of innocent people is that it derived at least in part from the existential situation of a persecuted minority that, especially in the 1930s, found itself under an attack of unprecedented dimensions led by nazism, the "native" fascist movements of East Central Europe, and by less powerful but nonetheless frightening forces in America.

Of course, the vast majority of Jews in Europe and in America were not socialists, not to mention Communists (and those who were had no monopoly on that peculiar blindness that permitted them to praise a regime that specialized in mass murder). Nonetheless, a chapter dealing with the sources of appeal to Jews of various political movements must emphasize the tremendous power of the vision of an alliance between Jews and all progressive mankind—Polish and Russian workers, American blacks, all the dispossessed and powerless, struggling together for a better world, for a just society, against the forces of evil embodied by nazism. It was, I believe, one of the great heroic visions of modern Jewish politics, and if it had, to put it mildly, its unpleasant side, so did the others.

Nationalism

"I am no nationalist—I am for all mankind," says Leache in Hazaz's novel, and she adds: "I am a communist."[43] But it was possible, of course, to be a member in good standing of the left and also to be a Jewish nationalist, thus avoiding the potentially unhappy fate of those Jewish socialists who spent their time "dancing at someone else's wedding," allied with potential or actual antisemites, running the risk of ending up like Nahman the baker—abandoned and despised by all. Indeed, in the struggle for the hearts and minds of Jews, and in particular in the struggle for the hearts and minds of East European Jewish youth, the appeal of nationalism, whether combined with socialism or not, was by far the strongest. It won the support of the East European masses, and it won the support of some of the most illustrious of Jewish intellectuals. Kafka was taken with it, and Einstein was one of its chief propagandists. Schoenberg, a convert who reconverted to Judaism, became a strong Jewish nationalist, and Freud went on record in 1935, in a letter to the Hebrew poet Leib Jaffe: "I want to assure you that I know full well how powerfully and beneficently effective an instrument this foundation [the Foundation Fund for Palestine] has become for our people in the endeavor to found a new home in the old fatherland."[44] Even Leopold Bloom, the most famous of all Jewish fictional characters, was interested, though not converted. On reading a prospectus of a society calling on Jews to buy land in Palestine, a society called Agendath Netaim, he thinks to himself, "Nothing doing. Still an idea behind it."[45]

Why all this support? One already knows some of the reasons—the end of American immigration in the 1920s and the growing tragedy of European Jewry in the 1930s. I have tried to show that in Eastern Europe, at least, Jewish nationalism made perfect sense because the Jews there did possess many if not all of the characteristics of a modern nation and because a modern national Jewish identity was the obvious solution for a Jewish youth that was dissatisfied with the ghetto but could not, or did not want to, claim the national identity of the gentile nations among whom they lived. Nationalism, I have said, allowed them to be both Jewish and modern, a heady combination. But there was more to it than this, and I want to consider here some of the subtexts of the appeal of Jewish nationalism in general and Zionism in particular.

It is perfectly obvious that nationalism held out the priceless gift of dignity and self-respect to those who perceived themselves as the victims of humiliation and discrimination. The Zionist revisionists, with their famous emphasis on *hadar* (dignity or splendor in Hebrew) understood this very well. And Jewish nationalism also fought to win for the Jews something no less important—the respect of their nationalist-minded neighbors. In this connection the cultural work of the Jewish national movement was particularly important. One of the great sources of appeal of the Bund, for example, was its championing of the (secular) Yiddish language, which it helped elevate to the dignity of a true national language possessing a great national culture, just like Polish.[46] Zionism labored with remarkable success to make of Hebrew a language in which young Jews might not only pray and learn religious texts but also study physics, mathematics, and—more important—Jewish history. National dignity was exemplified by the new, modern Jewish national school, which taught all subjects in one (or both) of the Jewish national languages. Consider the tale of a young person from Volhynia in eastern Poland (the *kresy*) who began his educational career in a *heyder* and was then sent to a Polish state school, which he despised. When he finally achieved his goal and was sent to a Tarbut (Zionist Hebrew) school, he felt "as though I had been reborn. . . . The Hebrew language, the teachers and the pupils, my brothers and sisters, greatly influenced me. . . . Here was planted in my heart a great love of my people and my motherland, and thus grew my enthusiasm to work in order to redeem our country [Palestine]."[47]

The gaining of self-esteem in a hostile environment and as a bonus winning the esteem of those who traditionally despised you—what could be more attractive? "Every people [*folk*]," writes a young Polish convert to Zionism, "carries a flag, holds it high." And he continues in terms immediately obvious to those familiar with East European nationalism: "Our flag is besmirched and made of rags. Only with blood can we purify our flag, our coming generations will have pure flags, they will breath and move freely."[48] Here is his definition of Zionism: "Zionism wishes to raise up the Jews from their lowly state. . . . Zionism must lead to the inner freedom of Jews, it must root out the traces of slavery, it must implant in the hearts and souls of Jews the desire for life, for air, for purity."[49] The Jews, it was generally felt, were in a lowly state (*shofeldike madreyge*), especially as compared with other nations. The appeal of Zionism and other forms of Jewish nationalism for them was associated with the promise to alter this situation: "Poland has been oppressed for 100 years, and they have understood that a people [*folk*] without land must go under. And we, 2,000 years without a home and without a language and without a country."[50]

The historical lesson was crystal clear. True dignity, respect, and self-esteem would come only when the Jews had all the necessary components of nationhood, like the Poles. In Tarbut schools maps of Palestine hung in the classrooms, an important source of pride.[51] In the local Betar organization a young man learned that the Jews, too, might have a fatherland, that one need not be ashamed of being Jewish,[52] and in Kołomyja, Poland, a boy who attended a state school and was subjected to antisemitic taunts and told to "go to Palestine" thought to himself, "Why shouldn't we Jews have our own country?"[53] A Polish Jewish tailor came to the conclusion that the Jews need "a home so that people will not treat us as they treat a dog without a leash, so that we will not be treated as worthless."[54]

I have said that an important aspect of the appeal of the left was that it represented an extremely attractive model of heroic action—cooperation with the oppressed of other nations in order to create a better world. Jewish nationalism did the left one better by actually producing two different, although complementary models of heroism and self-sacrifice closely attuned to the yearnings and aspirations of young people, and in particular economically depressed young people living in the highly nationalistic and antisemitic environment of Jewish Eastern Europe. The best known was the heroic model put forward by a number of movements of central importance in East European Zionism, in particular the youth movements, namely, that of the Pioneer (*halutz*).

The pioneer was the embodiment of "the new, national Jewish man (or woman)," a young person equipped with unquenchable optimism and prepared to undergo an internal revolution in order to transform himself (or herself) into a productive laborer serving the Zionist cause under the broiling Palestinian sun (see fig. 24). The pioneers in Mordecai Halter's novel *We Are Preparing* are youngsters made of iron, miraculously emerging from the wretched reality of the Jewish town; they are "new people" (*naye mentshn*) who are charged with "saving the youth."[55] Halter has the leader of the movement explain: "*Hakhsharah* [vocational training sponsored by the Pioneer movement] is not a school that ends after one year, the main thing is not moving from one place of residence to another, the most important thing is—to change the person."[56] These pioneers are the very opposite of the "Diaspora Jew." In contrast to the latter's sick individualism and wretched materialism the pioneers believe in the collective and prepare themselves for living in a commune where all resources will be equally shared among the comrades. They are neither full of despair nor "resigned."[57] They are imbued with boundless optimism. They work like gentiles, but theirs is a Jewish dream, a Jewish drama.

The other model of self-sacrifice and heroism put forward by the Jewish national (again Zionist) movement was that of the Jewish soldier, the legionnaire, the man in uniform fighting to liberate his country (Palestine, of course, not Poland or Lithuania) from foreign rule. It is hard to overestimate the appeal of this version of the proud, "new" Jew in countries like Poland and the Baltic states that owed their independence, or at least so they claimed, to the heroic military performance of their young people. "Poland," reads a column in a Betar journal, "achieved her independence thanks to the legions that were organized in Siberia and France, and at the right moment our country will be freed and the kingdom of Israel will be established by the legions of Betar that are being organized and are waiting everywhere in the Jewish exile."[58] Poles and Lithuanians died to free their lands, and so will Jews: "And if our fate is to sacrifice

Fig. 24: The Future Belongs to Us. The new man, an icon of the Zionist pioneering youth movements. (Fidus, *Prayer of Light,* as reproduced in *El Al,* publication of *Ha-shomer ha-tsair* [Warsaw, 1922].)

Jewish blood . . . it will be the blood of the heroes of war who will wage war for the honor of their people and their land, as befits a nation marching towards its rebirth and its emancipation through an uprising."[59] The Jewish soldier, the hero and potential martyr, was seen as a kind of latter-day knight—just as the medieval knight was prepared "to struggle and to die for his leader, his faith, his people, land, or honor," so the Jew of today must be prepared for a similar fate.[60]

    These two heroic models—the pioneer and the soldier—came together in the person of the greatest of all modern Zionist heroes and martyrs, Yosef Trumpeldor, who fell in 1920 in defense of a Jewish settlement in

Palestine. His cult was assiduously spread by the Zionist movement in Eastern Europe. It appealed, as we can readily imagine, to people like the "naive young boy dreaming of heroic acts" who describes in his auto-biography how he was taken by the idea of a "Jewish legion."[61] Another youngster from Horodenka loved the idea of "marching like a real soldier," adding: "I loved Trumpeldor more than anything else, we never tired of reading about him and honoring him. I was enthralled by the tales of the first pioneers, of the Jewish legion in the [First World] War."[62] In Halter's novel the pioneers hold a "Trumpeldor evening" during which the leader explains to his charges the real meaning of this martyr's life: "The greatness of Trumpeldor and his comrades . . . is, in my opinion, their heroic life. They had no despair, they were not resigned. Those who are resigned, those with despair, they cannot build!"[63]

The cult of the military hero, of discipline, and of military action—the great "legionary idea"—was propagated by various Zionist movements, but it was most developed within the Zionist right. To this the revisionists added the potent myth of Jewish unity—unity among the classes (seen as artificial constructs) and even unity between secular and religious Jews. In his "Letter to Jewish Parents" of 1934 Menachem Begin emphasized that his movement had "great respect for the religious foundations of Judaism," and it was also claimed that Trumpeldor himself "had absorbed the spirit of Judaism in the *heyder* and remained true to this spirit and to its national sentiments for his entire life."[64] This emphasis on Jewish unity, in addition to other characteristics of typical East European integral nationalism-statism, "historic" borders, absolute rejection of binationalism in favor of the need to establish a Jewish nation-state, with the emphasis on *Jewish*, also helps to explain the considerable appeal of revisionism in Eastern Europe.

I have spoken of three "models" of heroic political activism with great appeal to Jews, mostly young and more or less secular East European Jews (although, as I have noted, there were also Orthodox pioneers and Ortho-dox revisionists). As against these mainly secular models the antinational Orthodox camp boasted one of their own—that of the talmudic student, the *matmid*, poring over his texts day and night, devoting his life to study (see fig. 25). The talmudic student was no less heroic, no less self-sacrificing, than the socialist marching on May Day with the Polish workers, the pioneer working in the Polish stone quarry, or the soldier preparing himself for battle in the Jewish legion. But, of course, the same social forces in East European Jewish life that were producing more and more recruits for secular movements like Zionism and the Bund were reducing the number of young Jews willing to remain wholly within the traditional world of Jewish Orthodoxy. An Agudah report from 1922 speaks of a situation in which "every day thousands and tens of thousands of our young people are leaving us and fall into the camps of others whose programs are heresy and sectarianism to one degree or another."[65] Chaim Grade, in his fictional description of interwar Vilna, the "Jerusalem of

Fig. 25: *Not New, But Still Heroic.* The heroes of the Orthodox world. (Max Weber, *Students of the Torah,* 1939. The Phillips Collection, Washington, D.C.)

Lithuania," remarks that in a particular workers' synagogue in the city plenty of Torahs were available but few were reading them because "Workers of the modern generation were . . . forming unions and join- ing the Bund."[66]

But it was not only that the numbers of Orthodox Jews were diminish- ing. The point is that in the context of interwar East European Jewish history, characterized as it was by severe economic crisis and rising anti- semitism, the essentially passive figure of the *matmid,* the talmudic scholar who spent his life in the study hall, could scarcely compete with the activist models of heroism championed by the socialists and the nationalists. The fact that even Agudat Israel, the political party of East European Ortho- doxy, began to sponsor its own Palestinian activities (including *hakh- sharah*) in the 1930s was an admission that the prayers of the heroic *mat- mid* were not likely to solve the crisis, at least not in the short run (in the long run, of course, they would hasten the coming of the Messiah). There is no question that within East European Zionism the pioneer was the central figure, a man or woman who in the eyes of most adherents of this movement best symbolized the Zionist revolution, just as the Jewish worker marching with his fellow Poles and Lithuanians on behalf of social justice represented the central figure within the Bund. The Agudah, how- ever, could not help but realize that its heroic Jew, the eternal talmudic student, was something of an anachronism in Poland and other East European countries of the 1920s and 1930s. Indeed, the very existence of the Agudah, a modern political party, implied this. The *matmid* as an ideal type continued to be glorified, and continued to exist, but in the hurly-burly of East European Jewish life the Orthodox party could offer no real alternative to the pioneer training to transform the swamps of Palestine into flourishing agricultural settlements in which no man would exploit the labor of his brother, the soldier acquiring the necessary military discipline and knowledge in order to conquer the land by force, and the socialist striving to transform Poland from a jungle of national and religious hatred into an island of tolerance and justice for all men, irrespective of nationality or faith.

If I am right in suggesting that the appeal of modern Jewish political movements was related to their promotion of heroic models of activism, it follows that the movement able to combine several of them would enjoy a certain advantage. This is my explanation for the tremendous success of those movements in the Jewish political world that combined nationalism of the Zionist variety and socialism. For only Zionist socialism was able to promote *both* the powerful notion of Jewish–Christian cooperation in the struggle for a better world and the heroic image of the pioneer. In short, I am suggesting that Zionist pioneering, since it combined both the ideal type of the heroic pioneer with the promise of an alliance with the non-Jewish progressive world, was the political movement with the greatest potential appeal to the secularizing Jewish youth of Eastern Europe and to a larger periphery, including people who might not have been ready or able to join the pioneering movement but who sympathized with its aims. In Haim Hazaz's novel the Jewish revolutionary Soroke is described as a man who "desires both the revolution and Israel."[67] This synthesis often led to tension, but no other political message on the "Jewish street" could match its power.

The synthesis between socialism and nationalism was, of course, much more common in Eastern Europe than in the West. But both in Eastern Europe and in the West, especially in the United States, an important source of Zionist appeal was that it served as a kind of Aladdin's lamp. I have already noted that Zionism was able to attract every sort of Jew, from Orthodox to secular, from socialist to antisocialist. And its chief product, the new Jewish community in Palestine (the *yishuv*) served as a source of hope and pride to every sort of Jew. Its great advantage, I would argue, was its very newness. Here was a brand new (or so it seemed) Jewish community; Palestine seemed to be a tabula rasa on which could be pinned the hopes, no matter how extragavant, of Jews of the most disparate sorts. For some Orthodox Jews, for example, it represented a great hope for the renewal of Torah life. The subtext of the appeal of Zionism for Orthodox Jews had to do with establishing a new Jewish society in Palestine that would offer ideal conditions for the flourishing of Torah-based Jewish life. If Orthodoxy was declining in the Diaspora—and there was little quarrel about that in Orthodox circles—it would flourish in the ancient Jewish homeland, where rabbis would regain their rightful place at the head of the Jewish people and where all Jews would obey Jewish law. In other words, the establishment of a Jewish homeland was seen as the salvation of Orthodox Jewry, which in the Diaspora was losing its best sons and daughters to secular creeds (see fig. 26). As I have already pointed out, for the non-Orthodox, but nonetheless religious Jews of the West, the new Jewish community in Palestine held out the hope of becoming a "light unto the gentiles," a society based on the prophetic teachings, inspired by Judaism (if not, necessarily, by what they regarded as its legalistic, closed Orthodox variety). As the hero of Ludwig Lewisohn's novel *Trumpet of Jubilee* puts it (a bit inaccurately), "There are no Fascists in Eretz Yisrael [the Land of Israel]; there are no Communists; there is neither hunger nor ignorance, neither rivalry nor hatred."[68] This theme had a powerful appeal in the West, especially for Reform and Conservative rabbis, who made it a cornerstone of their Zionist sermons in the synagogues. "In Palestine alone, among consciously Jewish forces, is social justice a reality," a Reform Rabbi announced in 1938.[69] The Jewish homeland would not be like other nation-states, filled with national and religious strife. It would be a country in which Jews would lead "an inspired and inspiring life as well."[70] And for secularists, of course, the Jewish society being established in Palestine had enormous appeal as a model for a more-or-less classless society, a society "without exploiters and without exploitation," a society where the principles of American progressivism would be realized (as Louis Brandeis hoped). For them, moreover, the very Zionist enterprise represented an affirmation of collective Jewish identity in a period when (let us remember the words of Henry Roth's *melamed*) large numbers of Jews were fleeing from Judaism. Here was a movement around which nonreligious Jews who wished to remain Jews could happily rally.

What I have been arguing, then, is that a major factor in the appeal of Zionism in both Eastern Europe and in the West was its promise to establish a wholly new Jewish society onto which all kinds of Jews and all varieties of Jewish groups could project their fondest hopes—even fantasies—for the Jewish future. No other Jewish political movement could compete with Zionism on this score.

And there was one other matter of great importance. I have argued that in Eastern Europe Jewish nationalism bore with it the gift of self-esteem and promised to its followers the esteem of others. This was true in America also, but in a slightly different way. In Poland one of the messages of Zionism was: We shall gain the esteem of the Poles, the Ukrainians, and all the others when we, by virtue of our heroic acts, go to Palestine and establish there our own national Jewish society. In the United States the message was: The Zionist movement and the eventual establishment of a Jewish national home will raise the prestige and hasten the successful integration of Jews in America. This, as I have already noted, was the Jewish version of a theme with many parallels among other American

Fig. 26: The Future Is in Palestine. The salvation of the Orthodox Jew resides in his transformation into a productive inhabitant of the Land of Israel. (E. M. Lilien, postcard for the Fifth Zionist Congress. The Zionist Archives, Jerusalem, Israel.)

ethnic groups. The potent combination of pride in Jewish achievements in Palestine and the expectation that these achievements would further the cause of American Jews *in America* was yet another reason for the considerable, even unbeatable appeal of Zionism.

In my discussion of the subtexts of the appeal of the Jewish left, I mentioned the perils of the celebrated nexus between the Jews and radicalism. By the "fatal attraction of the left" I meant its tendency to lead some Jews into two traps—an insensitivity to Jewish needs and Jewish suffering, and an alliance with the unholy forces of Stalinism and other extremely unpleasant movements of the left. Of course, the Jewish left was not alone in having its negative characteristics. If the heroic Jewish fighter against fascism and for equality marched side by side with the Stalinist, the heroic *matmid* of the Orthodox camp, devoted to the study of holy texts, did not usually possess much sympathy for the *goy* and all his works. As for the nationalists, some of them, like some of the socialists, indeed may be charged with a tendency to flirt with highly unpleasant political forces in the gentile world. Thus in the late 1930s Zionist leaders negotiated with right-wing Polish and Romanian national leaders who were, to put it mildly, no liberals and certainly not free of antisemitism.[71]

There is also something else, known today to all those who read newspapers and take an interest in current affairs. If the Jewish left was tainted by its link with some of the most unpleasant of all modern political movements, did not Jewish nationalism in some of its manifestations take on some of the most unpleasant aspects of general nationalism—disdain or even hatred of the "other" (in this case the non-Jew), chauvinism, and so forth? Of course, because Jewish nationalists failed to take over any territory during the interwar period, one would be hard pressed to test this. It is easy to accuse certain Poles—and even the interwar Polish state—of chauvinism, for we know Polish national regimes did not grant real equality to the various national minorities in that period. But Jews of the national persuasion—Bundists with their rather modest demands for national cultural autonomy or Zionists with their demands for a Jewish state—can hardly be accused of such crimes and misdemeanors as they ruled over no one. The autonomists, like the Bundists, had no territorial ambitions anyway, so they could hardly have oppressed anyone even if their demands for autonomy had been met.

As for the Zionists, the situation is a bit more complicated. Here there was a danger of *potential* oppression à la the Poles, the Romanians, and others. I have in mind, of course, the question of relations with the Arabs in Palestine. Now there were many attitudes toward the Arab question in the Zionist camp, and this is not a question I wish to deal with here. Nonetheless, it is a fact that the idea of a Jewish state obviously did bring up the problem of what to do with non-Jewish minorities in such a state. Moreover, if we assume that mainstream (meaning East European) Zionism was the Jewish version of mainstream East European nationalism, the likelihood of that problem becoming severe was very great simply because most national movements of East European provenance preached the necessity of establishing nation-states and not multinational states, whatever the ethnic situation on the ground happened to be.

The danger of Jewish nationalism establishing an oppressive, exclusivist Jewish nation-state, to the detriment of the non-Jewish inhabitants of Palestine, was very much on the minds of critics of Zionism, such as the Bund, and even of some of its friends. In 1934 the president of the Central Conference of American Rabbis stated:

> Realizing, then, as everyone of us should, that in the spread of intolerance, we Jews are always the first victims, it behooves us to be especially watchful of our own conduct and not commit the folly of believing that similar illiberalisms may not develop among ourselves. . . . We would be especially on guard against the development in Jewish circles of narrow and trivial conceptions of culture, of chauvinistic nationalism. . . .[72]

Whatever one may think of such sentiments, there is no doubt that here was located the Achilles' heel of Jewish nationalism of the Zionist type, a problem to which it really had (and has) no ready answer.

A few final remarks on the appeal of the various Jewish political forces are in order. It is clear that both the left and Jewish nationalism were the products of, and appealed to, deeply felt yearnings. Cyrus Adler, a hardheaded Jewish pragmatist and an enemy of political Zionism makes this point in an interesting letter to a friend in 1931 in which he explains why he cannot resist the appeal of the Jewish national movement: "You see, my dear Schulman, the real fact is that there is something mystical about the whole business [of Palestine], and when we go into the realm of logic and

philosophy we are just as apt to go astray as by following ou
itions."[73] This "mystical" dimension helps explain the respon.
Jews (not all but many) to the idea of rebuilding Jewish life in
For those Jews who wanted the Jews (however defined) to co
exist, the whole Palestinian affair was very difficult to resist. Log.
have indicated that it was impossible, that the British would never a   ..,
that the Arab question was intractable—as enemies of Zionism contended—but, as Adler says, logic was often no match for emotion.

I have mentioned in passing, in my discussion of the Jews and the left,
the issue of messianism. There is no question that both the left and the
Zionist version of nationalism evoked in many Jews something like messianic longings—for a perfect society, for a reign of justice, either in Palestine or in some other place, under the rule of rabbis or Communists. Of
course *messianism* is no easy term to define. All believing Jews are by
definition messianists, but among them were fierce anti-Zionists as well as
Zionists. For every Orthodox Jew who saw in the return of Jews en masse
to Palestine the beginnings of the messianic era, the beginning of the era of
redemption, there was an Orthodox Jew who regarded as a major disaster
the aliyah of secular Jews and the emergence in the Holy Land of a secular
Jewish society. For every Reform Jew whose messianism was expressed in
his (or her) belief in the mission of Israel, and who transferred this mission
theory to Palestine, looking to the creation there of a perfect society based
on the teachings of the prophets, there was a Reform Jew who denounced
Zionism and all its works. Nor can we assume that every Jewish Communist who believed, along with the hero of Varshaviak's novel, in "the idea
of liberating the world," was a messianist, or any more of a messianist than
any non-Jewish socialist.[74]

Nonetheless, it is obvious that the Jewish messianic tradition, along
with hopes for a renewed, healthy Jewish community and the desire to
satisfy profound psychological needs rendered Zionism, of all the competing Jewish political movements, the most attractive. But how successful
was it (and its competitors) in its efforts to solve the Jewish question? This
is the subject of chapter 5.

5

Success?

Futility

Nothing would be easier than to chronicle the many failures of the three schools of interwar Jewish politics in their efforts to impose their visions of the Jewish future on Jewish society and on the world. Consider the fortunes of the national camp. Diaspora nationalism, championed by the Bund and the Folkists and supported, for tactical reasons, by East European Zionists, was a definite flop. In Poland the state refused to fund Jewish national cultural activities. The modern Yiddish and Hebrew schools were funded by the Jews themselves, and the fact that they were forced to charge tuition naturally limited their appeal. Only in the Baltics was some regular state aid for national Jewish education forthcoming, but even in these ideal environments for Jewish nationalism the more grandiose demands of the Diaspora nationalists—a guaranteed number of Jewish representatives in parliament, the appointment of a minister for Jewish affairs to represent Jewish national interests in the government, a government-recognized and government-supported democratic Jewish national council speaking for the Jewish nation—were ultimately dashed. In a region characterized from the beginning by integral, intolerant nationalism and in the 1930s by the rapid decline of democracy, such schemes were doomed to failure, and the lack of Jewish unity, which made the establishment of all-Polish or all-Lithuanian Jewish national organizations very difficult, if not impossible, was no help either. Nor should one ignore the fact that even among the poverty-stricken Jewish population of backward Poland Yiddish was being replaced by Polish as the main spoken language of the young. True, its decline was much less striking in Eastern Europe than in America, but it was a fact nonetheless, with serious, even fatal consequences for the partisans of Yiddish-based Jewish nationalism.

What of the most important of all Jewish national movements, Zionism? Its appeal, as I have attempted to prove, was great. But did it succeed in solving, or at least ameliorating, the Jewish question in interwar Europe? Not really. If we consider Zionism to be first and foremost a movement of aliyah, seeking to save Jews by promoting their organized emigration to the Jewish national home-in-the-making in Palestine, the failure of the movement is perfectly evident. I have already said something about the Polish case. According to the first Polish census, there were approximately 2.8 million Jews in the state; by the eve of World War II, after twenty years of feverish Zionist activity in this, the greatest center of modern Jewish nationalism, that number had grown considerably, to well over 3 million— 3.5 million according to some experts. At the very time when the Zionists' most pessimistic pronouncements regarding the lack of a Jewish future in Central and Eastern Europe were actually coming true—in the middle and late 1930s—aliyah declined dramatically. And the relatively low level of aliyah was not exclusively the fault of the British. The fact is that most European Jews did not want to go to Palestine, even most East European Jews, not to mention German Jews. This was true not only of anti-Zionists but also of those who sympathized with the Zionist movement. The success story of Israel should not obscure this. There were a variety of reasons why such a tiny percentage of Polish, Romanian, and Baltic Jews went off to Palestine during the 1920s and 1930s, but it is clear that most Jews felt that they should or had to stay where they were. Here we encounter the formidable and even unique obstacle confronted by Zionism in its effort to win mass support.

All this does not mean that Zionism's Palestinian program was a total failure. From the point of view of the huge Polish Jewish community aliyah from that country was insignificant, but from the point of view of the Palestinian *yishuv* it was extremely important—even a lifesaver. The establishment of the State of Israel in 1948 would hardly have been possible without the emigration to that country of several hundred thousand Jews, mostly from Eastern and Central Europe, during the 1920s and 1930s. Nor should we forget that by going to Palestine these Jews were saved from Hitler's concentration and death camps (although some were killed in the Israeli war of independence). Moreover, to accuse Zionism of failure in the interwar period is to give the reader the impression that Zionists thought they could effect, in the period of twenty years, a mass transfer of Jews from Europe to the Holy Land. They did not. The failure of Zionism in the period under discussion is intimately connected with the incredible disaster of the Holocaust, which no one could possibly have foreseen or even imagined. In 1918, at the beginning of our period, most Zionists thought they had plenty of time. In the late 1930s, when some of them, like Jabotinsky, realized that time was running out, there was little they could do about it.

The failures of Jewish nationalism to solve the Jewish question were paralleled by the failures of Agudat Israel. If old-style Jewish Orthodoxy and the way of life it promoted was in trouble in 1918, it was in greater trouble in 1939. By that time it was evident that Agudah's vision of the Jewish future—a Jewish world ruled benevolently but sternly by rabbis and governed by Jewish law, whose faithful adherents were waiting patiently for the Messiah and cooperating with the gentile authorities in maintaining the status quo—was a vision shared by fewer people than at any previous period in East European Jewish history. And if this was true in the East, how much more was it the case in Western Europe and in the United States, where Orthodoxy appeared almost helpless in the face of the new, modern Jewish denominations—Reform and Conservative Judaism—and in the face of rampant secularism.

The only great success of Jewish politics in the interwar period was integrationism—but I hasten to add that this success was limited only to a few countries. It was most striking in the United States. Here, I would argue, developments in the 1920s and 1930s bore out the prognosis of the integrationist camp headed by such people as Louis Marshall and Cyrus Adler. The great majority of Jews acculturated, and the new, American-born generation abandoned Yiddish in favor of English. If they remained religious, they embraced modern versions of Judaism. By the 1930s they were busy integrating into the American political system. Above all, most—even the nonreligious—came more and more to identify themselves as Americans of the Jewish faith and were perceived as such by non-Jewish Americans. They thus successfully integrated as an *American* religious group, and if they were deeply concerned with the fate of their coreligionists abroad, this concern was, in the American multiethnic context, absolutely legitimate. So it was that the principles laid down and propagated by the mostly "German" Jews of the pre–World War I American Jewish Committee were adopted by the majority of *Ostjuden,* the East European Jews and their descendents, who by the interwar period constituted the vast majority of American Jewry.

Integrationism was successful in other Western countries as well—in England, for example. But the failures of this political camp were even greater than those of the nationalists and the Orthodox. Of course, in the inhospitable environment of Eastern Europe this doctrine never had much of a chance. True, one part of its platform—acculturation—was being achieved because among young Polish, Romanian, and Czech Jews more and more were adopting the language of the land as their own. But this was usually a case of acculturation without integration—the worst of all worlds, and no victory for the Poles and Romanians of the Mosiac faith. The greatest defeats of this political camp were suffered in Central Europe, above all in Germany, where the triumph of nazism signified the tragic end of the optimistic vision of Moses Mendelssohn and his followers, who constituted, after all, the majority of German Jews. From 1933 onward the idea that one might be German by nationality and Jewish by religion and feeling became totally untenable because the Jews were now defined by the rulers of Germany as a separate "race." A similar disaster occurred in Hungary, which I have already identified as a core area of Jewish integrationism. As early as 1920 Hungary passed a *numerus clausus* law aimed at restricting Jewish access to universities. Starting in 1938 the regime, now identified with the extreme right, passed a series of Jewish laws that also had the effect of ruling out the possibility that one might be a Hungarian of the Mosaic faith. In the very same year, Fascist Italy put an end to many years of highly successful Jewish–Italian integrationism by passing its own anti-Jewish law. Nothing in modern Jewish history and politics is more tragic, or pathetic, than the continued professions of patriotism on the part of the integrationist leaders of the acculturated German, Hungarian, and Italian Jewish communities in the face of the antisemitic onslaught. From the psychological point of view their failure was more profound than that of the nationalists and the Orthodox, who could hardly have been surprised by the worsening of Jewish–gentile relations (indeed, the Zionists had predicted it) and whose most fundamental beliefs—in the necessity to continue the process of Jewish nation building or to preserve the traditional Jewish religious community—were not dependent on the attitudes of the nations among whom the Jews lived.

The failures of modern Jewish politics are to be explained at least in part by the failures of the various alliance systems proposed by the various schools of modern Jewish politics. Zionist alliances with other minority groups in Eastern Europe did not result in the achievement of national minority rights; neither did close ties with the Polish antisemitic government in the late 1930s open the gates of Palestine. The authoritarian, integral nationalist regimes of East Central Europe could not deliver the goods to the Zionists despite their sympathy for this movement. These regimes also sympathized with Agudat Israel, whose adherents were perceived as conservative and law-abiding citizens who, unlike the Jewish socialists and Jewish partisans of national autonomy, did not wish to alter the basic nature of regimes under which they lived. Alliances between Agudah and integral nationalists in Poland and other countries did possess a certain value—Orthodox Jews were left alone to practice their religion and helped in their efforts to maintain control in the *kehilot*. But these alliances did not stem the decline of Orthodox Judaism.

The successes and failures of integrationism were, of course, the direct result of the fate of its alliance with liberal, progressive, and pluralist forces in the non-Jewish world. In America the political establishment remained true to its liberal tradition, thereby enabling and even encouraging all European immigrants to the country to become part of the American nation. In Germany, Hungary, Italy, and even France (albeit only during World War II, after part of the country had fallen under direct Nazi occupation) liberalism was destroyed by fascism. And the defeat of the left in Central and East Central Europe signified the failure of the Jewish left's alliance system. This alliance, like the alliance of Agudah with Piłsudski's moderate right-wing regimes in Poland during the years 1926–35, had its bright moments—one thinks of demonstrations against antisemitism in which both the Jewish and non-Jewish left participated and of the support for the Zionist project within the international socialist movement. It was doomed by the failure of social democracy to match the appeal of extreme nationalism and clericalism. In the Soviet Union the Jewish alliance with victorious communism, entered into with great enthusiasm by some sectors of Soviet Jewry, ended in the destruction not only of traditional Jewish life (something the Jewish left actually desired) but in the destruction of nearly all aspects of autonomous Jewish life.

Hope

But a totally negative answer to the question raised by this chapter would constitute a superficial and incorrect judgment on the significance of Jewish politics in the interwar period. Success can be measured in many ways. Jewish politics may not have solved the Jewish Question in Europe, but it did have a considerable impact on the Jewish population.

In his book on socialism in southern France Tony Judt wisely remarks, "Most people are not particularly interested in politics most of the time. They are certainly not as concerned with political life as the preoccupations of historians might lead us to believe."[1] This is true enough in the Jewish case, although much depends on what is meant by being "interested" in politics. In America, for example, one might well argue that most American Jews, by acculturating at "breakneck speed" (as Alfred Kazin puts it), were in fact expressing through their behavior their agreement, their "interest" in a well-defined Jewish political line—that of the integrationists.[2] From an organizational point of view this did not transform the American Jewish Committee into a mass organization, but hundreds and thousands of these Jews did join the Reform or Conservative Jewish denominations, which certainly did preach Jewish integration into American Jewish life. Active participation in organized Jewish political life, however, was not great. As I have already shown, membership in the Zionist movement declined after the flurry of excitement during and immediately following World War I, and this was also true of the specifically Jewish left.[3] To the extent that American Jews were actually joining political organizations, and not merely acting in a way that conformed with the ideological views of a particular Jewish political camp, they were getting involved in *American* political organizations, in particular the Democratic party. As Deborah Moore puts it, "Second generation Jews were ardent participants in the American political process. Democracy appeared to be the real religion of America and second generation Jews embraced the new faith."[4] Things were different in Eastern Europe. Even there it was doubtless the case that most Jews were not politically active (I emphasize the word *active*), but there is also no doubt that in at least some of the newly independent states of that region Jews actually participated on a mass scale in organized, specifically Jewish politics. This was certainly the case in Poland and in the Baltic states. One obvious reason was that here, in contrast to the West, Jews found it more difficult to play a role in general politics (the only important exception being the left). But there was more to it than that.

I have already quoted a passage in Yehudah Varshaviak's novel of Polish Jewish life after World War I in which the hero, Margolin, just back from service in the Polish army, is asked by a boyhood friend, "Well, and you . . . which organization will you join?"[5] What is interesting here, of course, is that there is no doubt in his friend's mind that Margolin will join some "organization" (meaning a political organization), never mind which. The notion that he might remain aloof from the political arena is unthinkable. We are reminded of Zangwill's description of the Polish shtetl, where virtually every Jew is identified with some sort of political group.[6]

There is no doubt that Varshaviak is decribing an important aspect of Polish (and general East European) Jewish reality. It really does seem to be the case that a very high percentage of young people joined Jewish political organizations (above all youth movements) of one kind or another. According to some contemporary reports it appears that in some places in Poland, particularly in the 1930s, almost all the young people did so. "Today," we read in a memoir from Warsaw, "one cannot find a single young person who does not belong to a movement. Almost all are political [*parteyish geshtimt*]."[7] I didn't want to join a youth movement, says another youngster in a memoir from 1934, "but that was very much the fashion, and most of the youth became party men [*partey-mentshn*]."[8] It was apparently quite common for classmates in Jewish schools to join a particular organization en masse. For example, in one town all the students in one of the grades of the local Tarbut school joined the famous Zionist youth movement Ha-shomer ha-tsair. In those days, we read, "Every young girl or boy had to be in an organization."[9] So common was it to join up that those who did not were sometimes regarded with astonishment or even suspicion. "In general," a youngster relates in his autobiography, "a person who did not belong to an organization was considered to be a stranger."[10] Indeed, at least some of those who did not join were greatly troubled by their inability to do so, "For a long time I was troubled with the question why do I isolate myself from society, why aren't I active in an organization?"[11]

The organizations these young people joined were often youth movements, which spread like mushrooms after the rain in the towns and cities of Jewish Poland. These youth movements were of all sorts. Some were officially connected to political parties (no Jewish political party worth its salt was without a youth component, whose graduates were supposed to join the ranks of the parent organization at the age of eighteen), others were not. In ideology they ranged from Orthodox traditionalism to the extreme secular left. They usually offered their members, along with a political weltanschauung, a healthy dose of pure, nonpolitical scouting activities and all manner of educational and social activities. Their appearance and rapid proliferation in interwar East Central Europe (they also existed elsewhere, but nowhere else did they have such an impact on Jewish life) was an extremely important event in the history of Jewish politics. For thousands of young people (by young I mean adolescents) this was the first stage in their political education, the very beginning of their transformation from innocent schoolchildren into adherents of some form of Bundism, Agudism, Zionism, and so on.

Why did these movements flourish? Why so many joiners? Those who did the joining were not always able to furnish coherent reasons. One youngster, who became a member of the Bundist youth group *Skif (Sotsialistisher kinder farband* [Socialist Youth Union]), tells us that he had no idea why he had done so; whatever the case, it had nothing to do with his "convictions" at that time.[12] Those who do try to explain often give reasons that were certainly valid, but they do not probe very deeply. They join because their friends do or because, as a student from Czortków says, "I myself was looking for friendship."[13] A youngster from Jezierzany, who joined Betar and eventually was taught that the ideological position of the organization was "to throw out all the Arabs from the country [Palestine] and establish a Jewish majority," joined the revisionist youth movement not because of its integral nationalism but because the *lokal* (the club where the members met) was better lit than that of the rival Gordonia (labor Zionist) youth movement.[14] A heyder student from Lublin joined the Bundist (Skif) group because all his friends did, even though his parents opposed the move, claiming that all Bundists were *goyim* (gentiles).[15] In Tłuste friends of a pupil in the local Polish state school tried to convince him to join Betar because it was "jolly" there, thanks to the presence of girls.[16]

These rather banal statements hint at a possible solution to the problem. I would argue that for hundreds and thousands of Jews in Eastern Europe the youth movement, and then the political party, was particularly attractive because it seemed to offer a happy alternative to grim Jewish reality. The rapid growth of the youth movements was a result of the Jewish crisis in interwar Eastern Europe—increasing economic misery, increasing antisemitism, the feeling that there was no future, and the belief that one's parents were at a loss to map out the path to a satisfying life. This crisis, much greater than the one that affected American Jews during the Great Depression, produced a vacuum into which stepped Betar, Hashomer ha-tsair, Skif, and all the other groups, promising not only friendship, not only relationships on an equal basis with people of the opposite sex, not only gaiety, but also something more profound. In the memoir literature one encounters descriptions of Jewish life in Poland that emphasize its "emptiness" (*pustkeyt*), its "grayness," its "disorder" (*umordnung*).

To escape from this one joined an *organizatsye*—the word itself is of great significance—a world that stood for a life that was "rational" and "planned,"[17] a world that emphasized the virtues of carrying out orders and bearing responsibility, a world of "strictness and punctuality."[18] Great emphasis was placed on outings to the countryside, where the young Jews were introduced to the harmony of nature, so different from the ugliness of the town.[19]

The organization also offered its new members new hope, a possible way out of the impasse. When a young man from Ostryna joined Ha-shomer ha-tsair he and his classmates "found, more or less, a goal for which [they] could struggle."[20] Previously they had seen through a glass, darkly, but now their eyes were opened, they received "a little window to the great world."[21] In short, by joining an organization these young people felt they were beginning a new era in their lives, an era characterized by new hope.

Any consideration of the achievements or the lack of achievements of interwar Jewish politics must take all this into account. It must also take into account the success of Jewish politics in creating satisfying subcultures, little worlds that supplied a wide range of services to their adherents.

Imagine, if you will, the situation in a medium-sized town in Eastern Poland, in Lithuania, or in Bessarabia. The leading Jewish educational establishments are the modern, Zionist-sponsored Tarbut Hebrew elementary and high schools. Most of the pupils in the elementary school are members of Zionist youth movements—of Betar, perhaps, or of its great adversary, Ha-shomer ha-tsair. At home they speak Yiddish, and they also learn the language of the land—Polish, Lithuanian, or Romanian (which their parents probably did not know very well, if at all); but both in school and in the movement modern Hebrew, as it was spoken in Palestine, is cultivated. So one may assume that many of the young people in town actually spoke Hebrew among themselves. At home it is likely that a traditional, religious (in Eastern Europe meaning Orthodox) Jewish life-style was followed, but in school and in the movement Orthodoxy was put aside in favor of modern secular nationalism, which emphasized that the Jews were a nationality with the same right to statehood as Poles, Lithuanians, or Romanians.

It is likely that many of the young people of the town were seriously hoping to go to Palestine, and in order to prepare themselves they joined, after "graduating" from the youth movement, the local He-halutz (Pioneer) organization. In the summers they went on trips (*tiyulim*) or to *hakhsharah* (vocational training) to prepare themselves for productive labor in Palestine. These young people were citizens of Poland, Lithuania, and Romania, but they lived in what might be called oases of Palestinianism, in a Hebrew-speaking Zionist world that offered them, along with a strong Jewish national identity, cultural nourishment, a satisfying social life, and, above all, hope for a happier future far away from the economic misery and anti-Jewish chauvinism of Eastern Europe.

Now consider the situation in a medium-sized industrial city in central

Poland. Here Jewish socialists, mostly Bundists, have succeeded in establishing a modern Yiddish-language school, where pupils are taught to
value both modern secular Yiddish culture and the benefits of proletarian
solidarity. Some of the youngsters might belong to youth organizations of
the Bund, and their parents to Bundist-dominated Jewish trade unions. On
May Day they parade through the streets of the city, joined (perhaps) by
their Polish comrades. They might congregate, after work, in Bundist
coffeehouses, and in the summer some might visit the Bundist-run sani-
torium for a bit of rest and recreation. This, too, was a world, a cultural–
political entity whose members were sustained by their faith in the historically determined, inevitable triumph of social justice and by their identification with a vibrant, militantly secular Yiddish-based Jewish national identity.

In the very same Polish city, probably not far from the Bundist school
and trade union *lokal,* one would certainly encounter a number of institutions established by Agudat Israel. This organization might not have succeeded in establishing a model of heroic activism to rival those of the
nationalists and the socialists, but it, too, managed to establish a complex
network of institutions that paralleled those of the secular Jewish parties.
In Poland, for example, its network of Orthodox schools attracted more
pupils than any other private Jewish educational system. Tens of thousands
of students attended its *Horev* schools (for boys), its *Bes Yaakov* schools (for
girls), and its yeshivas. Many of them were active in the chief youth organization of Agudah, *Tseirei agudat yisrael* (Agudat Israel youth). The educational, political, and social institutions of Agudah, no less than those of the
Jewish socialists and nationalists, constituted a little Jewish world of its
own, a world that aimed at preserving traditional East European Judaism.

The remarkable politicization of East European Jewish youth and the
establishment by the various Jewish political parties of impressive insti-
tutional—in particular educational—networks—all this has to be taken
into consideration in any discussion of the success or failure of modern
Jewish politics. Zionism may have failed to solve the Jewish Question in
interwar Eastern Europe, but it succeeded through its youth movements
and its educational institutions in enriching the lives of innumerable young
Jews, in offering them a way to cope with the grim reality of East European
life. And the same can be said of its ideological rivals.

But even on this level the story is not entirely rosy. Far from it. Many
joined political organizations only to leave them. Sometimes they wan-
dered about from one movement to another or gave up on this kind of
activity altogether. Youth movements may have sprouted like mushrooms
after the rain, but they were also likely to wither away and die; as I have
already pointed out, violent ups and downs were characteristic of Jewish
politics. There are many descriptions of party *lokaln* that existed only on
paper or were kept going by one man and a battered typewriter. In
I. B. Singer's novel *Shosha,* Haiml goes off to attend a conference of Poale
Zion in Warsaw in the 1930s, but soon returns, "The conference had been

canceled because a quorum wasn't present."[22] If some youngsters became convinced *shomrim* (members of the Shomer) and *betarim* (members of Betar), others tried, grew disillusioned, and gave up.

I have spoken of the failures of Jewish nationalism, socialism, and Orthodoxy to solve the Jewish Question. Inevitably, such failures in the great political arena were bound to have an impact on the hundreds and thousands of Jewish recruits to youth movements and parties, for the hope these organizations provided could not, over the long run, shut out the grim reality of little aliyah, of little success in the struggle against fascism, or even of little headway in the fight against growing secularism. It is hardly surprising that hope could easily give way to despair. Says the Jewish socialist Stach in Hazan's novel, "Often I am overwhelmed with despair. It seems to me that there is no hope for the world . . . there is no redemption, there is a void."[23] In the same novel Hannah Lea, a fanatic socialist betrayed by her comrades, commits suicide. A disillusioned youngster from Poryck, Poland, came to the conclusion that the whole Zionist enterprise had resulted in a Jewish community in Palestine consisting of 20,000 Jewish workers and 230,000 merchants, rabbis, beggars, and the like—"Such are the wretched achievements of fifty years of Zionist hullabaloo [*behole*]."[24] Finally, let me quote the words of I. B. Singer's happy Zionist who goes off to Palestine in the 1920s and soon returns to Poland. From there he writes a pathetic letter to a friend, "And tomorrow I shall begin my wanderings. . . . I shall go and never return . . . we are lost, my brother . . . there is no place for us, neither in the diaspora nor in Palestine."[25] The words of this disillusioned, despairing young pioneer indicate that for many recruits to Jewish politics failure on one level inevitably led to failure on another very personal one.

And yet, as I have already said, if the establishment of the State of Israel in 1948 is to be regarded as the greatest achievement of modern Jewry, then interwar Jewish politics cannot be counted a failure. It did, after all, create the crucial alliance between Zionists and integrationists in the West, along with dispatching enough immigrants (*olim*) to Palestine to make possible the military victory in 1948. Beyond that, the political struggle for Jewish national rights, for all its shortcomings and failures, did achieve one thing of great importance—it impressed upon contemporaries, both Jewish and non-Jewish, that in Eastern Europe at least the Jews did, indeed, constitute a legitimate national entity, for which some sort of national solution would have to be found. This was not forgotten in 1948, even after much of East European Jewry had been destroyed by the Nazis and their allies.

Another vital aspect of the legacy of interwar Jewish politics was its commitment to democracy, a result of the admittedly brief but supremely important experiment in democracy in Eastern Europe. Jews were able to participate, through the medium of specifically Jewish parties, in elections to parliaments, city councils, and *kehilot;* as a result the Jewish masses were educated in the rules and regulations of democratic politics. True, some

Jewish organizations were hardly committed to democratic principles—Agudat Israel, for example, or the Jewish Communists. But even the Agudah, by virtue of its participation in election campaigns, became the medium through which hundreds and thousands of Orthodox Jews were introduced to political pluralism. If democracy and political pluralism live on in the successor state of East European Jewry, Israel, part of the credit must be granted to the Jews' political experience in the interwar period.

6

Comparisons

Modern Jewish history, including modern Jewish politics, certainly possesses its unique characteristics. But in some ways at least Jewish politics in the interwar period had much in common with the politics of other peoples, and a comparative approach might well prove enlightening. It is perfectly obvious, for example, that the Jews were not the only people whose politics was characterized by bitter division; Yeats's famous lines, "Out of Ireland have we come / Great Hatred, little room / Maimed us at the start," certainly fit the Jewish case, with the Pale of Settlement, or Poland, substituted for Ireland.[1] More specifically, I would propose two general contexts in which the comparative approach is particularly appropriate—the politics of national minorities in Eastern Europe and the politics of various ethnic groups in the United States.

Eastern Europe

In interwar Eastern Europe the Jews were usually considered by themselves and by non-Jews as one of many national or national-religious minorities. All these minorities shared two obvious characteristics—a condition of relative or absolute political powerlessness and a perception of being oppressed, to one degree or another, by the majority nationality. In Jewish historiography it is almost an article of faith to claim that the Jews suffered more than anyone else—that in Poland, for example, although all the minorities suffered, the Jews were by far the worst off.[2] What interests me, however, is not who suffered the most, but rather that the political dilemmas of the other oppressed minorities were reminiscent of those confronted by the Jews.

To start with, many of these minorities shared with the Jews a basic uncertainty as to their identity. Just as not all Jews believed that the Jews constituted a proper, modern nation, so not all those considered by Belorussian nationalists to be Belorussians thought that there was such a thing as a Belorussian nationality. The same was true of the Ukrainians. To take one rather extreme case, some members of the Slavic minority inhabiting the easternmost province of Czechoslovakia, Subcarpathian Rus' (or Ruthenia), claimed to be Ukrainians, others believed themselves to be Russians, and yet others thought themselves to belong to a distinct "Rusyn" nationality.[3] Here, as in the Jewish case, different attitudes on the vexed question of self-identification led to different political camps.

True, the parallel is not quite exact, for a Rusyn who decided that he was a Russian or Ukrainian by nationality ceased being a Rusyn, at least in his own eyes, whereas a Jew who decided that he was not a Jew by nationality did not cease to be a Jew—he could, and in Eastern Europe almost always did, remain a Jew by religion, even if he was a nonbeliever. In other words, an unusual aspect of the Jewish case was that the Jews could reject membership in a modern Jewish nation with modern national rights and still remain strongly Jewish and deeply involved in Jewish politics. This option was not so readily available to other East European minorities, although I think it did exist among the numerous Germans (Volksdeutsche) of the region (and, to take a different example outside of Eastern Europe, among the members of the Greek Diaspora).

Granted this essential difference, similarities abound. In both the case of the Jews and other minorities in Eastern Europe modern politics was to a great extent the politics of nation building, meaning the effort to raise national consciousness and to convince the world that the minority in question was a bona fide nationality. If these efforts were sometimes opposed by the more traditional elements within the synagogue, they were also sometimes opposed by the churches of other Eastern European minorities, and for the same reason. Thus the conservative, loyalist, and antimodern nationalist stance of Agudat Israel is reminiscent of the attitude taken by some leaders of the Uniate (Greek Catholic) church (in some regions as much a "Ukrainian church" as Judaism was the "Jewish church") toward Ukrainian nationalism. In Subcarpathian Rus', for example, many Uniate clerics opposed Ukrainian or Rusyn nationalism and maintained a strongly pro-Hungarian attitude (in the pre-World War I period this region had been part of Hungary). Even in Galicia, where the Uniate church was historically very closely identified with Ukrainian nationalism, some members of this church opposed such nationalism.[4]

A critical aspect of nation building had to do with language; in Eastern Europe at least it was universally believed that a proper nation could not really exist without its own special language. Thus Belorussians demanded schools in Belorussian, Ukrainians schools in Ukrainian, and so forth.

Tremendous efforts were made to convince both members of the national group itself and outsiders that Ukrainian and Belorussian—despite the fact that no state in modern times claimed either of those tongues as its official language, and no army stood behind them—were proper languages, not merely dialects, exactly as some East European Jewish nationalists made tremendous efforts to elevate Yiddish from its lowly state as jargon to equal membership in the family of high, dignified languages.

Once again it will be said, fairly enough, that the parallel is not exact, because the Jews possessed two national languages, Yiddish and the much honored, but seldom spoken holy tongue, Hebrew. True, and yet not entirely true because the language war on the "Jewish street" between partisans of these two languages was far from unique. A scholar of the Rusyns of Subcarpathian Rus' reports that even the Rusyn nationalists "failed to come to agreement between themselves regarding the question of which language should be chosen as the national idiom."[5] Slovaks, and more famously Greeks, quarreled over which dialect of their language should be elevated to the status of *the* national language. According to an authority on Greek nationalism, "The problem of language came to be as hotly disputed as any political issue."[6] And when dialect was not an issue, the symbolically and politically important question of which alphabet to employ sometimes was. Thus the Ukrainian national movement in Galicia boasted advocates of the Cyrillic alphabet (as used in Russian) as well as advocates of the Latin, Western-oriented alphabet (as employed in Polish and by the Roman Catholic church).

As for the heroic Jewish national effort to revive Hebrew, the obvious parallel is to be found not in Eastern Europe but in Ireland and Wales, where some nationalists took the position that the creation of modern Irish and Welsh nations would be impossible without a process of deanglicization and the adoption of a proper national language. The politics of language divided Irish nationalism into Gaelic and English camps, and members of the former deplored the "contemptible indifference" of the Irish toward Gaelic, just as some Jewish nationalists deplored the indifference of some famous Zionists to Hebrew and the well-known revulsion many Jews felt toward Yiddish. If, as many Jewish nationalists believed, their people could not qualify for national rights without their own national language, so the Irish, without their own language, were regarded as "only half a nation."[7] As was the case with Hebrew, so Irish efforts to revive Gaelic often bordered on the absurd. When Douglas Hyde, the archpriest of Gaelic Irish nationalism, spoke at an Irish national meeting in Boston in 1905, "he began speaking in Gaelic to a partly delighted but mostly bewildered audience, then switched within a few minutes (to a roar of laughter and much applause) to English."[8] How often—at Zionist congresses, for example—was this embarrassing scene repeated, with Hebrew replacing Gaelic, and German (or Germanized Yiddish, or plain Yiddish) replacing English.

There were other obvious ways in which the Jews' national politics in

Eastern Europe resembled that of their non-Jewish neighbors. For example, within many of the national movements of the oppressed minorities in Eastern Europe there was a fundamental division between those who insisted on the absolute necessity of establishing a sovereign state and those who were willing to accept national autonomy as a solution to the national problem. And the synthesis of nationalism and some variety of socialism, which I have described as the most potent of all Jewish political movements, was by no means unique to the Jews. In Eastern Europe, after all, the oppressed minority *nations*—the Lithuanians, Latvians, Belorussians, Ukrainians, and so on—were often nearly identical with oppressed social *classes*—the peasantry and the proletariat. The national and socialist Jewish Bund represented the Yiddish-speaking Jewish laboring masses, who suffered, so it was claimed, from both national and social disabilities. In the Ukrainian case most speakers of the national language were peasants or workers because the gentry had either Russified (in the east) or Polonized (in the west). Such a situation was responsible for the fact that in the Russian Ukraine "there were no rightist or conservative Ukrainian parties, and most political groups holding the epithet Ukrainian were—in fact or in name—socialist."[9] The Jewish romance with the left was particularly dramatic, but the synthesis represented by the Bund and Poale Zion fits a well-known East European pattern.

I have already suggested that Agudah's opposition to Jewish nationalism was not unlike the attitude of various Christian churches toward secular nationalism in Eastern Europe. There are also striking parallels—both in Eastern Europe and in the West—to Jewish integrationist-type opposition to Jewish nationalism. For many sophisticated Jewish men (and women) of the integrationist persuasion the idea of a Jewish state implied a disgraceful retreat back into the dark ages of the ghetto from whence their parents or grandparents had quite properly fled. Such a state, they feared, would be chauvinistic, narrow, rabbi-ridden, gentile-hating—in short, everything they wished to put behind them forever. When, in a novel by Philip Roth, the hero decides to go off to Israel, his wife is horrified: "No—because my husband, who is an American, who I thought of as my generation, of my era, *free* of all that weight, has taken a giant step back in time, *that's* why I am dissolving the family."[10]

The observer of the present-day Israeli scene may or may not agree with her. What interests us, however, is that other potentially xenophobic national movements have provoked similar reactions among cosmopolitan-minded people who wished to combine, as did the Jewish integrationists, a certain group identity with a strong sense of belonging to a larger, multinational or multiethnic world. Not all Poles, for example, preferred the Polish nation-state of the 1918–39 period to the good old days of the Austro-Hungarian Empire, when the Poles of Galicia were part of a complex but relatively tolerant multinational world centered in Vienna. E. M. Forster describes the Greek poet Constantine Cavafy as "a loyal Greek, but Greece for him was not territorial. It was rather the influence that has flowed from his race this way and that through the ages, and that (since Alexander the Great) has never disdained to mix with barbarism, has indeed desired to mix."[11] This sounds a bit like the mission theory of those Reformed Jews who also did not believe that being Jewish had anything to do with territory and who wished to spread the enlightened message of Judaism among the gentiles. Along the same lines, one is told that the Greek poet George Seferis "had already lamented the narrowing of horizons once Hellenism became identified with the Greek state."[12] Finally, to take a West European example, an Irish historian writes that Yeats considered post-1922 Ireland to be a center of "cheap patriotism, demagoguery, internecine quarrels, threats to law and order."[13]

Of all the national minorities in Eastern Europe, the group bearing the closest similarity to the Jews was the so-called Volksdeutsche, the German minority.[14] As in the Jewish case, the Volksdeutsche were an extraterritorial minority who spoke their own language and often professed a religion (some variety of Protestantism) different from that of the majority among whom they lived. During the interwar period many moderate Germans wished to integrate to a certain degree and to become, say, Hungarians but retain a German identity—to become, if one stretched a point, Hungarians of the German persuasion. They were severely challenged by more extreme types who rejected this option in favor of strident German nationalism.[15] The latter were aided, and the former hampered, by the attitude of the East European regimes that not only took a dim view of German separatism but wished the German minorities to assimilate and disappear altogether. Until the 1930s the inherent similarity in the condition of Jews and Germans led, in Poland and elswhere, to a political alliance based on demands for an end to national discrimination and for national minority rights. But during the 1930s more and more East European Germans, faced with oppressive regimes at home, came to look outside the borders of their countries—to Germany—for salvation, just as many Jews, also faced with oppression, looked to Palestine. In the case of the Volksdeutsche, of course, this led to their disastrous nazification, ending in the willingness of some of them to play a role in Nazi Germany's horrific policy in the East during World War II.

I wish to make one final point with regard to the East European context, a point I have already alluded to (see pp. 111–112). I have reiterated throughout this book that the East European regimes of the interwar period tended to be intolerant and even oppressive, though never totalitarian. Above all they had difficulty coping with their numerous national minorities. How could a Polish state successfully cope with a huge non-Polish population comprising something in the nature of 40 percent of all its citizens? By the same token Zionism, chiefly an East European phenomenon, was never able to devise, and still has not devised, an adequate policy for dealing with the problem of non-Jews in a Jewish state. The post-1948 State of Israel is not interwar Poland or interwar Lithuania. Poland was never totally surrounded by hostile Ukrainians or Belorussians who threatened—and even attempted—to push her into the sea. But it is hard to deny that Israel shares with most East European nation-states of the 1920s and 1930s a basic dilemma, with no solution in sight.

The United States

The comparative approach is particularly useful, I think, in understanding Jewish politics in the United States and above all the phenomenon of American Zionism. As I have already argued, the attitude of many American Jews toward the Palestinian movement was quite reminiscent of the attitude of other so-called ethnic groups toward the national movements of their oppressed compatriots in Europe. Poles in America took a great interest in the struggle for independence and statehood in the old home, as did Irishmen, Czechs, and immigrants belonging to other subjugated groups. America was a center of Irish nationalism and Polish nationalism, just as it was a center of Zionism. According to one authority, Irish nationalism may have been stronger in America than in Ireland.[16] Indeed, among some of these groups national consciousness actually increased after arrival in multiethnic America. In the Polish case, for example, "It was in America . . . that many of the immigrants became fully conscious for the first time that they were Poles."[17] Oscar Wilde, very much the Englishman in England, gloried in his Irishness in America. It was in the United States, in 1882, that "he rediscovered himself as an Irishman."[18]

Now the Jews did not have to come to America to discover their Jewishness. But their adherence to a peculiar version of Zionism—one that combined elements of acculturationism and integrationism with support for the national struggle of their compatriots left behind—fits a recognizable American pattern. I have already noted the unwillingness of Irish American nationalists to speak Gaelic. Nor did many of them wish to go back to Ireland to fight for Irish freedom and to live in a free Irish state. Some Poles did return to fight with the Polish forces fighting for independence during and immediately after World War I, but, of course, the great majority by then regarded America as their home and had no desire to leave it.[19] And precious few American blacks returned to Africa, despite the urgings of some black nationalists. The nationalism of these groups, like that of the vast majority of American Zionists, was basically platonic in nature.

Of particular interest here are the reasons why members of the various American ethnic groups, who clearly desired to Americanize, so strongly identified with, and offered material support for, the national movements of their comrades back home. Of course, a sympathetic response to appeals from one's oppressed countrymen is perfectly natural, and should not surprise. But it was more complicated than that. The fact is that for many ethnics in America the successful resolution of the struggle for national independence and freedom back home was regarded as crucial in the struggle for successful *integration* into American society. Total acceptance as a good American was associated with the existence, somewhere, of a national base in whose political and cultural achievements one might take legitimate pride.

Therefore, for many American ethnic groups support for nationalism abroad and integration at home was not contradictory, but in fact perceived to be complementary. The Irish nationalist Michael Davitt explained the nexus between the two during a lecture to an Irish audience while on a tour of the United States in 1880: "Aid us in Ireland to remove the stain of degradation from your birth . . . and [you] will get the respect you deserve [here in America]."[20] As for the Poles and their support of Polish independence, we are told, "It makes, of course, much difference with regard to the *standing of Poles in America* [italics added] whether they are wanderers without a country of their own or have the background of a strong and independent state." The PNA supported Polish independence at home but, "Not Poland but the Polish-American group is the ultimate object of interest of the [Polish] National Alliance."[21] The NAACP was, of course, an integrationist organization par excellence, but one of its most famous leaders, W.E.B. Du Bois, was an enthusiastic Pan-Africanist and took a great interest, during the interwar period, in African affairs. When he visited Liberia in 1923, he explained:

> The unswerving loyalty of Negro Americans to their country is fitly accompanied by a pride in their race and lineage, a belief in the potency and promise of Negro blood which makes them eager listeners to every whisper of success from Liberia, and eager helpers in every movement for your aid and comfort. In a special sense, the moral burden of Liberia and the advancement and integrity of Liberia is the sincere prayer of America.[22]

Now I realize that the Jewish case is not quite the same as the case of the blacks, or the Irish, or the Poles, or anyone else. American Jews did not come from Tel-Aviv or Jerusalem—the homeland whose establishment some of them supported was a place where they and their immediate forebears had never been. But this is mere detail. In fact American Jewish willingness to support Zionism fits very well into the pattern of American ethnic behavior that I have been describing—behavior that was considered absolutely legitimate in the United States. And the Zionists were perfectly aware of this. American Zionists, who like Zionists everywhere worried about charges of double loyalty, were delighted to point out that they were behaving just as other ethnic groups behaved—their support of Jewish nationalism abroad in no way conflicted with their intense Americanism at home, just as Americans of Irish origins who fought to oust England from Ireland were perfectly good Americans.[23]

Louis Brandeis, American Jewry's greatest Zionist, summed it all up in his famous formulation of Zionist faith: In 1914 he declared, "To be good Americans, we must be better Jews, and to be better Jews, we must become Zionists."[24] And another celebrated American Zionist, Horace Kallen,

wrote the following in 1919: "The re-establishment of the Jewish homeland . . . is thus an essential element in the 'harmonious adjustment of
the Jew to American life.'"[25] In the Jewish case, then, as in the case of the
other ethnic minorities, the successful conclusion of the national movement abroad—the achievement of a free Poland, a free Ireland, a free
Africa, a free Palestine—was seen as a condition for truly successful Americanization at home. The fact that this approach was adopted by leaders of
many American ethnic groups in the new immigration that began in the
1880s surely helps to explain the success of Zionism in finding a home in
America.

I am not the first person to suggest that of all the comparisons to be
made between Jewish politics and the politics of other peoples the most
striking is that with the American blacks.[26] Harold Cruse has written,
"American Negro history is basically a history of the conflict between
integrationist and nationalist forces in politics, economics, and culture, no
matter what leaders are involved and what slogans are used."[27] If Jews
could not always agree on what term best described them, sometimes
preferring *Hebrew* or *Israelite* to the rather prosaic *Jew,* nineteenth-century
American blacks considered and employed the following terms, "African,
Ethiopian, Free African, Colored, Negro, Children of Africa, Sons of
Africa, Colored American, people of color, free people of color, blacks,
Anglo-African, Afric, African-American, Afro-American, Afmerican,
Aframerican, Africo-American, and Afro-Saxon."[28] The choice of a proper
name (now settled in the case of American Jews, but not in the case of
American blacks) was, of course, a political choice. In 1905 Du Bois re-
jected the term "Afro-American" because it was too alien and championed
the use of the word "Negro American" in a way that reminds us of Louis
Marshall, who argued for the use of the word "Jew" as opposed to terms
like "Israelite," which seemed to hint at the continued existence of a full-
fledged Jewish nation.[29]

Both among Jews and blacks the profusion of terms implied a confusion as to *what* these groups were—bona fide nations or something else: In
the Jewish case a religious group of one kind or another, in the black case a
race (albeit a race with its own church, at least in the South) fully capable
and desirous of complete integration into American society. Integration
but not assimilation—not only because assimilation was practically impossible but because, as with the Jewish case, it was deemed undesirable.
According to some of its leaders the blacks "as a race have a contribution to
make to civilization and humanity which no other race can make."[30] Here
was the black version of the Jewish mission theory as propagated by the
Reform movement within Judaism.

The black integrationists, like the Jews, emphasized the deep American
roots of their community and its splendid American patriotism, exemplified by its heroic deeds during World War I. They believed, again like
the Jewish integrationists, that their problem would be solved *here,* in the

United States, the result of a successful, courageous, uncompromising campaign for equality under law. Thus the NAACP, although rejecting the conciliatory strategies of Booker T. Washington (a kind of black *shtadlan*, who acquiesced in black inferiority in the short run), also rejected out of hand the utopian fantasies of its critics from the national camp.

Black nationalism, unlike Jewish nationalism in Eastern Europe, could not be based on language, because the American blacks were monolingual and had no memories of, and less interest in, their ancestral tongues. Their nationalism was based on a common cultural heritage: a glorious history (the heroes of this camp were the leaders of the slave revolts, the black Bar Kokhbas); great cultural achievements, real or imagined; and a strong belief that hatred of the blacks would never diminish, that black integrationism in America was as much an illusion as Jewish integrationism in Germany or Poland was an illusion in the eyes of Zionists. Like Jewish nationalism, it was divided on the question of *where* the black question might be solved: some promoted American black emigration to Africa, in particular Liberia; others thought in terms of Central America or Haiti (the equivalent of the Jewish territorialists); still others thought in terms of national autonomy somewhere in the United States (a program calling for black national autonomy in the southern "black belt" was adopted by the American Communist party in the late 1920s).[31] Marcus Garvey, the most celebrated American black nationalist of the interwar period, promoted emigration to Africa, although he—like American Zionists but unlike Eastern European Zionists—surely did not believe that most of his followers would actually go there.

Black nationalism in America denounced the rich and wealthy elite, the "mulatto" element that blindly strove for the unattainable—"assimilation and miscegenation"—the equivalent in the black world to the assimilationist "German Jews" of the Upper East Side of Manhattan.[32] Like the Zionists, Garvey practiced high-profile protest politics as opposed to the "accommodationism" of his enemies, who (he claimed) curried favor with whites just as Jewish "assimilationists" curried favor with the gentiles.[33] In his search for allies in the white world Garvey saw nothing wrong with negotiating with racists; indeed, he respected them for telling the truth, for agreeing with him in thinking integrationism to be both impossible and undesirable, and for despising the weak-kneed and hypocritical white liberals who founded the NAACP (many of them Jews, by the way). Thus his famous (or infamous) meeting in 1922 with a leader of the Ku Klux Klan, which was violently denounced by black integrationists as an act of betrayal and madness, just as many Jews viewed with horror Jabotinsky's tête-à-tête with Polish semi-Fascists.[34]

Black nationalism and American Zionism both flourished in the early 1920s. They were inspired by the rise in violence directed against Jews and blacks—pogroms in Eastern Europe, race riots and lynchings in America—and in a more positive sense by the postwar settlement that had led to the establishment of new nation-states in Eastern Europe. In fact, black nationalists pointed out that although the Great Powers "gave to the Jew Palestine," and independence to the Irish and the Poles, the blacks had received nothing.[35] Both Zionism and black nationalism sought and received support from the poorer, less acculturated elements within the community—Jewish immigrants from Eastern Europe, black migrants from the South.

If there are striking similarities between black politics and Jewish politics, there are also great differences, particularly apparent in the different reaction of the two groups to the clarion call of nationalism. For all of Du Bois's enthusiasm on reaching the shores of Liberia, it is nonetheless the case that Africa had less resonance among black Americans than Palestine among Jews. "What is Africa to me" asked the poet Countee Cullen,[36] and the answer given by the masses was—not too much, or at least not as much as Zion was to the Jews, even the American Jews. If the Jewish church urged its members to remember Zion, if not actually to go there, the black churches, though called African, were part and parcel of American Christianity. Emigrationism, the idea of solving the black question *there* in Africa (or in the Caribbean), was perhaps associated in many black minds with white efforts to expel the blacks from America; Liberia, after all, was originally a white scheme to rid America of its freed slaves. Some Polish Jews also believed that Zionism, if not invented by antisemitic gentiles, was strongly favored by them as a means to cleanse their country of unwanted Jews. But this fear was not a major factor in diminishing the appeal of Zionism among the Jewish masses in Eastern Europe and was no factor at all in America, where the relatively smooth acceptance of Jews into society made it much easier for them to support the Jewish nationalism of the *Ostjuden*.

There is one other way in which black politics and Jewish politics appear to be strikingly similar—in their tilt to the left. I have already cited Auden to the effect that black politics must be left-wing politics. What other group had less stake in the status quo and more interest in drastic change? In America the left was not alone in opposing antisemitism—this doctrine was never accepted by the political establishment and was opposed by both major parties. But black subjugation, at least in the South, was supported or tolerated by both Democrats and Republicans. Where else could the blacks look than to socialism and communism, which had the added attraction of opposing colonialism in Africa and of claiming, at least, to represent the poor working class in which blacks were so heavily represented. Moreover, the Communists, spurred on by the Comintern, made a tremendous effort to recruit blacks, an effort that derived from the assumption that this large minority might transform communism from a sect dominated by foreign immigrants into a mass movement for radical change.

It is, therefore, hardly surprising that many prominent blacks were identified with the left, in particular with the Communist party. According to one estimate some 75 percent of all "black cultural figures" were associated with that party in New York City in the 1930s, among them such great figures as Paul Robeson and Richard Wright.[37] Du Bois joined the Socialist party before World War I, and, like many a Jewish fellow traveler, he was enthralled by the Soviet Union, which he visited in 1926: "There lay an unforgettable spirit upon the land, in spite of almost insurmountable obstacles; in the face of contempt and chicanery and the armed forces of the civilized world, this nation was determined to go forward and establish a government of men, such as the world had never seen."[38] There was, Du Bois noted, no racism in that country, "If I happened to sit beside a white woman no one seemed to notice me. Singular country this."[39]

Here, too, however, as in the case of nationalism, the parallel between the black and the Jewish political experience breaks down at a certain point. What is striking is that the blacks, despite their much greater poverty and much greater oppression, proved much more immune to the temptations of the left than did the more prosperous, less despised Jews, thus giving the lie to Auden's prediction. A number of fairly obvious factors explain this. Although the left has traditionally championed the downtrodden, the downtrodden have not always been attracted to the left. There were, after all, not that many black intellectuals, and the black masses were very much under the influence of their politically conservative churches and highly suspicious of the white world, even the white radical world.[40] If the Jews produced many more intellectuals than the blacks, there was also no real parallel in the black world to the secularized, highly literate Jewish working class, sections of which had been politicized in the czarist school of hard knocks before coming to America. Nor was trade unionism nearly so great a force among blacks as among Jews, partly because so many unions refused to accept blacks as members. As against the mighty needle trades' unions, the backbone of the Jewish left in America, there was only A. Philip Randolph's union of sleeping car porters.

In interwar Jewish politics those organizations that combined nationalism with socialism and allied themselves with the world socialist movement were particularly successful. Among blacks, however, nationalism and socialism did not mix as well. Marcus Garvey, the greatest of all black nationalists, was strongly antisocialist—he was an advocate of capitalism, which was "necessary to the progress of the world"—and rejected out-of-hand any alliances between blacks and the general white left. "I am of the opinion," he wrote, "that the group of whites from whom Communists are made, in America, as well as trade unionists and members of the Worker's party, is more dangerous to the Negro's welfare than any other group at present. Lynching mobs and wild time parties are generally made up of 99 percent of such white people."[41] It is true enough that to the extent that the American left had the interests of blacks at heart, its message, at least in the North, was the message of integration, which the black nationalists opposed.[42] Rejected both by Garveyism and by the black churches (the two mass black organizations), as well as by the liberal and moderate NAACP, socialism had much less of an impact on black politics than it did on Jewish politics.

Along with the structural similarity between black and Jewish politics we have the well-known perception on the part of leaders of both groups that they shared common interests, that their fates were somehow intertwined. From the black point of view the Jews were a group to be admired and emulated—their love of Zion was extolled by black admirers of Africa, their success in moving up the ladder of success in America was lauded by black integrationists, their "unity, pride, and love of race" was respected by both groups.[43] Jews probably did not admire blacks very much, but they did sympathize with their suffering, and they did establish a kind of alliance with them. It should be emphasized, however, that this famous alliance between Jews and blacks was based on the belief of Jews of various political persuasions—integrationists and nationalists, liberals and socialists—that the only solution to the black problem was integration. Here were sown the seeds of future conflict. At the criminal trial of Marcus Garvey in 1923 the judge was Julian Mack, a leader of American Zionism but no supporter of black nationalism. He was, in fact, a member of the NAACP and his integrationist stance moved Garvey to protest that Mack was prejudiced against him.[44] Much later Harold Cruse claimed that the Jewish Communists in New York, although allowing for the existence of autonomous Jewish cultural activity, ruthlessly suppressed any signs of autonomous black activity and insisted on the virtues of black assimilation into white culture.[45] The reasons for the post–World War II collapse of the Jewish–black alliance are complex, but the roots of this collapse go back into the interwar period and are doubtless related to the fact that antisemitism has had much less power in America than antiblack racism. Integration has been (so far) *the* success story of Jewish politics in America, but not of black politics.

I have tried to demonstrate that Jewish Diaspora politics had much in common with the politics of other minority groups, in particular extraterritorial minority groups like the East European Volksdeutche or the American blacks. It is useful to bear in mind, however, that the most important of all interwar Jewish political movements—Zionism—was unique. After all, it aimed at nothing less than creating an almost wholly new national center for the Jewish people in a place where, prior to the inception of the movement, relatively few Jews (and certainly very few modern national Jews) lived. Polish nationalists may have argued among themselves as to where the borders of Poland should be fixed, as did Greek nationalists and Ukrainian nationalists. There were advocates of a greater Poland and of a smaller ethnic Poland—similar disputes divided Greek nationalists. But Polish nationalism, Greek nationalism, and Ukrainian nationalism were all aimed at restoring or establishing national sovereignty in a region where most or at least many members of the nationality already resided. Even in the case of the blacks, Liberia, Haiti, and Ethiopia were already inhabited by members of their race, and American black emigration to those independent black republics was therefore a rather different proposition than the transformation of Palestine, with its majority Arab population and its minuscule number of Jewish residents, into a modern Jewish nation-state. Merely to state this is to demonstrate the tremendous handicap under which Zionism labored and to emphasize the nearly incredible nature of its ultimate success in the post–World War II era.

7

Conclusions: Then and Now

During the more than fifty years since the beginning of World War II the Jewish world and Jewish politics have undergone a sea change. Two dramatic and unexpected events, one horrific, the other miraculous (at least in the eyes of many Jews) have much to do with this change. I refer, of course, to the Holocaust and to the establishment of the Jewish state. The Nazis and their local allies destroyed forever the Yiddish-speaking Jewish nation that had inhabited Poland, Romania, parts of Czechoslovakia, and the Baltic states. As a result several pieces fell out of the Jewish political puzzle. Those political movements based exclusively or largely on this nation were doomed. As I have already pointed out, Yiddish-oriented Diaspora nationalism, championed by the Bund, the Folkists, and the Zionists of Eastern Europe, was already a doctrine in decline before the war. It could not survive the war, and is today only a memory. The Bund itself—of all the major East European Jewish political parties the one most closely linked to *doikeyt* (hereness), to the Yiddish-speaking East European "masses,"—was shattered forever.

The disappearence of the Bund was part of a larger phenomenon of great consequence—the decline of the Jewish left in general. It is hard to believe in 1992 that Jewish political movements of the left once played so great a role in the Jewish world. Of course, Hitler destroyed not only the Bund but also the Zionist socialist movement of Poland and its neighboring countries that had dominated world Zionism in the 1930s—Poale Zion, the Pioneer, and the various left-wing Zionist youth movements like Ha-shomer ha-tsair. Beyond Hitler's domains upward social mobility and the end of mass immigration were burying Jewish socialism well before

1939. By that year the Jewish left in America was but a shadow of its former self; after the war its decline continued apace.

Such a decline is, of course, part and parcel of the general weakening of the left in postwar Europe and America, which in turn is closely associated with disillusionment with the Soviet Union. In the Jewish case it is true that the terrible shock of the Soviet–Nazi pact of 1939 was soon almost forgotten as a result of the Nazi invasion of the U.S.S.R. at the end of June 1941. For a while Jewish Communists and fellow travelers in America and elsewhere could revel in their alliance with the Soviet Union, the great power that had defeated the Jews' greatest enemy in modern times and had helped to establish in Eastern Europe the various "progressive," presumably anti-antisemitic "peoples' republics" in place of the old fascist or semi-fascist, anti-Jewish regimes of the interwar period. The Soviet Union was even willing to recognize and aid Israel in her early years, icing on the cake to many Jews.

But this did not last. In the 1950s revelations about Stalinist terror and antisemitism along with McCarthyite persecution combined to weaken what remained of the organized pro-Communist Jewish left. The next decade witnessed a new flourishing of Jewish left-wing activity—in the protest movements of the so-called new left. But this was mostly the activity of individuals, not of specifically Jewish left-wing organizations. And it, too, is but a distant memory today.

The attraction of Jews to socialism and communism was partly based on the idea that the left stood for the noble ideals of the brotherhood of man and the united struggle of the oppressed of all nations and ethnic groups—ideas of great potency and appeal for the weak, powerless Jewish minority. The Holocaust not only destroyed many of the Jewish organizations that cleaved to these ideals but also made it rather more difficult for many Jews to retain a belief in the ideals themselves. So, once its horrors were proved beyond the shadow of a doubt, did Stalinism. Within the Jewish world the notion that Jews can rely only on themselves, that the gentiles, including even the socialist gentiles, are not to be trusted, has surely been strengthened. This view has certainly taken hold in Israel; in fact the existence of the Jewish state has had a good deal to do with the decline of the Jewish left in recent times.

At first glance this would appear to be a peculiar statement. After all it was precisely the Jewish left—albeit a moderate, anti-Soviet, and highly national version—that had dominated first Jewish politics in the immediate prestate era of British Palestine and then Israeli politics (up to 1977). But the very circumstances of Israel's establishment in 1948 and its precarious situation thereafter—surrounded as it was by enemies bent on throwing the Jews into the sea—heightened, I believe, the appreciation in the Jewish world that, in the final analysis and despite the obvious need for external aid, Jews can count only on themselves, not on left-wing so-called allies. All the more so was this the case when the general left began to abandon Israel. The Soviet Union—after a very brief period of support (motivated by the desire to see the British ousted from the Middle East, not by any particular feelings of friendship for the Jews)—turned into a great center of anti-Israel and anti-Zionist (and antisemitic) propaganda. To be sure, the Soviet Union had been ideologically opposed to Zionism from the very beginning, so this development was not very surprising. But after 1967, in the wake of Israel's great military triumph and occupation of the West Bank, the Gaza Strip, and the Sinai, the non-Communist left also began to turn against her. Elements within both the new left and the old condemned Israel's occupation policies—Israel was accused of imperialism and racism. She became a second South Africa, a target of endless attacks by the Third World and its radical allies (a factor, of course, in the decline and fall of the Jewish–black alliance).

All this occurred before the revolutionary victory of revisionism's Israeli successor, the Likud, in the elections of 1977. This is not the place to go into the reasons why in Israel, in contrast to Poland, the Jewish secular right, allied with the religious right, finally took power on the "Jewish street." For my purposes what is important is that the Diaspora Jewish world rallied around this new antileft government, as it had previously rallied around Mapai. Thus we have, from 1977 to 1992, the existence of a right-wing Israeli regime supported by the world Jewish community and under attack from at least some elements of what remained of the left (much depleted, of course, by the collapse of East European and Soviet communism).

Once upon a time, when nazism and facism endangered the world, especially the Jews, many Jews believed in the slogan "no enemies on the left"—and with good reason. Today there has been a certain realignment of forces. Along with Stalinism the radical right has declined (though by no means disappeared) in Europe; if the left denounces Israel the moderate (by which I mean, among other things, not antisemitic) right is strongly pro-Israel. If Christian fundamentalists and some elements in the right wing of the Republican party in the United States defend Israel to the hilt, who can blame some Jews for saying, today: "No enemies, or almost no enemies, on the right."

Has the decline of the Jewish left been accompanied by the rise of an organized Jewish new right? Not so organized, perhaps, but certainly a not insignificant part of the American Jewish community identifies with this point of view. A number of outstanding American Jewish intellectuals, some of them former left-wingers, have become supporters of the Republican right—their journal is *Commentary*, which is published by the American Jewish Committee.

Rightist views are also generally held by the Orthodox Jewish community, which amazingly is now on the rise. During the interwar period Orthodoxy was generally on the defensive and was certainly declining. And since its political arm, Agudat Israel, was centered in Eastern Europe (in particular in Congress Poland), it, too, was shattered by nazism. Nonetheless, unlike Bundism, Orthodoxy survived the war—in Israel, of course, but also in the United States. A sizable number of Orthodox survivors emigrated to America after the war, and their success in preserving Orthodoxy—a success that certainly would have astonished Abraham Cahan's David Levinsky and other prophets of the inevitable demise of strict Judaism in secular America—has certainly given a boost to the Jewish right-wing bloc. In this area, too, the situation in Israel is important—the great role that Orthodox Jews have played and are playing in Israeli politics is certainly an inspiration to the Orthodox community of the United States.

I have linked the collapse of the Jewish left and the rise of a strong body of right-wing Jewish political opinion to events in Israel (it is, of course, too early to say whether the surprise victory of the Labor party in the elections of 1992 will reverse this trend). Indeed, there can be no doubt that the most significant event in the post-1948 Jewish world and in post-1948 Jewish politics is the growing hegemony of Israel. In 1939 the Jewish community of British Palestine numbered nearly half a million— considerably less than the Jewish community of Romania, not to mention Poland, Soviet Russia, or the United States. Today there are over 4 million, and the number is growing rapidly. The percentage of world Jewry residing in Israel has been steadily increasing, both because of a relatively high Jewish birthrate in the Jewish state (where there is virtually no intermarriage) and because Israel continues to attract Jewish immigrants (*olim*) from countries of oppression—most dramatically from the former Soviet Union and from Ethiopia. This is not the only reason for the ever-increasing weight of Israel in the Jewish world, but it is an important one.

The centrality of Israel has had the effect of reducing to a minimum those once powerful Jewish political forces opposed to Jewish nationalism and to Zionism. The anti-Zionist Jewish left is as dead as a doornail. The Orthodox of the Agudah type have made their peace with the Jewish state—they are not supporters of the ideology of Zionism, but most of them fervently support the existence of Israel, as well they might, because Israel is now a great center of Orthodox Judaism, and the expectations that it might well become a truly Orthodox state, a state based on religious law (*halakhah*), have never been higher.

As for integrationists—Americans, Englishmen, and Frenchmen of the Jewish persuasion—they, too, are now totally identified with Israel and most, if not all of her works. We have traced this development back into the interwar period with the emergence of the Zionist-integrationist alliance. Today this alliance has reached complete fruition. The Reform movement is 100 percent pro-Israel, as is the American Jewish Committee. Pro-Israelism, it is often said, is the civil religion of organized American Jewry. Plenty of American Jews are critical of Israel, of course, or indifferent—but organized Diaspora Jewry, led by American Jewry, supports the Jewish state to the hilt.

In this sense Jewish politics today is much much simpler than it was in the days when Zangwill wrote his story "Samooborona," quoted at the beginning of this work. True, the basic division between Jews who see themselves chiefly as a religious or ethnic group and Jews who regard themselves as members of the Jewish political *nation* still very much exists. It lies at the heart of what some observers believe to be the ever-growing dichotomy in the Jewish world between the national community in Palestine and the religious-ethnic community in the United States.[1] But the old political fault line in the Diaspora between Zionists and anti-Zionists is gone, as is the old language war between partisans of Hebrew and Yiddish. Integration "here," in the Western Diaspora, and a fierce loyalty to the still-embattled homeland "there," a homeland in which few American, English, or French Jews wish to live, is today's watchword. The kind of normalization much hoped for by American Zionists of Brandeis' type has now been reached.

The simplicity of Jewish politics today, at least in the framework of the terms of reference employed herein, may or may not be a source of rejoicing. One may or may not regret the demise of the Yiddish-speaking Jewish left, the old anti-Zionist Orthodox movement, militant antinational integrationism, and so forth. One thing is clear—what we have here is the Jewish version of a familiar twentieth-century story, namely, the triumph of nationalism. In Jewish politics, as in the politics of so many groups in the twentieth century, the nation-state has enjoyed great triumphs, even if it is not entirely victorious. The cosmopolitan, culturally and religiously divided Jewish people is united today in support of the Hebrew-speaking Jewish nation-state where an ever-growing number of Jews actually lives, and where many more visit in order to gain inspiration. Who would have believed this possible in 1918?

NOTES

Chapter 1

1. Israel Zangwill, "Samooborona," published in the collection *Ghetto Comedies* (New York: 1907; rpt. London, 1929), pp. 429–87. The title is the Russian word for self-defense, in this case meaning Jewish self-defense (*zelbshuts* in Yiddish) against the pogromists.

2. Ibid., p. 481.

3. Aron Zeitlin, *Veytsman der tsveyter* [Weizmann the Second], in *Drames* (Tel-Aviv: 1980), vol. 2, pp. 279–80. All translations are my own unless otherwise indicated.

4. Ibid., p. 271.

5. "The Influence of the Jews on the Progress of the World" [1888] in *Selected Addresses and Papers of Simon Wolf* (Cincinnati, Ohio: 1926), p. 74.

6. Quoted in Ernest Samuels, *Bernard Berenson: The Making of a Legend* (Cambridge, Mass.: 1987), p. 443.

7. Henry Miller, *Sexus* (New York: 1987), p. 425.

8. Ibid.

9. Darius Milhaud, *Notes Without Music: An Autobiography* (New York: 1970), p. 3.

10. Cited in Charles Reznikoff, ed., *Louis Marshall: Champion of Liberty*, (Philadelphia: 1957), vol. 2, pp. 797–98. From a letter to the editor of the *Jewish Daily News,* 7 February 1906.

11. Ibid., p. 806. Letter of Louis Marshall to Fred B. Smith, 5 November 1928.

12. *Pamietnik pierwszego walnego zjazdu zjednoczenia Polaków wyznania mojżeszowego wszystkich ziem polskich,* [Proceedings of the first all-Polish conference of Poles of the Mosaic faith] (Warsaw: 1919).

13. *U.O.B.B. Bericht über den 1. Logentag des IX. Distriktes abgehalten in Czernowitz am 15. und 16. Juni 1924* (Cernăuţi, Rom.: 1924), p. 46.

14. *Yearbook of the Central Conference of American Rabbis* [1895] (Cincinnati, Ohio: 1896), vol. 3, p. 8.

15. Artur Rubinstein, *My Young Years* (New York: 1973), p. 365.

16. Eliza Orzeszkowa, *Meir Ezofowicz* [1878] (Warsaw: 1939), vol. 2, p. 103.

17. Letter of Cyrus Adler to Lucien Wolf, 22 August 1922, in Ira Robinson, ed., *Cyrus Adler: Selected Letters* (Philadelphia: 1985), vol. 2, p. 52.

18. "Zehn Minuten Diskussionsrede! Ein Vorschlag," in *Anti-Anti: Tatsachen zur Judenfrage* (n.p.: 1932?).

19. Quoted in Robert Blumenstock, "Going Home: Arthur Koestler's Thirteenth Tribe," *Jewish Social Studies* 48, no. 2 (1986), 98–99.

20. "The American Jew as Soldier and Patriot" [1895], in *Selected Addresses and Papers of Simon Wolf,* p. 95; Wilhelm Filderman, *Adevarul asupra problemei evreesti din România in lumina textelor religioase si a statisticei* [The truth concerning the Jewish problem in Romania] (Bucharest: 1925), pp. 3–21.

21. See *Ksiega pamiatkowa ku czci Żydów bojowników sprawy polskiej 1905–1918* [Memorial Book in Honor of Jewish Fighters for the Polish Cause] (Warsaw: 1936).

22. Magdalena Opalski and Israel Bartal, *Poles and Jews: A Failed Brotherhood* (Hanover, N.H.: 1993), pp. 117–18.

23. *Yearbook of the Central Conference of American Rabbis* [1901] (n.p., 1901), vol. 11, pp. 24–25.

24. Reiner Bernstein, *Zwischen Emancipation und Antisemitismus; die Publizistik der deutschen Juden am Beispiel der 'C.V.-Zeitung,' Organ des Centralvereins deutscher Staatsbürger jüdischen Glaubens, 1924–1933* (Berlin: 1969), p. 29.

25. "The Influence of the Jews on the Progress of the World" [1888], in *Selected Addresses and Papers of Simon Wolf,* p. 50.

26. See the speech of N. Bakst at a meeting of the Society for the Spread of Enlightenment Among the Russian Jews in *K stoletnemu dniu konchiny Moiseia Mendelsona* [The hundredth anniversary of the death of Moses Mendelssohn] (St. Petersburg: 1886).

27. Deborah Dash Moore, *B'nai B'rith and the Challenge of Ethnic Leadership* (Albany: 1981), p. 4.

28. Abram Isaacs, *Step by Step: A Story of the Early Days of Moses Mendelssohn* (Philadelphia: 1929). Isaacs emphasizes Mendelssohn's spiritual debt to Maimonides.

29. *The Alliance israélite universelle: Publication of the Twenty-fifth Anniversary of Its Foundation* (Paris: 1885), p. 6.

30. Yearbook of the Central Conference of American Rabbis (n.p.: 1899), vol. 9, p. 172.

31. Marjorie Lamberti, *Jewish Activism in Imperial Germany* (New Haven, Conn.: 1978), pp. 23–54.

32. Cyrus Adler, *Jacob Schiff: His Life and Letters* (New York: 1928), vol. 1, pp. 314–17.

33. See the interesting analysis by David Levering Lewis, "Parallels and Divergences: Assimilationist Strategies of Afro-Americans and Jewish Elites from 1910 to the Early 1930s," *Journal of American History* 71, no. 3 (December 1984), 543–64.

34. Letter of Cyrus Adler to Jacob Schiff, 15 June 1920, in Robinson, *Cyrus Adler: Selected Letters,* vol. 2, p. 9.

35. Letter of Louis Marshall to Judah Leon Magnes, 10 October 1908, in Reznikoff, *Champion of Liberty,* vol. 1, p. 33.

36. George Eliot, *Daniel Deronda* [1876] (London: 1913), p. 363.

37. In the seminar on Jewish politics at the Hebrew University of Jerusalem, the Hebrew word *mishtalvim* was used, the equivalent of integrationists.

38. Letter of Cyrus Adler to Israel Zangwill, 25 October 1923, in Robinson, *Cyrus Adler: Selected Letters,* vol. 2, p. 86.

39. Arthur Koestler, *Arrow in the Blue* (New York: 1952), p. 110.

40. See Emanuel Goldsmith, *Architects of Yiddishism at the Beginning of the Twentieth Century* (Rutherford, N.J.: 1976), pp. 183–222.

41. *Three Cities,* trans. Willa and Edwin Muir (New York: 1933), p. 333.

42. See Yaacov Shavit, *Jabotinsky and the Revisionist Movement 1925–1948* (London: 1988), p. 383, n. 4.

43. See Koppel Pinson's introduction to Simon Dubnow's *Nationalism and History* (New York: 1970), pp. 48–9.

44. Shlomo Avineri, *The Making of Modern Zionism: Intellectual Origins of the Jewish State* (New York: 1981), pp. 170–71; Orest Subtelny, *Ukraine: A History* (Toronto: 1988), p. 299.

45. Yitskhak Katzenelson, *Dos lid funem oysgehorgetn yidishn folk* [The poem of the murdered Jewish people] (New York: 1948), p. 46.

46. *Zygelboym-bukh* (New York: 1947), p. 365.

47. *Vos vil agudas ha-ortodoksim? [What does the Orthodox union want?]* (Warsaw: 1916), p. 11.

48. Isaac Breuer, *Die Idee des Agudismus* (Frankfurt a/M: 1921), p. 4.

49. A free translation of the Hebrew verses in *Unzer entshtehung: musterhafter tetikeyts-berikht fun tseirei agudas yisroel in yastromb* [Our development: report on the activities of Agudat Israel youth in Jastrzab] (Jastrzab Pol.: 1931–32).

50. See Mordechai Breuer, *Jüdische Orthodoxie im Deutschen Reich, 1871–1918: Sozialgeschichte einer religiösen Minderheit* (Frankfurt a/M: 1986), pp. 61–90.

51. *Di organizirung fun bnos agudas yisroel* [The organizing of Agudah girls] (Łódź: 1929–30), p. 20].

52. *Der yud,* 19 February 1920.

53. Letter of Adar 1936 in Haim Ozer Grodzenski, *Ahiezer: Kovets igerot* (Tel-Aviv: 1970), vol. 2, p. 541.

54. Mendel Piekarz, *Hasidut polin: megamot ra'ayoniyot bein shtei milhamot uve-gezerot tash-tashah ("ha-shoah")* [Polish Hasidism: ideological tendencies between the two world wars and during 1939–1945 ("the Holocaust")] (Jerusalem: 1990), p. 229.

55. From a political tract read by a character in Isaac Bashevis Singer's novel *The Family Moskat,* trans. A. H. Gross (New York: 1950), p. 242.

56. Quoted in Zvi Gitelman, *Jewish Nationality and Soviet Politics: The Jewish Sections of the CPSU, 1917–1920* (Princeton, N.J.: 1972), pp. 322–23.

57. Michal Bursztyn, *Iber di khurves fun ployne* [Over the ruins of ployne] (Buenos Aires: 1949), pp. 56–57.

58. Gershon Bacon, "Agudath Israel in Poland, 1916–39: An Orthodox Jewish Response to the Challenge of Modernity" Ph.D. diss., Columbia University, 1979, pp. 130–67.

59. Barukh Charney Vladeck, *Moyshe rabeynu,* in Yefim Yeshurin, *Vladek in lebn un shafen* [Vladeck's life and work] (New York: 1936), pp. 183–216.

60. Isaac Mendelsohn, *Slavery in the Ancient Near East* (New York: 1949), p. 123.

61. Alfred Kazin, *A Walker in the City* (New York: 1951), pp. 162–63.

62. For example Raphael Mahler, "Hasidism and the Jewish Enlightenment,"

in Gershon David Hundert, ed., *Essential Papers on Hasidism* (New York: 1991), p. 405. This is an English translation of a section of Mahler's book *Ha-hasidut ve-ha-haskalah* [*Hasidism and haskalah*], which was published in 1961.

63. Singer, *The Family Moskat,* p. 242.

64. Vladimir Jabotinsky, *Ideologja bejtaru,* [Betar's ideology] (1934), pp. 12ff.

65. Bacon, *Agudath Israel,* pp. 130–67.

66. Arnold Zweig, *De Vriendt Goes Home,* trans. Eric Sutton (New York: 1933), p. 29.

67. Shavit, *Jabotinsky,* pp. 24–26.

Chapter 2

1. The best guide to this complex situation is Hillel J. Kieval, *The Making of Czech Jewry: National Conflict and Jewish Society in Bohemia, 1870–1918* (New York: 1988).

2. I. J. Singer, *Of a World That Is No More,* trans. Joseph Singer (New York: 1970), p. 74. It should be noted that in Poland the word "Litvak" could mean any "Russian" Jew, and not merely "Lithuanian."

3. Ibid., p. 221.

4. I. J. Singer, *The Brothers Ashkenazi,* trans. Maurice Samuel (New York: 1936), p. 254.

5. Asch, *Three Cities,* p. 325.

6. In 1935 about one-third of all Lithuanian Jews purchased the shekel, a higher percentage than anywhere else in the Diaspora.

7. Quoted in *El al, iton ha-shomrim* [El al, Journal of the shomrim] (Warsaw, 1924), p. 24.

8. Nissan Oren, *Revolution Administered: Agrarianism and Communism in Bulgaria* (Baltimore, Md., 1973), p. 123.

9. Gideon Shimoni, *Jews and Zionism: The South African Experience, 1910–1967* (Oxford: 1980), p. 4.

10. Michel Abitbol, *Les Deux Terres promises: Les Juifs de France et le sionisme, 1897–1945* (Paris: 1989), p. 202.

11. See the remarks of Eugene Weber, "Reflections on the Jews of France," in Bernard Wasserstein and Frances Malino, eds., *The Jews in Modern France* (Hanover, N.H.: 1985), pp. 8–27. See also Pierre Birnbaum, *Un mythe politique: "La république juive" de Léon Blum à Pierre Mendès-France* (Paris: 1988), pp. 76–78.

12. Dan Vittorio Segre, *Memoirs of a Fortunate Jew: An Italian Story* (New York: 1987), p. 19.

13. As quoted in Meir Michaelis, *Mussolini and the Jews: German-Italian Relations and the Jewish Question in Italy, 1922–1945* (London: 1978), p. 3.

14. See Alexander Ron, "Dmutah shel yahadut hungariyah ve-hashpa'atah al yahas yehudei hungariyah la-tsiyonut" [Hungarian Jewry's attitude to Zionism], Master's thesis, Hebrew University of Jerusalem, 1991.

15. Abraham Cahan, *The Rise of David Levinsky* [1917] (New York: 1966), p. 110.

16. Hayyim N. Bialik, *Complete Poetic Works of Hayyim Nahman Bialik,* trans. Maurice Samuel (New York: 1948), p. 35.

17. Reuven Asher Braudes, *Ha-dat ve-ha-haim: Roman* [Religion and life: A novel] [1885] (Jerusalem: 1974), vol. 1, pp. 78, 186; vol. 2, pp. 192–93.

18. See Bacon, *Agudath Israel,* p. 116; in general see pp. 115–17.

19. M. Breuer, *Jüdische Orthodoxie im Deutschen Reich,* supplies the background to this development.

20. Moshe Mishkinsky, "Regional Factors in the Formation of the Jewish Labor Movement in Czarist Russia," *Yivo Annual of Jewish Social Science,* vol. 14 (1969), pp. 27–52. Mishkinsky emphasizes the connection between the multinational character of the Lithuanian lands and the success of the Bund in that region.

21. Isaac Bashevis Singer, *Shosha,* trans. Joseph Singer (New York: 1978), p. 185.

22. Ibid., p. 185.

23. Shimoni, *Jews and Zionism,* p. 186.

24. See Jehuda Reinharz, *Fatherland or Promised Land, The Dilemma of the German Jew, 1893–1914* (Ann Arbor, Mich., 1975); Yehuda Eloni, *Zionismus in Deutschland: Von den Anfangen bis 1914* (Stuttgart: 1987), p. 122.

25. Quoted in Y. Sh. Herts, *50 yor arbeter-ring in yidishn lebn* [50 years of Workmen's Circle in Jewish life] (New York: 1950), p. 232.

26. *Ideological Development of Habonim: Documents, 1922–1957* (New York: 1942), p. 238.

27. Shmuel Yosef Agnon, *Orayah natah lalun* [A guest for the night] (Tel-Aviv: 1960), p. 283.

28. Marvin Lowenthal, *Henrietta Szold: Life and Letters* (New York: 1942), p. 238.

29. Israel Zangwill, "The Jewish Trinity," in *Selected Works of Israel Zangwill,* (Philadelphia: 1938), p. 122.

30. Shimoni, *Jews and Zionism,* p. 36.

31. Letter of Wyndham Deedes to Leib Jaffe, 17 July 1928, Central Zionist Archives, Jerusalem, KH4/B/2153.

32. On this dispute between "Pinsk" and "Washington," see Benjamin Halpern, *A Clash of Heroes: Brandeis, Weizmann, and American Zionism* (New York: 1987).

33. See the report *Congresul Uniunei evreilor pământeni tinuit in Zilele de 18, 19 si 20 Februarie 1923* [Congress of the Union of Native-Born Jews . . .] (Bucharest: 1923).

34. G. B. Sliozberg, *Dela minuvshikh dnei* [Things of the past] (Paris: 1933), vol. 1, p. 4; vol. 2, p. 293. See also M. Vinaver, *Nedavnee (Vospominaniia i kharakteristiki)* [From the recent past (memoirs and descriptions)] (Paris: 1926), p. 258.

35. Sliozberg, *Dela minuvshikh dnei,* vol. 2, pp. 301–2.

36. *III-ci walny zjazd delegatów związku Żydów uczestników walk o niepodległość Polski w Krakowie dnia 5,XII.1937 r* [Third conference of delegates of the union of Jewish participants in the struggle for Polish independence, in Cracow, 5.XII. 1937] (Cracow: 1937), p. 1. The speaker was Zd. Zmigryder-Konopka.

37. Ludwig Holländer, *Deutsch-jüdische Probleme der Gegenwart: Eine Auseinandersetzung über die Grundfragen des Central-Vereins deutscher Staatsbürger jüdischen Glaubens* (Berlin: 1929), p. 9. See also Bernstein, *Zwischen Emancipation,* pp. 52 ff.

38. Quoted by Sholem Aleichem in *Why do the Jews Need a Land of Their Own?,* trans. Joseph Leftwich and Mordecai S. Chartoff (New York: 1984), p. 37.

Chapter 3

1. I. B. Singer, *Shosha*, p. 131.

2. Idem, *Lost in America*, trans. Joseph Singer (New York: 1981), p. 4.

3. Ibid.

4. Ibid.

5. See Nahum Sokolow's remarks in *Haynt*, 26 December 1933, quoted in Ezra Mendelsohn, "Jewish Politics in Poland: An Overview," in Israel Gutman, Ezra Mendelsohn, Jehuda Reinharz, and Chone Shmeruk, eds., *The Jews of Poland Between Two World Wars* (Hanover, N.H.: 1989), p. 13.

6. Bursztyn, *Iber de khurves fun ployne*, p. 89.

7. *Haynt*, 29 April 1920.

8. Yehuda Varshaviak, *Orot me-ofel: Roman* [Lights from the Darkness] (Warsaw: 1931?), p. 70.

9. Bursztyn, *Iber di khurves fun ployne*, p. 93.

10. Agnon, *Orayah natah lalun*, pp. 263. But, he adds, "they come to pray like Jews."

11. On the election campaigns and results in 1919 and 1922, see Shlomo Netzer, *Ma'avak yehudei polin al zekhuiyotayhem ha-ezrahiyot ve-ha-leumiyot* [The Struggle of Polish Jewry for civil and national rights] (Tel-Aviv: 1981), pp. 73–103, 283–314.

12. Yitshak Bashevis [I. B. Singer], "Tsurikvegs," *Literarishe bleter* 47 (23 November 1928), 927.

13. See Bacon, *Agudath Israel*, pp. 410–13.

14. Y. Bashevis: "Tsurikvegs," *Literarishe bleter* 48 (30 November 1928), 947.

15. Report of 17 October 1928, Central Zionist Archives, Jerusalem, KH/B/2154.

16. I. B. Singer, *The Family Moskat*, p. 518.

17. Bacon, *Agudath Israel*, pp. 299–300.

18. For data on the Bund's showing in city council elections in Łódź, Poland's second city, see Robert Moses Shapiro, "Jewish Self-Government in Poland: Łódź, 1914–1939," Ph.D. diss., Columbia University, 1987, appendixes.

19. Leib Rashkin, *Di mentshn fun godlbozhits* [The people of Godlbozhits] (Warsaw: 1935), p. 495.

20. Leib Hazan, *Geula: roman* [Redemption: a novel] (Kowel Pol.: 1930), pp. 4–5.

21. Mordecai Halter, *Mir greyten zikh* [We are preparing] (Warsaw: 1937), p. 23.

22. Joseph Schechtman and Yehuda Benari, *History of the Revisionist Movement* (Tel-Aviv: 1970), vol. 1, p. 390.

23. As quoted in Allon Gal, *David Ben-Gurion: likrat medina yehudit* [David Ben-Gurion: toward a Jewish state] (Sde Boker, Isr.: 1985), p. 78.

24. M. Burshztyn, *Bay di taykhn fun mazoviye* [By the rivers of Mazovia] (Warsaw: 1937), p. 27.

25. Antony Polonsky, "The Bund in Polish Political Life, 1935–1939," in Ada Rapoport-Albert and Steven Zipperstein, eds., *Jewish History: Essays in Honour of Chimen Abramsky* (London: 1988), pp. 547–77.

26. Delmore Schwartz, "The Ballad of the Children of the Czar," *Selected Poems: Summer Knowledge 1938–1958* (New York: 1967), pp. 21–22.

27. Henry Roth, *Call It Sleep* (New York: 1934), p. 507.

28. Michael Gold, *Jews Without Money* (New York: 1946), p. 29.

29. Cahan, *David Levinsky*, p. 337.

30. Jacob R. Marcus and Abraham J. Peck, *The American Rabbinate* (Hoboken, N.J.: 1985), pp. 62–63. See also Jenna Weisman Joselit, *New York's Jewish Jews: The Orthodox Community in the Interwar Years* (Bloomington, Ind.: 1990); note that the index does not even mention the Agudah.

31. Abraham Cahan, *Bleter fun mayn lebn* [Pages from my life] (New York: 1931), vol. 5, p. 44.

32. R. Zaltsman, *Tsu der geshikhte fun der fraternaler bavegung* [On the history of the fraternal movement] (New York: 1936), p. 204.

33. As quoted in Franklin Jonas, "The Early Life and Career of B. Charney Vladeck, 1886–1921: The Emergence of an Immigrant Spokesman," Ph.D. diss., New York University: 1972, p. 85.

34. Robinson, *Cyrus Adler: Selected Letters,* vol. 1, pp. 73–74.

35. Adler, *Jacob Schiff,* pp. 169–72.

36. Letter of Cyrus Adler to Louis Marshall, 7 July 1916, in Robinson, *Cyrus Adler: Selected Letters,* vol. 1, p. 313.

37. On this movement see Jonathan Frankel, "The American Jewish Congress Movement," in *Essays on the American Jewish Labor Movement*, ed. Ezra Mendelsohn, *Yivo Annual of Jewish Social Science* (1976), vol. 16, pp. 202–341.

38. Letter of Louis Marshall to Woodrow Wilson, 6 August 1919, in Reznikoff, *Champion of Liberty*, vol. 2, pp. 599–600. See, in the same source (pp. 715–16), the statement of the American Jewish Committee on the Balfour Declaration.

39. See Menahem Kaufman, *An Ambiguous Partnership: Non-Zionists and Zionists in America, 1939–1948* (Detroit, Mich.: 1991), pp. 11ff.

40. *Yearbook of the Central Conference of American Rabbis* [1909] (New York: 1910), vol. 19, p. 200.

41. *Yearbook of the Central Conference of American Rabbis* [1917] (Cincinnati, Ohio: 1917), vol. 27, p. 132.

42. Cyrus Arfa, *Reforming Reform Judaism: Zionism and the Reform Rabbinate 1885–1948* (Tel-Aviv: 1985), pp. 16–53.

43. *Yearbook of the Central Conference of American Rabbis* [1923] (Richmond, Va., 1923), vol. 33, p. 105.

44. *Yearbook of the Central Conference of American Rabbis* [1930] (n.p.: 1930), vol. 40, p. 101.

45. *Yearbook of the Central Conference of American Rabbis* [1936] (n.p.: 1936), p. 91.

46. Melvin I. Urofsky, *American Zionism from Herzl to the Holocaust* (New York: 1975), p. 305.

47. Ludwig Lewisohn, *Trumpet of Jubilee* (New York: 1937), pp. 301–2.

48. Isaac Rosenfeld, *Passage from Home* (New York: 1946), p. 80.

49. Budd Schulberg, *What Makes Sammy Run?* (New York: 1952), p. 238.

50. Gal, *David Ben-Gurion,* pp. 15, 86, 88.

51. See Hillel Rogoff, *An East Side Epic* (New York: 1930), pp. 55–60.

52. See Irving Howe, *World of Our Fathers* (New York: 1976), pp. 349ff; Ronald Sanders, *The Downtown Jews: Portraits of an Immigrant Generation* (New York: 1969), pp. 437–53.

53. Sholem Aleichem, *Motel Paysi dem khazens,* vol. 2, *In amerike* (New York: 1937), p. 106.

54. William Gropper, *The Little Tailor* (New York: 1955).

55. See Arthur Liebman, *Jews and the Left* (New York: 1979), pp. 357–443.

56. Joseph Freeman, *An American Testament: A Narrative of Rebels and Romantics* (New York: 1936), pp. 122, 160.

57. Arthur Miller, *Timebends* (New York: 1987), p. 70.

58. Alfred Kazin, *New York Jew* (New York: 1978), p. 4.

59. See Alexander Bloom, *Prodigal Sons: The New York Intellectuals and Their World* (New York: 1986) and David Hollinger, *In the American Province: Studies in the History and Historiography of Ideas* (Baltimore, Md.: 1985), pp. 56–73.

60. David Prudzon, "Ha-komunizm u-tenuat ha-poalim ha-yehudit be-artsot ha-brit" [Communism and the Jewish labor movement in America], Ph.D. diss., University of Tel-Aviv, 1985, pp. 252 ff; Melech Epstein, *The Jew and Communism* (New York: n.d.), pp. 223–33.

61. Matthew Josephson, *Sidney Hillman: Statesman of American Labor* (New York: 1952), p. 373.

62. Ibid., p. 400.

63. David Dubinsky and A. H. Raskin, *David Dubinsky: A Life with Labor* (New York: 1977), p. 263.

64. James Thrall Soby, *Ben Shahn: Paintings* (New York: 1963), pp. 13–14.

65. Yaacov Goldstein, "Heroine or Traitor? The Controversy over Manya Vilbushevich-Shohat and Her Links with Zubatov," in *Arts and Its Uses: The Visual Image and Modern Jewish Society,* ed. Ezra Mendelsohn, *Studies in Contemporary Jewry* (New York: 1991), vol. 6, pp. 285–89.

66. Moses Rischin, unpublished lecture on Abraham Cahan's trip to Palestine at the Conference on American Jewish History in honor of Professor Arthur Goren at Columbia University, March 1990.

67. Quoted in Norma F. Pratt, *Morris Hillquit: A Political History of an American Jewish Socialist* (Westport, Conn., 1979), p. 160.

Chapter 4

1. Evelyn Waugh, *The Ordeal of Gilbert Pinfold* (Boston: 1957), p. 152.

2. I. B. Singer, *Shosha,* p. 171.

3. I. B. Singer, *The Family Moskat,* p. 517.

4. Daniel Bell, *Marxian Socialism in the United States* (Princeton, N.J.: 1973), p. 98. Harvey Klehr, *The Heyday of American Communism: The Depression Decade* (New York: 1984), pp. 382–83.

5. R. Zaltsman, *Tsu der geshikhte fun der fraternaler bavegung,* p. 239.

6. Binyamin Lubelski, *Yidn in shpanishn birgerkrig* [Jews in the Spanish Civil War] (Tel-Aviv: 1984), pp. 195ff. Lubelski claims that some 20 percent of all the foreign volunteers were Jews.

7. Moshe Mishkinsky, "The Communist Party of Poland and the Jews," in Gutman, et al., eds., *The Jews of Poland,* pp. 56–74; Dov Levin, "The Jews in the Soviet Lithuanian Establishment, 1940–41," *Soviet Jewish Affairs,* 10, no. 2 (May 1980), 24.

8. Alfred Kazin, *Starting Out in the Thirties* (Boston: 1965), p. 3; idem, *Walker in the City,* p. 61.

9. Quoted in an interview in *Tikkun* (May/June 1989), 76.

10. For a good summary see Liebman, *Jews and the Left*.

11. Alan Anson, *The Table Talk of W. H. Auden*, ed. Nicholas Jenkins (Princeton, N.J.: 1990), p. 83.

12. Quoted in John D. Morse, ed., *Ben Shahn* (New York: 1972), p. 29.

13. Quoted in Bloom, *Prodigal Sons*, p. 109.

14. Philip Roth, *The Facts* (New York: 1988), p. 25.

15. Letter of 6 May 1926, in Ernst L. Freud, ed., *Letters of Sigmund Freud* (New York: 1961), p. 220.

16. Klehr, *Heyday of American Communism*, p. 163.

17. Howard Fast, *Being Red* (Boston: 1990), p. 243.

18. Haim Hazaz, *Daltot nehoshet* [Gates of bronze] (Tel-Aviv: 1956), p. 12.

19. Cited in Gerald Sorin, *The Prophetic Minority: American Jewish Immigrant Radicals, 1880–1920* (Bloomington, Ind.: 1985), p. 3, who quotes from Morris Winchevsky, "On Talmud, Torah, Scepticism and Isaiah," *Jewish Currents* (Sept. 1978), 32.

20. Sholem Asch, *Ist river* [East River] (New York: 1946), p. 269.

21. Ibid., p. 274.

22. Sidney Hook, *Out of Step* (New York: 1987), p. 307.

23. Lionel Trilling, *The Middle of the Journey* (New York: 1947), p. 115.

24. Vasily Grossman, *Forever Flowing*, trans. Thomas P. Whitney (New York: 1972), p. 185.

25. Gold, *Jews Without Money*, p. 65.

26. Ibid., p. 309.

27. Peysakh Novik, *Palestine on a paroykhes: Erets yisroel in yor 1932* [Palestine revealed: the Land of Israel in 1932] (Piotrków-Trybunalski, Pol.: n.d.), p. 72.

28. Kazin, *Walker in the City*, p. 142.

29. *Zigelboym-bukh* [Zigelboym book] (New York: 1947), p. 91.

30. Freeman, *An American Testament*, p. 246. See Hollinger, p. 64.

31. I. J. Singer, *Khaver Nahman* [Comrade Nahman] (New York: 1959), p. 145.

32. Ibid., pp. 258, 261.

33. Yivo Autobiographies, no. 3623 (Wilno, 1934), p. 136676.

34. Ibid., no. 3664 (Zdzieciól, Pol., 1934), p. 138856.

35. See, e.g., Hazaz, *Daltot nehoshet*, p. 149.

36. David Vital, *The Future of the Jews* (Cambridge, Mass.: 1990), p. 126.

37. Varshaviak, *Orot me-ofel*, p. 158. In the original this reads, "Ma lanu lekhol zeh?"

38. Ibid., p. 177.

39. Hazan, *Geulah*, p. 180.

40. Kenneth Kann, *Joe Rapoport: The Life of a Jewish Radical* (Philadelphia: 1981), p. 110.

41. See the remarks of Moses Soyer, art editor of the pro-Communist *New Masses* magazine, in that journal's 23 May 1944 issue, p. 28. Soyer describes the work of the sculptor Adolphe Wolfe and writes, "A gentle, kindly man, loved by his fellow artists and admired by many thousands of the working people whose houses are decorated with his plaques of Debs, Lincoln, Lenin, Stalin, and other beloved figures."

42. The writer is the well-known Jewish American radical Matthew Joseph-

son, quoted in David Shi, *Matthew Josephson: Bourgeois Bohemian* (New Haven, Conn.: 1981), p. 165. This remark was made in 1933.

43. Hazaz, *Daltot nehoshet*, p. 89.

44. Quoted in Peter Gay, *A Godless Jew: Freud, Atheism, and the Making of Psychoanalysis* (New Haven, Conn.: 1987), p. 123.

45. James Joyce, *Ulysses* (New York: 1952), p. 60.

46. See Y. Y. Trunk, *Poyln: Zikhroynes un bilder* [Poland: memoirs and images] (New York: 1953), vol. 7, pp. 196–97.

47. Yivo Autobiographies, no. 3869 (Tel-Aviv: 1939), pp. 149907–8.

48. Ibid., no. 3712 (Łanowice, Pol.: [?]), p. 141684.

49. Ibid., p. 141685.

50. Ibid., no. 3520 (Ostróg, Pol.: 1932), p. 130882.

51. Ibid., no. 3589 (Warsaw: 1934), p. 134546.

52. Ibid., no. 3712, p. 141688.

53. Ibid., no. 3816 (Kołomyja, Pol.: 1934), p. 146636.

54. Ibid., no. 3873 (n.p.: 1934), p. 150313.

55. Halter, *Mir greytn zikh*, p. 23.

56. Ibid., p. 204.

57. Ibid., p. 115.

58. *Menorah*, no. 1, Nissan 1936, p. 5.

59. Ibid., no. 2, Iyar 1936, p. 1.

60. *Hovrot betar, be-hotsa'at ha-mifkadah ha-rashit le-vrit trumpeldor be-folaniyah* [Betar pamphlets, issued by the chief headquarters of the Trumpeldor Union in Poland], 1 (n.d.), p. 31.

61. Yivo Autobiographies, no. 3542 (Bielsk Podlaski, Pol.: n.d.), p. 131952.

62. Ibid., no. 3571 (Horodenka, Pol.: 1939), p. 133600.

63. Halter, *Mir greyten zikh*, p. 115.

64. Menachem Begin, *Der betar un zayn vort tsu di idishe eltern* [Betar's message to Jewish parents] (Warsaw: 1934), p. 9. *Mazkeret le-vnei brit trumpeldor be-erets yisrael* [A memorandum to the Trumpeldor Union in Palestine] (Tel-Aviv: 1927–28), p. 6.

65. Quoted in Piekarz, *Hasidut polin*, p. 26.

66. Chaim Grade, *The Agunah,* trans. Curt Leviant (New York: 1974), pp. 69–70.

67. Hazaz, *Daltot nehoshet*, p. 169.

68. Lewisohn, *Trumpet of Jubilee*, p. 306.

69. *Yearbook of the Central Conference of American Rabbis* [1938] (Philadelphia: 1938), vol. 48, p. 287.

70. Ibid.; also see Maurice Eisendrath, in *Yearbook of the Central Conference of American Rabbis* [1937] (Philadelphia: 1937), vol. 47, p. 220. See on this phenomenon Allon Gal, "Independence and Universal Mission in Modern Jewish Nationalism: A Comparative Analysis of European and American Zionism (1897–1948)," in *Israel State and Society, 1948–1988,* ed. Peter Y. Medding, *Studies in Contemporary Jewry* (New York, 1989), vol. 5, pp. 242–55.

71. Lawrence Weinbaum, "Jabotinsky and the Poles," *Polin* 5 (1990), 156–72. Howard (Hanoch) Rosenbaum, "Promoting an International Conference to Solve the Jewish Problem: The New Zionist Organization's Alliance with Poland, 1938–1939," *Slavonic and East European Review* 69, no. 3 (July, 1991), 478–501.

72. *Yearbook of the Central Conference of American Rabbis* [1934] (n.p.: 1934), vol. 44, p. 152.

73. Letter of 13 January 1931 in Robinson, *Cyrus Adler: Selected Letters*, vol. 2, p. 209.

74. Varshaviak, *Orot me-ofel*, pp. 186–87.

Chapter 5

1. Tony Judt, *Socialism in Provence, 1871–1914* (Cambridge, Eng.: 1979), p. 53.

2. Kazin, *Starting Out in the Thirties*, p. 79.

3. Naomi Cohen, *The Year After the Riots: American Responses to the Palestine Crisis of 1929–1930* (Detroit, Mich.: 1988), p. 57.

4. Deborah Moore, *At Home in America: Second Generation New York Jews*, p. 201.

5. Varshaviak, *Orot me-ofel*, p. 70.

6. See chap. 1, n. 1.

7. Yivo Autobiographies, no. 3589 (Warsaw: 1934), pp. 134517–8.

8. Ibid., no. 3710 (Lomża, Pol.: 1934), p. 141627.

9. Ibid., no. 3758 (Miedzyrzecz, Pol.: 1939), p. 143946.

10. Ibid., no. 3803 (Płońsk, Pol.: 1934), p. 145970.

11. Ibid., no. 3605 (Wilno: 1932, 1939), p. 135595.

12. Ibid., no. 3528 (Biała Podlaska, Pol.: 1934), p. 131268.

13. Ibid., no. 3678 (Czortków, Pol.: 1934), p. 139537a.

14. Ibid., no. 3687 (Jezierzany, Pol.: 1934), p. 140342.

15. Ibid., no. 3720 (Lublin, Pol.: 1939), p. 142061.

16. Ibid., no. 3675 (Tłuste, Pol.: 1934), p. 139338.

17. Ibid., no. 3613 (Wilno: 1932), p. 136211.

18. Ibid., no. 3819 (Kosów, Pol.: 1939), p. 146822.

19. Ibid., see n. 13.

20. Ibid., no. 3518 (Ostryna, Pol.: 1934), p. 130778.

21. Ibid., no. 3720 (Lublin, Pol.: 1939), p. 142062.

22. I. B. Singer, *Shosha*, p. 28.

23. Hazan, *Geulah*, pp. 228–29.

24. Yivo Autobiographies, no. 3794 (Poryck, Pol.: 1934), p. 145603.

25. I. B. Singer, "Tsurikvegs," *Literarishe bleter* 50, 14 December 1928, p. 988.

Chapter 6

1. W. B. Yeats, "Remorse for Intemperate Speech," in *The Collected Poems of W. B. Yeats* (New York: 1958), p. 249.

2. See, e.g., Pawel Korzec, "Antisemitism in Poland as an Intellectual, Social and Political Movement," in Joshua Fishman, ed., *Studies on Polish Jewry, 1919–1939* (New York: 1974), p. 12.

3. On this see Robert Paul Magocsi, *The Shaping of a National Identity: Subcarpathian Rus', 1848–1948* (Cambridge, Mass: 1978), pp. 17–18.

4. Subtelny, *Ukraine,* p. 440; Magosci, *Shaping of a National Identity,* p. 187; John-Paul Himka, "The Greek Catholic Church in Nineteenth-Century Galicia," in Geoffrey A. Hosking, ed., *Church, Nation and State in Russia and Ukraine* (London: 1991), pp. 60–61.

5. Maria Mayer, "Some Aspects of the Development of the National Movement Among the Ruthenes of Hungary (Sub-Carpathian Ruthenia)," in Keith Hitchins, ed., *Studies in East European Social History* (Leiden, Neth.: 1977), vol. 1, p. 179.

6. Douglas Daken, *The Unification of Greece, 1770–1923* (New York: 1972), p. 256.

7. David George Boyce, *Nationalism in Ireland* (London: 1982), pp. 232, 155.

8. Quoted by Conor Cruise O'Brien in the *Times Literary Supplement,* 21 June 1991, p. 10, as cited in Janet Egleson Dunleavy and Gareth W. Dunleavy, *Douglas Hyde: A Maker of Modern Ireland* (Berkeley: 1991), p. 270.

9. Jurij Borys, "Political Parties in the Ukraine," in Taras Hunczak, ed., *The Ukraine, 1917–1921: A Study in Revolution* (Cambridge, Mass.: 1977), p. 129.

10. Philip Roth, *The Counterlife* (New York: 1986), p. 154.

11. Quoted by Henry Gifford in the *Times Literary Supplement,* 24–30 August 1990, p. 887.

12. Ibid., 12 December 1986, p. 1392.

13. Quoted by Boyce in *Nationalism in Ireland,* p. 339.

14. See Ezra Mendelsohn, "German and Jewish Minorities in the European Successor States Between the World Wars: Some Comparative Remarks," in Ezra Mendelsohn and Chone Shmeruk, eds., *Studies on Polish Jewry: Paul Glikson Memorial Volume* (Jerusalem: 1987), pp. li–lxiv.

15. Thomas Spira, *German-Hungarian Relations and the Swabian Problem: From Karolyi to Gombos 1919–1936* (New York: 1977); idem, *The German-Hungarian-Swabian Triangle 1936–1939: The Road to Discord* (New York: 1990), pp. 1–17.

16. Lawrence J. McCaffrey, ed., *Irish Nationalism and the American Contribution* (New York: 1976), "Introduction," unpaginated.

17. Donald E. Pienkos, *PNA: A Centennial History of the Polish National Alliance of the United States of North America* (New York: 1984), p. 43.

18. Richard Ellmann, *Oscar Wilde* (London: 1988), p. 185.

19. On this see Adam Walaszek, *Reemigracja ze stanów zjednoczonych do Polskiej po I wojnie światowej, 1919–1924* [Reemigration from the Unites States to Poland after World War I, 1919–1924] (Warsaw: 1983).

20. Quoted in Thomas N. Brown, *Irish-American Nationalism 1870–1890,* (Philadelphia: 1966), p. 24.

21. William I. Thomas and Florian Znaniecki, *The Polish Peasant in Europe and America* (New York: 1958), pp. 1598–99, 1600.

22. W. E. Burghardt Du Bois, *Dusk of Dawn* (New York: 1968) [1940], p. 125.

23. Urofsky, *American Zionism,* p. 90; Marc Lee Raphael, *Abba Hillel Silver: A Profile in American Judaism* (New York: 1989), pp. 25–26.

24. Melvin I. Urofsky and David W. Levy, eds., *Letters of Louis Brandeis* (Albany, N.Y.: 1973), vol. 3, p. 355.

25. Horace Kallen, "Zionism and Liberalism" [1919], in *Judaism at Bay,* (New York: 1932), p. 119.

26. John H. Bracey, August Meier, and Elliot Rudwick, eds., *Black National-ism in America* (Indianapolis: 1970), p. liii; Jonathan Frankel, *Prophecy and Politics: Socialism, Nationalism and the Russian Jews, 1862–1917* (London: 1981), p. 4.

27. Harold Cruse, *The Crisis of the Negro Intellectual* (New York: 1984), p. 564.

28. Sterling Stuckey, *Slave Culture: Nationalism Theory and the Foundations of Black America* (New York: 1987), pp. 199–200.

29. Elliot M. Rudwick, *W.E.B. Du Bois: A Study in Minority Group Leadership* (Philadelphia: 1960), p. 96.

30. This is Du Bois's formulation in 1897; see his *Dusk of Dawn*, p. 116, which quotes his 1897 pamphlet.

31. For the debate on emigrationism in the nineteenth century see Kwando M. Kinshasa, *Emigration vs. Assimilation: The Debate in the African American Press* (Jefferson, N.C.: 1988).

32. Quoted in John Henrik Clarke, ed., *Marcus Garvey and the Vision of Africa* (New York: 1974), p. 249.

33. The terms *protest* and *accommodationist* as applied to black political behav-ior are employed by Gunnar Myrdal in his classic study *An American Dilemma; The Negro Problem and Modern Democracy* [1944] (New York: 1962), pp. 720–56.

34. Edmund David Cronon, *Black Moses: The Story of Marcus Garvey and the Universal Negro Improvement Association* (Madison, Wis.: 1968), pp. 189–90; Judith Stein, *The World of Marcus Garvey: Race and Class in Modern Society* (Baton Rouge, La.: 1986), pp. 154–61.

35. Garvey, quoted in Clarke, *Marcus Garvey*, p. 291.

36. Countee Cullen, "Heritage," in Houston A. Baker, Jr., *Black Literature in America* (New York: 1971), p. 154.

37. Mark Naison, *Communists in Harlem During the Depression* (Urbana, Ill.: 1983), p. 193.

38. Du Bois, *Dusk of Dawn*, p. 287.

39. Quoted in Rudwick, *Du Bois*, p. 256.

40. Naison, *Communists in Harlem*, pp. 279–83.

41. Marcus Garvey, "The Negro, Communism, Trade Unionism and his (?) Friend," and "Capitalism and the State," in Amy Jacques Garvey, ed., *Philosophy and Opinions of Marcus Garvey* (New York: 1969), pp. 70, 72.

42. During the 1930s the American Communist party, spurred on by the Comintern, embraced the principle that the blacks in the South represented a national group and should enjoy national rights. But in the North, where virtually all Jewish Communists were active, this position was never adopted.

43. The quotation is from Booker T. Washington, writing in 1899, in Bracey, Meier, and Rudwick, *Black Nationalism*, pp. 233–34. See also Benjamin Neu-berger, "W.E.B. Du Bois on Black Nationalism and Zionism," *Jewish Journal of Sociology* (28 2 December 1986), 139–44.

44. Cronon, *Black Moses*, pp. 112–13.

45. Cruse, *Crisis of the Negro Intellectual*, pp. 147–70.

Chapter 7

1. Vital, *Future of the Jews*, pp. 101–44.

INDEX

Printed in the United States
2853